Wavelets in Soft Computing

WORLD SCIENTIFIC SERIES IN ROBOTICS AND INTELLIGENT SYSTEMS

Editor-in-Charge: C J Harris (*University of Southampton*)

Published:

More information on this series can also be found at https://www.worldscientific.com/series/wssris

World Scientific Series in Robotics and Intelligent Systems – Vol. 29

Wavelets in Soft Computing

2nd Edition

Marc Thuillard

Belimo Automation AG, Switzerland

 **World Scientific**

NEW JERSEY · LONDON · SINGAPORE · BEIJING · SHANGHAI · HONG KONG · TAIPEI · CHENNAI · TOKYO

Published by

World Scientific Publishing Co. Pte. Ltd.

5 Toh Tuck Link, Singapore 596224

USA office: 27 Warren Street, Suite 401-402, Hackensack, NJ 07601

UK office: 57 Shelton Street, Covent Garden, London WC2H 9HE

British Library Cataloguing-in-Publication Data
A catalogue record for this book is available from the British Library.

World Scientific Series in Robotics and Intelligent Systems — Vol. 29
WAVELETS IN SOFT COMPUTING
Second Edition

ISBN 978-981-126-398-9 (hardcover)
ISBN 978-981-126-399-6 (ebook for institutions)
ISBN 978-981-126-403-0 (ebook for individuals)

For any available supplementary material, please visit
https://www.worldscientific.com/worldscibooks/10.1142/13074#t=suppl

Printed in Singapore

To Claudia, Estelle, and Xavier

Foreword

The main goal of *Wavelets in Soft Computing* is to furnish a synthesis on the state of integration of wavelet theory into soft computing. Wavelet methods in soft computing can be classified into five main categories that form the backbone of the book:

- Preprocessing methods
- Automatic generation of a fuzzy system from data
- Wavelet networks
- Wavelet-based nonparametric estimation and regression techniques
- Multiresolution genetic algorithms and search methods.

The main new contributions of *Wavelets in Soft Computing* to these topics are the automatic generation of a fuzzy system from data (fuzzy wavelet, fuzzy wavenets for online learning), wavelet networks, and wavelet estimators (extension to biorthogonal wavelets) and multiresolution search methods. These new methods have been implemented in commercial fire detectors or used during development. Although over 2000 articles have combined elements of wavelet theory to soft computing, no book has been dedicated to that topic yet. The topic has grown to such proportions that it is not possible anymore to offer an exhaustive review. For that reason, the emphasis is placed on topics that are not specific to a particular application. A special place is given to methods that have been implemented in real-world applications. It is especially the case of the different techniques combining fuzzy logic and neural networks to wavelet theory. These methods have been implemented during the development of several products and have found applications in intelligent systems, such as fire detection.

The industry is certainly one of the driving forces behind soft computing. In many industrial products, very extensive computations are not feasible because it would make the product too costly, too slow, or sometimes the limitation may be the power consumption, for instance, in devices powered with batteries. Despite all these limitations, many products, such as sensors, require complex algorithms for data processing, and this is where soft computing finds one of its best fields of applications.

Multiresolution analysis and wavelet theory are a natural complement to soft computing methods. Soft computing solves computationally intensive problems with limited computing power and memory by giving up some precision, and multiresolution analysis can determine how and where to give up the precision. Also, several standard methods in the multiresolution analysis could be easily classified as part of soft computing. It is the case of algorithms such as the *matching pursuit* or of some wavelet-based regression and denoising methods.

The multiresolution analysis is of central importance in the mechanisms of perception and decision. Humans are particularly good at such tasks. Image processing in the brain relies heavily on analyzing the signals at several levels of resolution. Extracting details of importance out of a flow of information is an essential part of any decision process. Soft computing covers a range of methods somewhat tolerant of imprecision, uncertainty, and partial truth. Hybrid methods combining soft computing methods with wavelet theory have the potential to accommodate two central elements of the human brain, select an appropriate resolution to the description of a problem, and be somewhat tolerant of imprecision.

The main goal of this book is to present the state of integration of wavelet theory and multiresolution analysis into soft computing, represented here schematically by three of its main techniques.

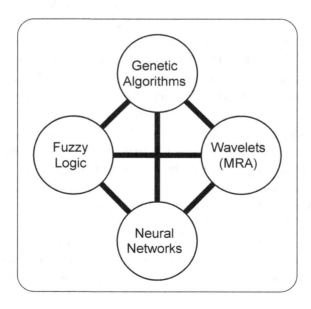

Different factors can explain the success of wavelet theory and multiresolution analysis. Wavelet theory offers both a formal and practical framework to understand problems that require the analysis of signals at several resolutions. Although several aspects of multiresolution analysis precede the development of wavelet theory, wavelet theory furnishes a unifying platform for the discussion of multiresolution signal processing. It is certainly one of the great merits of wavelet theory. From the point of view of applications, wavelet analysis possesses a very nice feature of being easily implementable.

There are several excellent books on wavelet theory (see Chui, 1992; Daubechies, 1992; Kaiser, 1994; Mallat, 1998; Meyer, 1992; Vetterli, 1995; Wickerhauser, 1994). In this book, we have deliberately chosen the view of presenting wavelet theory quite pragmatically, and the theory is limited to the minimum necessary to understand the ideas behind wavelet theory to apply them correctly. The same holds for the different soft computing techniques.

Learning is a central theme in that book. A significant development in recent years has been the recognition of the complementarity and similarities between neural networks, wavelets analysis, and fuzzy logic. The degree of maturity of the different hybrid techniques combining two or more soft computing methods is quite different. On the one hand, neuro-fuzzy has been used in numerous industrial projects. On the other hand, the combination of wavelet theory with fuzzy logic is emerging: only a few products using fuzzy wavelet techniques are now commercialized. Excellent books on neuro-fuzzy techniques have been written (see, for instance, Brown and Harris, 1994; Babuska, 1998; Jang, 1997; Kosko, 1992; Nauck, 1992; Nie and Linkens, 1995; a large range of applications can be found in recent proceedings of EUFIT or TOOLMET). As our approach follows the line of the book by Brown and Harris (1994), we refer especially to that book for an introduction to neuro-fuzzy. The main theme is the integration of wavelet theory into neuro-fuzzy methods. These hybrid techniques are referred to as fuzzy wavenets or as fuzzy wavelet networks, depending on the details of the applied method.

Overview of the book

Wavelet theory is presented in a self-contained manner, adding new concepts as they become necessary to comprehend the different hybrid methods combining wavelet theory with soft computing.

Part 1 presents wavelet theory from different complementary perspectives. It explains the first wavelet theory in simple terms by discussing the differences and the similarities between Fourier analysis and wavelet theory. In particular, the short-time Fourier transform is compared to the wavelet transform. Fundamental definitions (wavelet, orthogonality, biorthogonality, multiresolution, nested spaces) are given. After introducing multiresolution analysis from the mathematical perspective, the signal processing approach, also called subband coding, is presented. The most important algorithm, the fast wavelet decomposition algorithm, is then presented in the framework of filter theory. A wavelet decomposition can be carried out using a cascade of filters. The final sections present several examples showing the power of wavelet analysis for data compression, data analysis, and denoising. More recent developments of wavelet theory, for instance, the lifting scheme or nonlinear wavelets, are presented gradually in the following parts.

The majority of publications on applications of wavelet analysis in soft computing are in the domain of preprocessing. Wavelet preprocessing is used in many applications, from signal denoising and feature extraction to data compression. Part 2 is dedicated to wavelet theory in preprocessing. The first sections focus on two central problems in signal processing: the curse of dimensionality and the complexity issue. The curse of dimensionality is an expression that characterizes the sample size needed to estimate a function often grows exponentially with the number of variables. The complexity issue refers to the increase in computing power to solve hard problems with many inputs. In hard problems in many dimensions, both the curse of dimensionality and the complexity issues are relevant, and one can speak of a double curse. Different methods for reducing the dimension of an input space are briefly presented. The classical dimension reduction based on the Karhunen-Loève transform is explained. An important section discusses the contributions of wavelet theory to dimension reduction. The two main methods, the matching pursuit and the best basis, are presented. Wavelet theory also finds applications to exploratory knowledge extraction to discover nonlinear interactions between variables or non-significant variables. In the last sections, several representative applications combining wavelet pre-processing and soft computing are reviewed, emphasizing classification problems and applications to intelligent sensing.

Parts 3-6 are dedicated to wavelet-based methods suited to automatically developing a fuzzy system from data. It introduces first the reader to offline methods for data on a regular grid (fuzzy wavelet). In subsequent parts, online learning schemes are explained in the framework of wavelet-based neural networks and nonparametric wavelet-based estimation and regression techniques. Part 3 gives an overview of wavelet-based spline approximation and compression algorithms. Part 3 is a pre-requisite to parts 4-6 on learning. After introducing splines, the main families of spline-based wavelet constructions are presented.

Emphasis is set on approximation and compression methods based on the matching pursuit algorithm and wavelet thresholding.

Part 4 explains the connection between wavelet-based spline modeling and the Takagi-Sugeno fuzzy model in so-called fuzzy wavelet methods. It shows how wavelet modeling can automatically develop a fuzzy system from a set of data on a regular grid. One starts from a dictionary of pre-defined membership functions forming a multiresolution, and the membership functions are dilated and translated versions of a scaling function. Appropriate fuzzy rules are determined by making a wavelet decomposition, typically with B-wavelets, and keeping the most significant coefficients. Part 4 treats several issues central to applying fuzzy wavelet methods in applications (boundary processing, interpretability, and transparency of the fuzzy rules).

Part 5 is on wavelet networks. After presenting wavelet networks and wavenets and their applications, the methods in part 4 are extended to online learning. The resulting multiresolution neuro-fuzzy method permits the determination and validation of fuzzy rules online with very efficient algorithms using elements of wavelet theory. The data are modeled by an ensemble of feedforward neural networks using wavelet and scaling functions of a given resolution as activation functions. Rules are validated online by comparing the results at two consecutive resolutions with the fast wavelet decomposition algorithm. When only a few data points are known, the fuzzy rules use low-resolution membership functions. With increasing points, more rules are validated, and the fuzzy system is refined by taking higher resolution membership functions. Different approaches are explained that have in common to be easily implementable.

Part 6 presents an alternative method to the neural network approach using nonparametric wavelet-based estimation and regression techniques. After introducing (orthogonal) wavelet estimation and regression techniques, we show how to extend these techniques to biorthogonal wavelets. The main motivation is that these regression techniques may determine appropriate fuzzy rules describing an incoming flow of data points. Advantageous of that technique is that the data points do not have to be stored, and the wavelet-based validation methods described in part 5 are still applicable.

Part 7 discusses our experience with wavelet-based learning techniques pragmatically. Some reflections are made on developing optimally intelligent products using multiresolution-based fuzzy techniques. We explain how important it is to keep the man in the loop. It is vital to have a clearly defined interface between the computer-assisted learning method and the development team that allows the verification of all automatically generated rules. We show further how template methods can be applied to compare and validate the knowledge of different experts. These methods facilitate the fusion and the comparison of information from different sources (human, databank,...). With the help of this computer tool, new rules can be proposed to reconcile conflicting experts.

Part 8 explores the connections existing between genetic algorithms and wavelets. The first sections reformulated the classical discussion on deceptive functions based on Walsh partition functions within the multiresolution analysis framework. In the following sections, a very simple genetic algorithm is presented. The algorithm uses a single operator that tries to catch into a single operator some of the main features of the crossover and mutation operators in the standard genetic algorithm. Analytical results on the expected population distribution are expressed in terms of the wavelet coefficients of the fitness function. This simple model permits the discovery of some important relationships between sampling theory and multiresolution analysis. The model is generalized to multiresolution search methods at the end of this part.

Introduction to the Second Edition

This new edition is significantly enhanced compared to the original version. Many of the topics presented in the first edition have grown to full-fledge subfields with monographs on many very specialized cases. Multiresolution analysis and neural networks underwent a development similar to many other fields. After an explosive phase of rapid discovery, the area consolidated over the years with more and more specialized topics. Wavelet analysis is a well-established field, and signal compression using wavelets analysis belongs today to the classical signal processing toolbox. New and better wavelets also extended the toolbox. While wavelet analysis significantly impacts signal processing, the ideas behind multiresolution research permeate almost all fields. Multiresolution is ubiquitous today in science, and one now experiences several important developments in science in which multiresolution play a key role. For instance, algorithms integrating multiresolution techniques contributed to detecting gravity waves.

Another example is the field of deep learning. Many deep learning applications incorporate a wavelet decomposition stage to better capture features at different resolutions, a quite sensible step as the size of an object in an image may greatly vary. A fascinating aspect that we discuss in a new chapter is that multiresolution is at the heart of the functioning of deep learning.

Neural networks on graphs are important in studying communication networks and analyzing internet data. Here also, multiresolution permits a better analysis. The research community has broadly integrated the idea that the integration of multiresolution often improves algorithms. This new edition aims to capture some of these exciting new developments.

A new chapter covers multiresolution analysis in the analysis of networks, particularly of phylogenetic networks, with applications in classification going from the study of the structure of galaxies to the analysis of world myths.

This edition keeps the spirit of the original book by targeting an audience searching for an introduction to multiresolution and wavelets in soft computing. The book is structured so that the reader may rapidly start developing his applications, and each part includes the most recent developments in the field. The chapters have been slightly reorganized and extended compared to the first edition.

Part 1 contains a general introduction to wavelet theory. Several multi-resolution transformations efficiently extract smooth contours in an image. Contourlets, curvelets, and shearlets are steerable multiscale transformations that are particularly suited to the multiresolution analysis of edges. Steerable filters are central to wavelet scattering, a transformation similar to those found in convolutional neural networks but simpler to understand. Wavelet scattering networks conceptually facilitate understanding of how a convolutional neural network (CNN) works. We include a section on Empirical Wavelet Decomposition (EWD), a simple adaptive wavelet decomposition technique that found many applications (bearing fault diagnosis or wind speed prediction). It decomposes a signal into the sum of modes corresponding to the wavelet filtering of the signal on the bands associated with the main frequencies. An introduction to wavelet cross-correlation analysis completes part 1. Wavelet cross-correlation methods are powerful in identifying a correlation between frequency-rich signals. The method led to the detection of a strong correlation between severe monsoon and El Niño episodes.

Part 2 focuses on multiresolution's major contributions to preprocessing and introduces the main wavelet processing algorithms.

Part 3 introduces spline wavelets in the context of wavelet theory and fuzzy logic.

Part 4 shows how to generate automatically linguistically interpretable fuzzy rules from data using multiresolution techniques. A new section describes important developments in Neuro-Fuzzy systems, including Type-2 fuzzy logic, an approach already proposed by Zadeh in the early days of fuzzy logic to argue against the critics that the definition of fuzzy membership functions should also include uncertainty. He proposed membership functions containing the possibility of including uncertainty directly in their definition per design. Type-2 fuzzy logic became a practical method after the development of simple algorithms that allowed for better dealing with uncertainty in neuro-fuzzy and fuzzy wavelet approaches.

Part 5 (first ed. Part 6) is on Nonparametric Wavelet-Based Estimation and Regression Techniques and discusses applying the techniques to initialize wavelet or fuzzy wavelet networks.

Part 6 (first ed. Part 5) is on hybrid Neural Networks combining soft computing techniques. It extends fuzzy wavelet approaches to online learning, focusing on the rules automatic rule validation. The network is improved during learning by adaptively adding new validated rules. The part includes an overview of the main applications of fuzzy wavelet networks. A new section introduces 'Extreme Learning Machines,' an innovative approach for training neural networks suited to online learning and wavelet networks.

Part 7 is a new chapter that explains the main contributions of multiresolution analysis to deep learning. The development of deep convolutional networks, a type of neural network that uses multiple layers and many adaptable convolution filters, triggered deep learning. The field is progressing so fast that important articles are sometimes cited several thousand times a few months after being first published in archives and still unreviewed. Due to their importance, such references are also discussed.

Part 8 (first ed. Part 7) is on developing intelligent Sensors with fuzzy logic and multiresolution analysis.

Part 9 is a new chapter on the contributions of multiresolution analysis to graph analysis. The applications focus on classification using trees and networks with examples as diverse as the classification of galaxies or world myths' motifs.

Part 10 (first ed. Part 8) has a new section explaining nature-inspired search and optimization algorithms like bee swarms in the context of multiresolution analysis.

My scientific path is embedded in industrial research with its constraints bound to the feasibility and robustness of the different solutions. Many algorithms in this book are implemented in real applications. I greatly encourage young scientists and Ph.D. students to pursue their work in industrial research. Applied industrial research offers great opportunities to an open and interested mind. I always recommend that young researchers develop skills independently of their present employment to keep a fresh mind. Some chapters are not related to the companies I worked for, and I thank them greatly for their open mind. I am expressing my gratitude to the researchers who inspired me during this book's writing, with my warm thanks to Jean-Paul Marchand, Esko Juuso, Gregor Henze, Didier Fraix-Burnet, Jean-Loic Le Quellec, Julien d' Huy, Roz Frank, and Yuri Berezkin. This second edition is dedicated to Prof. Jean-Paul Marchand (Denver University) and my parents, who sadly passed away.

Contents

Introduction to Wavelet Theory

Part 1

Chapter 1

Introduction to Wavelet Theory

1.1.   A short overview of the development of wavelet theory

Wavelet analysis started in the '80s. Scientists processing recordings of seismic waves recognized the need for methods to analyze signals at different resolutions.

Multiresolution analysis has become a standard tool in signal processing. Many scientific fields benefit from multiresolution analysis, from quantum mechanics and econometrics to social sciences. Despite the large variety of wavelet applications, the primary domain of applications is still image processing. The image processing community has been using multiresolution analysis algorithms for years, and the JPEG 2000 standard uses wavelet data compression schemes.

Historically, one generally finds the roots of wavelet theory in the work of Morlet, a scientist by Elf-Aquitaine, who worked in the domain of oil research. Morlet recognized the need for signal processing techniques beyond Gabor's short-time signals analysis and modified Gabor's Gaussian window. To palliate a drawback of Gabor's approach, namely the bad resolution obtained at high frequencies due to the constant window size, he used variable-sized windows. He tagged the name wavelet, meaning little wave [Hubbard, 1998]. Due to his company's lack of funding and interest, no real-world applications appeared then. Grossmann grasped the potential of Morlet's s wavelet rapidly and contributed significantly to further developments.

Wavelet theory is an excellent example of the importance of cross-fertilization between different fields in science. An example is the development of perfect reconstruction algorithms within the filter theory community. Perfect reconstruction allows splitting a signal into downsampled subband signals and reconstructing it perfectly. After the pioneering work by Morlet and Grossmann [1984], the subsequent significant development was the axiomatic formulation of wavelet theory, mostly carried out within the mathematical community. It turned out that subband coding and wavelet theory are essentially equivalent. Possibly as important, it offered a view on multiresolution analysis that was more familiar to the signal processing community than the mathematicians' approach. The equivalency between subband coding and wavelet theory has permitted the development of efficient algorithms for wavelet decomposition and reconstruction.

The discovery of fast wavelet decomposition and reconstruction algorithms marks the beginning of a new era for wavelets. A fast wavelet decomposition consists of the iterative decomposition of a signal into coarse and detailed approximations. The fast wavelet decomposition algorithm efficiently computes the wavelet coefficients using a cascade of filters. This algorithm initially proposed by Mallat [1999] reduces the computing burden of a wavelet transform. The possibility of reconstructing the signal after decomposition has resulted in several applications in noise reduction and data compression. Complete wavelet decomposition is invertible in O(N) operations, making the wavelet transform well suited to lossless signal compression.

Wavelets of the second generation completed the wavelet toolbox. They are more flexible and permit solving significant problems, such as decomposing a signal on an irregular grid or a sphere. Second-generation wavelets are closely related to multiresolution methods used in computer graphics. An essential asset of second-generation wavelets is their geometric interpretation of wavelet theory. Second-generation wavelets furnish elegant solutions to the problem of endpoint processing that plagued wavelet methods for years.

Soft computing is now a well-established subject in computer science. It deals with solving computationally intensive problems with a limited amount of computing power and memory by giving up some of the precision. Soft computing is also often defined by its techniques, mainly neural networks, fuzzy logic, and genetic algorithms. One of the significant developments has been recognizing the complementarity and similarities between neural networks and wavelets analysis. This field is very active in connection to convolutional neural networks. Soft computing and multiresolution are, in many aspects, very complementary. Everyday experience teaches that the difference between two actions often lies in small details. Finding the crucial details is difficult since experience shows that focusing only on details leads to a tremendous waste of time and unproductive work. Finding the right balance between details and coarse features or actions is a highly human activity that finds its mathematical expression in the combination of wavelet theory and soft computing.

In part 1, we introduce the wavelet transform, an extension of the Fourier transform, following the historical development of wavelet theory. The premise of wavelet theory emerged in the context of seismic waves analysis. Before wavelet theory, the 'short-time Fourier transform' was the primary tool for processing non-stationary signals (also called the Gabor transform). Wavelet theory offers a very flexible alternative to the short-time Fourier transform. Wavelet decomposition is

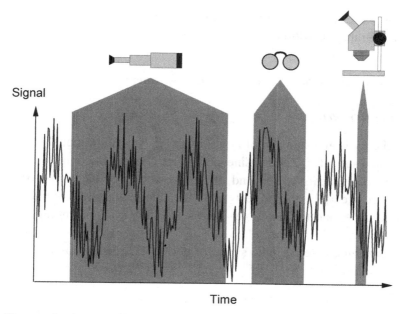

Fig. 1.1. The wavelet decomposition of a signal corresponds to a multiresolution analysis of the signal, and wavelet decomposition is a kind of mathematical microscope.

a type of mathematical microscope (Figure 1.1) in which each resolution level corresponds to a magnification factor.

The analogy between wavelet and Fourier theory offers a simple framework to grasp the main ideas behind the multiresolution analysis and wavelet theory. Both a discrete wavelet transform and a continuous wavelet transform can be defined. In a discrete wavelet decomposition, the signal is projected on a series of translated and dilated versions of a wavelet. The analogy to the discrete Fourier transform is apparent. The Fourier coefficients in the discrete Fourier transform correspond to the projection of a signal onto a series of dilated sine and cosine (the cosine is a translated version of the sine function!).

This first part will present the standard wavelet approach based on the analogy to Fourier formalism. We subsequently present wavelet theory more formally based on the axiomatic formalism of multiresolution analysis and in the framework of subband coding. The annex presents second-generation wavelets and nonlinear constructions (Annex A-B). At the end of the chapter, we present several standard and historical applications of wavelet theory, such as the compression of the FBI fingerprint data files. Quality enhancement of the only recording of Brahms playing a sonata is another early application [Berger, Coifman, and Goldberg, 1994]. The recording was of lousy quality, and transposing the music was impossible. After processing with multiresolution techniques, it became possible to compare Brahms partition with its interpretation.

1.2.   Wavelet transform versus Fourier transform

1.2.1.   Fourier series

Wavelet theory is an extension of Fourier theory. A periodic signal is represented by a weighted sum of sine and cosine in a discrete Fourier decomposition. The sine and cosine coefficients correspond to the projection of the signal on sine and cosine. More precisely, the projection on the sine and cosine is orthogonal. It is therefore unique, and the functions $\{sin(k \cdot i), cos(k \cdot i)\}$ form an orthonormal basis.

A square-integrable periodic signal of period T is decomposed into a sum of sine and cosine:

$$f(t) = \sum_k a_k \cdot sin(k \cdot i) + b_k \cdot cos(k \cdot i) \tag{1.1a}$$

with $a_k = 2 \int_0^T f(t) \cdot sin(2 \cdot \pi \cdot k \cdot t) \cdot dt;$

$$b_k = 2 \int_0^T f(t) \cdot cos(2 \cdot \pi \cdot k \cdot t) \cdot dt \tag{1.1b}$$

The below functions form an orthonormal basis:

$$\int_0^1 sin(m \cdot 2 \cdot \pi \cdot x) \cdot sin(n \cdot 2 \cdot \pi \cdot x) \cdot dx = 0, m \neq n \tag{1.2a}$$

$$\int_0^1 cos(m \cdot 2 \cdot \pi \cdot x) \cdot cos(n \cdot 2 \cdot \pi \cdot x) \cdot dx = 0, m \neq n \tag{1.2b}$$

$$\int_0^1 sin(m \cdot 2 \cdot \pi \cdot x) \cdot cos(n \cdot 2 \cdot \pi \cdot x) \cdot dx = 0, m \neq n \tag{1.2c}$$

The Fourier decomposition is invertible. A limited number of coefficients is sufficient to compute a good signal approximation in many cases. In a wavelet decomposition, one uses orthogonal time and frequency-limited functions instead of sine and cosine, intending to analyze non-periodic signals. Figure 1.2 shows an example of such a function, a so-called Daubechies wavelet [Daubechies, 1992]. The function is well localized and has a zero integral. Such a function is called a mother wavelet. A wavelet decomposition projects the signal on a series of dilated and translated versions of a mother wavelet. Similar to the Fourier transform, the projection is unique and invertible.

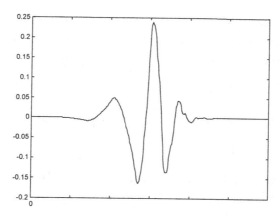

Fig. 1.2. Example of a wavelet.

1.2.2. *Continuous Fourier transform*

A second important category of Fourier transform is the continuous Fourier transform. The Fourier transform of an absolutely integrable function f(t) is defined by

$$F(\omega) = \int_{-\infty}^{\infty} f(t) \cdot exp(-i \cdot \omega \cdot t) \cdot dt \tag{1.3}$$

The inverse Fourier transform is given by

$$f(t) = \frac{1}{2\pi} \cdot \int_{-\infty}^{\infty} F(\omega) \cdot exp(i \cdot \omega \cdot t) \cdot dt \tag{1.4}$$

The power spectrum of the function f(t) is $|F(\omega)|^2$. The power spectrum measures the energy content of the signal at the different frequencies ω. The continuous Fourier transform can also be generalized to the continuous wavelet transform.

1.2.3. *Short-time Fourier transform versus wavelet transform*

Practical applications of the Fourier transform request some adaptation of the method. The main problem encountered is that a signal is seldom stationary, and the signal period tends to infinity. The signal must be integrated from 0 to infinity to satisfy the Fourier condition for convergence. Several approaches permit analyzing the signal to extract information on the local energy content of the signal or to decompose the signal so that a good signal reconstruction is possible with a limited number of coefficients. The classic approach is the short-time Fourier transform, also called the Gabor transform [Gabor, 1946].

A short-time Fourier transform is obtained by first multiplying the signal by a window function $G(t - \omega)$ and then performing the Fourier transform of the acquired signal.

$$SF(\omega, t) = \int_{-\infty}^{\infty} G^*(t - \tau) \cdot f(t) \cdot exp(-i \cdot \omega \cdot t) \cdot d\tau \qquad (1.5)$$

The window used by Gabor is the Gaussian window (Figure 1.3):

$$G(t) = a \cdot exp(-b \cdot t^2) \qquad (1.6)$$

The result of the transform depends on the time t, but also the frequency ω. The parameter b controls the width or the spread in time. Its Fourier transform is given by

$$G(\omega) = a \cdot (\pi/b)^{0.5} \cdot exp(-(\omega - \omega_0)^2/4b) \qquad (1.7)$$

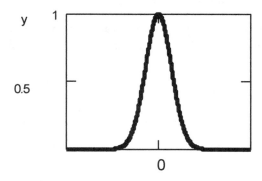

Fig. 1.3. Example of a Gaussian window (or Gabor window) used in windowed Fourier transform.

The function G(t) spread is the same as one of its translations. Similarly, the half-width of $G(\omega)$ is independent of the frequency ω_0. The signal is projected on a series of windowed functions to conduct a time-frequency analysis. Perfect reconstruction from the projection is possible, provided one uses many windows. The projection is then very redundant. Perfect reconstruction requires $O(N^2 \log_2 N)$ operations for a signal of period N [Mallat, 1999].

The short-time Fourier transform contains one of the main ideas of wavelet theory, namely the decomposition of a signal on dilated and translated versions of a basis function. Figure 1.4 compares the windows of the short-time Fourier transform to the wavelet transform. The main difference between the wavelet and the Gabor transform is that the time-frequency window of the Gabor transform is independent of the position and dilation of the window. In contrast, for the case of a wavelet transform, the time-frequency window depends on the dilation factor of the wavelet. The time window is much larger at higher frequencies than at low frequencies. This property of wavelets is, in many applications, a useful feature. Indeed, it is often desirable to have a result on the high-frequency part of the signal with a good time resolution, while a less good resolution for the low frequencies is not a problem in most applications.

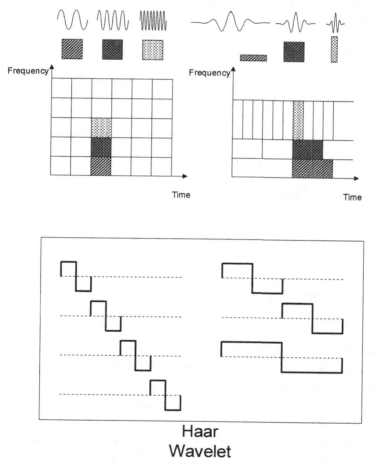

Fig. 1.4. Time-frequency tiling of the time-frequency domain. Left: Fourier transform, Right: Wavelet transform. Below: an example of dilated and translated wavelets.

1.2.4. *Discrete wavelet decomposition*

Let us start with a definition of wavelets englobing both orthogonal and non-orthogonal constructions.

Definition:
A function ψ is called a wavelet if there exists a dual function $\tilde{\psi}$ such that a function $f \in L^2(\Re)$ can be decomposed as

$$f(x) = \sum_{m,n} <f, \tilde{\psi}_{m,n}> \psi_{m,n}(x) \tag{1.8}$$

The series representation of f is called a wavelet series. The wavelet coefficients $c_{m,n}$ are given by

$$c_{m,n} = <f, \tilde{\psi}_{m,n}> \tag{1.9}$$

A function $\psi \in L^2(\Re)$ is called an orthogonal wavelet, if the family $\{\psi_{m,n}\}$ is an orthonormal basis of $L^2(\Re)$ that is

$$< \psi_{m_1,n_1}, \psi_{m_2,n_2} >= \int_{-\infty}^{\infty} \psi_{m_1,n_1}(x); \psi^*_{m_2,n_2}(x) \cdot dx = \delta_{m_1,m_1} \cdot \delta_{n_1,n_2}$$

and every $f \in L^2(\Re)$ can be written as

$$f(x) = \sum_{m,n} c_{m,n} \cdot \psi_{m,n}(x) \tag{1.10}$$

with

$$\psi_{m,n}(x) = 2^{m/2} \cdot \psi(2^m \cdot x - n) \tag{1.11}$$

$m,n \in Z$.

The wavelet coefficients $c_{m,n}$ of orthogonal wavelets are given by $c_{m,n} = <f, \psi_{m,n}>$. It follows that for an orthogonal wavelet, the dual function $\tilde{\psi}$ is identical to the wavelet ψ.

The definition of an orthogonal wavelet is quite similar to the Fourier series. The only difference lies in the candidates' functions for the projection. By projecting the signal on wavelets, the condition that the function must be periodic to guarantee perfect reconstruction is unnecessary. In a Fourier series, cosine and sine form the basis functions together with integer dilated of the two basis functions $cos(2\omega t)$ and $sin(2\omega t)$. In orthogonal wavelets, dilated and translated versions of a function are taken: $\psi_{m,n}(x) = 2^{m/2} \cdot \psi(2^m \cdot x - n)$. The dilation factor is also different (m versus 2^m).

The simplest example of an orthogonal wavelet is the Haar wavelet (Figure 1.5), defined as

$$\psi_H(x) = \begin{array}{ll} 1 & 0 < y \leq 1/2 \\ -1 & 1/2 < x \leq 1 \\ 0 & otherwise \end{array} \tag{1.12}$$

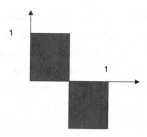

Fig. 1.5. An example of an orthogonal wavelet: the Haar wavelet.

The orthogonality of the Haar wavelet can be easily verified, as schematically explained in Figure 1.6.

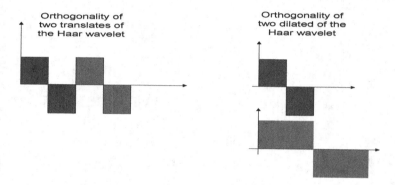

Fig. 1.6. The Haar wavelets form an orthonormal basis.

1.2.5. *Continuous wavelet transform*

As for the Fourier analysis, there is a continuous wavelet transform. The integral wavelet transform is defined by

$$W_\psi f(a, b) = 1/\sqrt{a} \int_{-\infty}^{\infty} f(x) \cdot \psi^*(\frac{x-b}{a}) dx \tag{1.13}$$

Contrarily to the wavelet series, the factor a is continuous. The interpretation of the wavelet transform is generally tricky and not too intuitive. Figure 1.7 shows an example of a continuous wavelet transform. The values of the wavelet transform are grey-coded.

Applications of continuous wavelet analysis followed theoretical break-throughs in multiple domains like vibration monitoring [Staszewski, 1997], heart rhythm perturbations monitoring [Thonet *et al.*, 1998], power system waveform analysis [Pham and Wong, 1999], ship detection [Magli, Olmo, and Presti, 1999].

Atmospheric and oceanographic modeling [Torrence and Compo, 1998] is crucial in El Nino's studies. El Nino corresponds to a phase in which warm water poor in nutrients surges along the south American coast due to the periodic variation of the water currents. The analysis of sea surface temperature with the continuous wavelet analysis has shown that the El Nino-southern oscillation index was significantly higher during some periods (1880-1920 and 1960-90). Considering the devastating effects of El Nino, such studies are of vital importance to the future of many South American countries. An increase in El Nino due to pollutants might ruin the economy of these countries by causing enormous problems to fishery and agriculture.

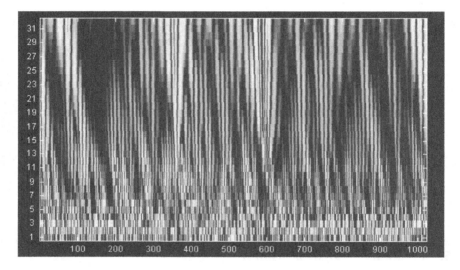

Fig. 1.7. Continuous wavelet transform of the logistic map: $x(n + 1) = 4 \cdot x(n) \cdot (1 - x(n))$.

1.3.   The fast wavelet transform

The Fast Fourier Transform is probably one of the algorithms that most influenced science and engineering. The main idea of the FFT is already in a paper by Gauss, and James Cooley and John Tukey formulated it in 1965. The FFT reduces from N^2 to $N \log_2 N$ the number of necessary operations for a Fourier transform of a signal with N values. We will show that a fast wavelet transform exists similarly to the Fourier transform.

From a practical point of view, the fast wavelet transform is the most important algorithm in multiresolution analysis. Before using it in an application, good knowledge of the fast wavelet transform algorithm is recommended.

The fast wavelet transform permits the computation of the wavelet transform; at each level of the transform, a low-pass and a high-pass filter process the data. The high-pass filtered data are known as the detail wavelet coefficients. The result of the low-pass transform is used as input data to compute the next level of detail wavelet coefficients.

To explain the fast wavelet transform algorithm, we will first introduce new concepts representing multiresolution analysis foundations.

1.3.1. *The dilation equations (or two-scales relations)*

We will not discuss here in many details how to construct wavelets, and we will restrict our discussion to the main ideas behind the construction scheme. From the practical point of view, it is generally sufficient to know the main properties of the different wavelet families to choose the best wavelet family appropriately for an application. As we will see in the next chapter, a wavelet analysis reduces to a cascade of filters. It is therefore essential to understand the properties of the filters. The properties of the wavelet family associated with the filter determine the symmetry of the wavelet coefficients.

One of the essential concepts of multiresolution analysis is the definition of nested spaces. Nested spaces are like Russian dolls. The larger dolls contain the smaller ones. Figure 1.8 shows an example of a nested space, together with a representation of the complementary spaces W_0 and W_{-1}.

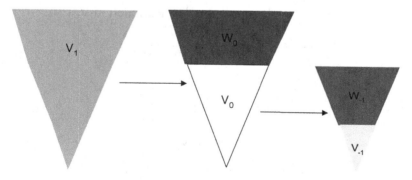

Fig. 1.8. Example of nested spaces: $V_{-1} \subset V_0 \subset V_1$. The space W_{-1} is the complementary space of V_{-1} with $W_{-1} \oplus V_{-1}$. Similarly, $V_0 = W_0 \oplus V_0$.

The concept of nested spaces [Daubechies, 1992] is applied to spaces generated by linear combinations of a function, say ϕ. We define V_1 as the space generated by $\varphi(2x)$, and its integer translates. The space V_1 corresponds to all possible combinations of ϕ and its integer translates: V1: $\{\varphi(2x - n)\}$. Let us now consider a second space, V_0, generated by the 2x dilated function $\phi(x)$ and its translates: V_0: $\{\varphi(x - n)\}$. The space V_0 is nested in V_1 if $V_0 \subset V_1$. Generally speaking, it follows from $V_0 \subset V_1$ that any function in V_0 is a linear combination of the functions generating V_1.

$$\varphi(x) = \sum_n g_n \cdot \varphi(2x - n) \tag{1.14}$$

Since $V_0 \subset V_1$, the space V_0 is so as $V_1 = V_0 \oplus W_0$. The space W_0 is the complement of the space V_0. Following the same line of thought as previously, we have $W_0 \subset V_1$ which follows that any function ψ in W_0 is a linear combination of the basis functions in V_1.

$$\psi(x) = \sum_n h_n \cdot \varphi(2x - n) \tag{1.15}$$

The two equations are the so-called dilation equations or two-scales relations. These two equations are central to reconstructing a signal starting from the wavelet coefficients (or detail coefficients) and the lowest level of approximation coefficients. Also, most constructions of new types of wavelets start from the dilation equations (we come back to this point as we will sketch how to build wavelets).

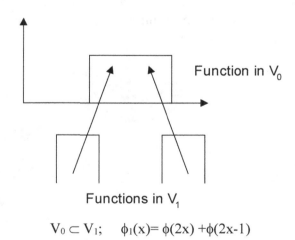

$$V_0 \subset V_1; \quad \phi_1(x) = \phi(2x) + \phi(2x-1)$$

Fig. 1.9. Example illustrating the dilation equation for the characteristic function.

For example, let us take the characteristic function, then V_0 is the space of piecewise constant functions consisting of zero-order polynomials defined on [n,n+1] with n an integer. In Figure 1.9, the 2x dilated characteristic function generates a space V_0 nested in V_1: $V_0 \subset V_1$. Any function in V_0 is a linear combination of the generating functions in V_1. Figure 1.10 shows another example using a second-order spline function.

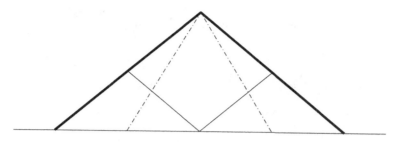

Fig. 1.10. Illustration of the two-scales relation for the second-order B-spline. The triangular spline function is the sum of translated triangular functions at the higher level of resolution.

1.3.2. *Decomposition and reconstruction algorithms*

Since $V_1 = V_0 \oplus W_0$, a function in V_1 is the sum of two functions with the first function in V_0 and the second function in W_0. It follows that a basis function in V_1 is the weighted sum of the basis functions of V_0 and W_0 (for an exact derivation of the relation below, see Chui [1997])

$$\varphi(2x - k) = \sum_k p_{k-2n} \cdot \varphi(x - n) + q_{k-2n} \cdot \psi(x - n) \tag{1.16}$$

$k \in Z$.

This relation is called the decomposition relation. The function ϕ is the scaling function, while the function ψ is the mother wavelet.

The decomposition algorithm of a function $f \in V_1$ is computed from the decomposition relation (Figure 1.11). One obtains

$$c_{m-1,n} = \sum_k p_{k-2n} \cdot c_{m,k} \tag{1.17a}$$

$$d_{m-1,n} = \sum_k q_{k-2n} \cdot c_{m,k} \tag{1.17b}$$

$$f_{m-1}(x) = \sum_k \sum_n c_{m.k} \cdot p_{k-2n} \cdot \varphi_{m-1.k} + d_{m.k} \cdot q_{k-2n} \cdot \psi_{m-1.k} \tag{1.18}$$

The decomposition algorithm can be used iteratively in a cascade of filters so that a function f becomes:

$$f = g_0 + g_{-1} + g_{-2} + \ldots + g_{-N} + f_{-N} \tag{1.19}$$

with $g_{-j} \in W_{-j}$.

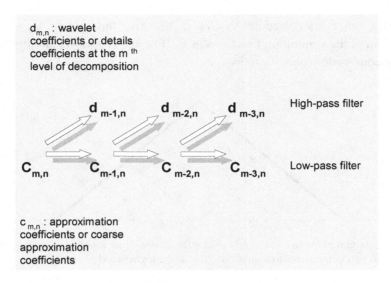

Fig. 1.11. Decomposition algorithm.

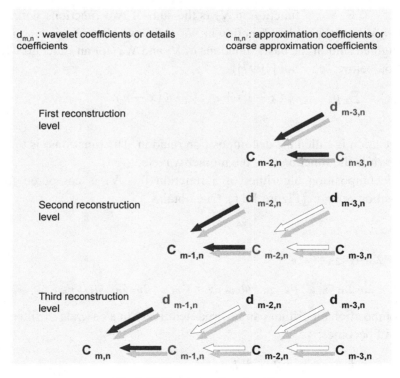

Fig. 1.12. Reconstruction algorithm.

The following algorithm gives the reconstruction algorithm:

$$c_{m,n} = \sum_k g_{n-2k} \cdot c_{m-1,k} + h_{n-2k} \cdot d_{m-1,k} \qquad (1.20)$$

The two-scale relation defines the coefficients g and h. The proof is similar to the decomposition algorithm, and we will skip it.

The fast wavelet decomposition corresponds to a cascade of filters. A low-pass and high pass filter iteratively process the signal. The detail coefficients correspond to the high-passed signal coefficients, while the approximation

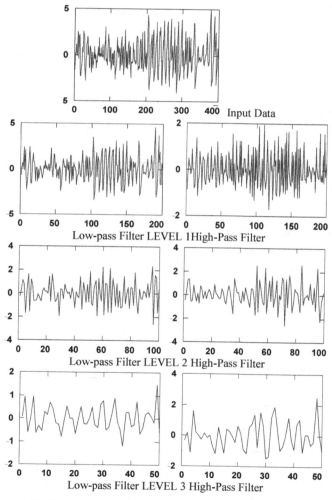

Fig. 1.13. Example of a wavelet decomposition with a Haar wavelet.

coefficients result from the low-pass filtering. The low-pass coefficients are then decimated by a factor of two and used as an input signal at the next level of resolution. After the decimation, one processes the data with the same two filters. The decomposition is invertible. The signal can be reconstructed iteratively from the detail coefficients and the last level coefficients of the low-pass filter, as shown in Figure 1.12.

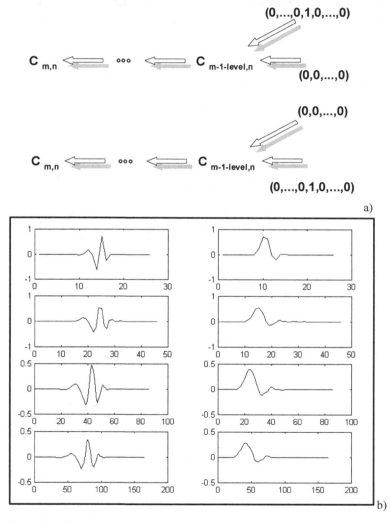

Fig. 1.14. The scaling function and wavelet are computed with the reconstruction algorithm setting all but one value to zero as input. a) Top: wavelet; Bottom: scaling function; b) Left: Approximation of the Daubechies-4 wavelet at the four first levels; right: Approximation of the Daubechies-4 scaling function at the four first levels.

The filter coefficients corresponding to an orthogonal wavelet family are generated from a single filter defined by its Fourier transform. The filter coefficients for the decomposition and the reconstruction algorithms are the same, making the filter very simple and efficient. An orthogonal decomposition is often optimal for data compression since there is no redundancy in an orthogonal decomposition. Figure 1.13 shows an example of a wavelet decomposition using orthogonal wavelets.

The associated wavelet is constructed by setting a unique value to one at the lowest level of the wavelet decomposition. The wavelet approximation is refined at each reconstruction level, as shown in Figure 1.14.

1.4. Definition of a multiresolution

In the previous section, we presented some of the main concepts behind multi-resolution informally. As a complement, we will give an exact definition of a multiresolution following Daubechies' book, Ten Lectures on Wavelets [1992]. This definition is broadly accepted and forms the foundation of wavelet theory. A multiresolution analysis consists of a sequence of embedded closed subspaces $\dots V_2 \subset V_1 \subset V_0 \subset V_{-1} \dots$ with the following properties:

- Upward completeness
  $\bigcup_{m \in Z} V_m = L_2(R)$ (the ensemble of square-integrable functions on R in a Hilbert space)
- Downward Completeness
  $\bigcap_{m \in Z} V_m = \{0\}$
- Scale Invariance
  $f(x) \in V_m \Leftrightarrow f(2^m x) \in V_0$
- Shift invariance
  $f(x) \in V_0 \Leftrightarrow f(x - n,) \in V_0$ for all $n \in Z$
- Existence of a Basis
  There exists $\phi \in V_0$ such that
  $\{\phi(x - n) | n \in Z\}$
  is an orthonormal basis for V_0.

The above definition is axiomatically fundamental, as it permits to define and verify in practice if a basis forms a multiresolution.

1.5. Biorthogonal wavelets

A second central definition in wavelet theory is the definition of a Riesz basis [Mallat, 1999].

A family $\{\phi_n\}$ of a Hilbert space H is a Riesz basis if for any $y \in$ H, there exists A>0, B>0 such that

$$A\|y\|^2 \le \Sigma_n|< y, \phi_n >|^2 \le B\|y\|^2 \tag{1.21}$$

and $\{\phi_n\}$ are linearly independent.

A Riesz basis is a basis with relaxed orthogonality conditions. The usefulness of the concept of the Riesz basis will become apparent soon. A theorem [Mallat, 1998] states that if $\{\phi_n\}$ is a Riesz basis; then there exists a dual basis $\{\tilde{\phi}_n\}$ such that a function y in H is decomposed as

$$y = \Sigma_{n \in Z} < y, \tilde{\phi}_n >\cdot \phi_n = \Sigma_{n \in Z} < y, \phi_n >\cdot \tilde{\phi}_n \tag{1.22}$$

From this expression, one shows that the bases $\{\tilde{\phi}_n\}$ and $\{\phi_n\}$ fulfill the following biorthogonality condition. Biorthogonality is obtained from (1.22). Setting $y = \phi_p$, one gets

$$\phi_p = \Sigma_{n \in Z} < \phi_p, \tilde{\phi}_n >\cdot \phi_n \tag{1.23}$$

Since the basis is formed of linearly independent functions, the equation follows

$$< \phi_p, \tilde{\phi}_n >= \delta(p - n) \tag{1.24}$$

This relation is called the biorthogonality condition. For an orthogonal basis function, $\phi_p = \tilde{\phi}_p$ and the expression reduces to the orthogonality condition. A second important theorem states that if a sequence of subspaces satisfies the definition of a multiresolution, then there exists an orthogonal basis $\{\psi_{m,n}\}$ for the orthogonal complement of V_m in V_{m-1} with

$$\psi_{m,n} = 2^{m/2} \cdot \psi(2^m x - n) \tag{1.25}$$

In other words, the space spanned by V_m and its orthogonal complement W_m is the space V_{m-1}: $V_m \oplus W_m = V_{m-1}$.

In the orthogonal case, the function ψ is constructed by writing

$$\varphi(x) = 2^{-1/2} \cdot \Sigma_{n \in Z} g[n] \cdot \varphi(2x - n) \tag{1.26}$$

$$\psi(x) = 2^{-1/2} \cdot \Sigma_{n \in Z} h[n] \cdot \varphi(2x - n) \tag{1.27}$$

Taking the Fourier transform, one obtains, after some manipulation, an expression relating the Fourier transform of g to the Fourier transform of h:

$$H(e^{j\omega}) = -e^{-j\omega} \cdot G^*(e^{j(\omega+\pi)}) \tag{1.28}$$

or in the time domain:

$$h[n] = (-1)^n \cdot g[-n+1] \tag{1.29}$$

Inserting (1.29) in (1.25), one obtains

$$\psi(x) = 2^{-1/2} \cdot \sum_{n\in\mathbb{Z}}(-1)^n \cdot g[-n+1] \cdot \varphi(2x-n) \tag{1.30}$$

A wavelet $\psi(x)$ function decomposes into a weighted sum of scaling functions $\varphi(2x-n)$.

1.6. Wavelets and subband coding

Researchers with a background in physics and mathematics invented wavelet theory. Subband coding was developed mainly within the electrical engineering community [Croisier, 1976] by designing filters to split a signal into downsampled subband signals. The process is invertible, which allows a perfect signal reconstruction, and these filters are called perfect reconstruction filters. Both communities realized the similarity between the two subjects [Vetterli, 1984; Vetterli and Herley, 1992]. The recognition that the wavelet series formulation and the theory of perfect reconstruction filter banks are deeply related is a significant achievement in signal processing. From the practical point of view, the understanding that subband coding was equivalent to wavelet theory had significant practical implications by relating multiresolution analysis to filter theory. Figure 1.15 shows an example of perfect reconstruction filters associated with Daubechies wavelet. The two filters have complementary powers summing up to one.

We will present subband coding briefly, emphasizing the similarities to the approach presented in the previous sections. We will introduce some new aspects better explained within the framework of subband coding. In particular, we describe the conditions on the filters to ensure perfect reconstruction.

Let us show the close connection between wavelet theory and filter theory by looking first at series expansions of discrete-time series. As illustrated in Figure 1.15, an orthogonal expansion conserves the signal energy. This property is

$$|\,T(\omega)|^{\,2}$$

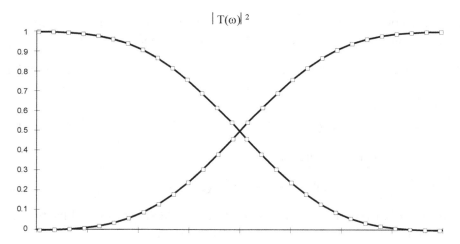

Fig. 1.15. Filter characteristics of two filters satisfying the power complementarity condition (Daubechies-4.).

very useful for spectral analysis, as the energy in the different subbands equals the total signal energy. Biorthogonal expansions extend series expansions to a large number of filters. Several methods require the use of biorthogonal expansions. Wavelet-based fuzzy methods discussed later in the book are such an example. Consider a signal x[n]. An orthogonal expansion of x[n] on an orthogonal basis $\{\phi_k\}$ is

$$x[n] = \sum_{k \in Z} X[k] \cdot \phi_k[n] \tag{1.31}$$

with

$$X[n] = \sum_{k \in Z} \phi_k^*[n] \cdot x[n] = < \phi_k^*, x[n] > \tag{1.32}$$

Energy conservation is expressed under the form:

$$\|x\|^2 = \|X\|^2 \tag{1.33}$$

For dual bases $\{\phi_k\}, \{\tilde{\phi}_k\}$ satisfying the biorthogonality condition

$$< \phi_k[n], \tilde{\phi}_l[n] > = \delta[k - l] \tag{1.34}$$

the biorthogonal expansion is given by one of the two expansions:

$$x[n] = \sum_{k \in Z} X[k] \cdot \phi_k[n] \tag{1.35a}$$

$$x[n] = \sum_{k \in Z} \tilde{X}[k] \cdot \tilde{\phi}_k[n] \tag{1.36a}$$

with

$$X[n] = \sum_{k \in Z} \phi_k^*[n] \cdot x[n] = < \phi_k^*, x[n] > \tag{1.35b}$$

$$\tilde{X}[n] = \sum_{k \in Z} \tilde{\phi}_k^*[n] \cdot x[n] = < \tilde{\phi}_k^*, x[n] > \tag{1.36b}$$

Similarly to the continuous series expansion, the expansion is stable provided there exists A>0 and B>0 such that

$$A \cdot \sum_n |X[k]|^2 \le \|x\|^2 \le B \cdot \sum_n |X[k]|^2 \tag{1.37}$$

In the biorthogonal case, energy conservation (1.33) is replaced by a different energy conservation relation:

$$\|x\|^2 = < X[k], \tilde{X}[k] > \tag{1.38}$$

The link between filter banks and wavelet theory permits efficient implementations of the wavelet ideas in practical applications. Following the line of presentation by [Vetterli and Kovacevic, 1995], let us discuss these algorithms.

Consider the four filters P, Q, G, H with the impulse responses p, q, g, h satisfying the relations

$$\phi_{2k}[n] = g[2k - n] \tag{1.39a}$$

$$\phi_{2k+1}[n] = h[2k - n] \tag{1.39b}$$

$$\tilde{\phi}_{2k}[n] = p[n - 2k] \tag{1.39c}$$

$$\tilde{\phi}_{2k+1}[n] = q[n - 2k] \tag{1.39d}$$

The filters P Q correspond to the decomposition filter coefficients (1.17-18), while the filters G H are the reconstruction filters. After some manipulations, one may show that perfect reconstruction is achieved if the following relation is fulfilled:

$$\sum_{k \in Z} g[k] \cdot p[2n - k] = \delta[n] \tag{1.40}$$

$$\sum_{k \in Z} h[k] \cdot q[2n - k] = \delta[n] \tag{1.41}$$

In other words, perfect recognition is achieved if the biorthogonality relations (1.34) are fulfilled.

All the filter coefficients can be derived from just one filter for an orthogonal basis. The impulse responses p, q, g, h are given by

$$h[n] = (-1)^n \cdot g[2K - 1 - n] \tag{1.42a}$$

$$p[n] = g[-n] \tag{1.42b}$$

$$q[n] = h[-n] \tag{1.42c}$$

with K the filter length.

Wavelet construction uses the Fourier approach, the lifting scheme, or the z-transform. The z-transform is defined as $F(z) = \sum_{n=0}^{\infty} f[n] \cdot z^{-n}$. Using the z-transform, the perfect reconstruction condition is:

$$P(z) \cdot G(z) + Q(z) \cdot H(z) = 2 \tag{1.43a}$$

$$P(z) \cdot G(-z) + Q(z) \cdot H(-z) = 0 \tag{1.43b}$$

Many wavelet constructions start from the above expression [Mallat, 1999].

The diagram in Figure 1.16 describes a two-channel filter bank. The symbol with the arrow pointing towards the bottom represents downsampling, while the reverse arrow is for upsampling.

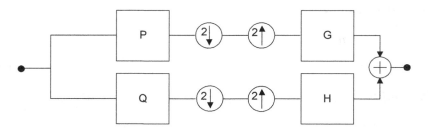

Fig. 1.16. Two channels filter bank with analysis filters P, Q and synthesis filters G, H.

1.7. Contourlets and shearlet

The 2-D wavelet decomposition is not always optimal for image processing tasks. The dyadic transform is not shift-invariant, and the transform has difficulties capturing discontinuities such as lines or curves. They are not ideal for recognizing continuous boundaries. Simoncelli and Freeman [1995] developed steerable filter multiscale pyramids. The filters are steerable by using rotation operators. The decomposition is invertible. Contourlets [Do and Vetterli, 2005] and curvelets [Candes and Donoho, 2000] are steerable multiscale transformations particularly suited to the multiresolution analysis of edges. The contourlet is a multiresolution transform that efficiently extracts smooth contours in an image. The transformation is invertible, and a filter bank makes it quite efficient. The contourlet cascades

Laplace transforms and directional filters. The number of directional filters (a power of two) decreases at low resolution. Figure 1.17 shows the Laplacian operator's filter bank structure and directional filters at the top. The bottom images show the high-resolution shearlet of the 'thinker' of Hamangia, an old Neolithic site in Romania.

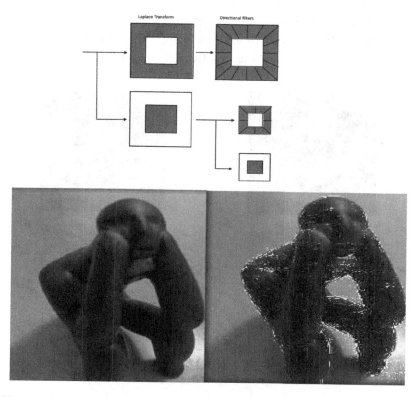

Fig. 1.17. Top: the filter bank structure comprising a Laplacian operator and directional filters. Bottom left: test image; right: high-resolution contourlet fused with it. The contourlet cascade Laplace transforms with the directional filters. The number of directional filters (a power of two) decreases at a low resolution. The white points indicate the position of the most significant contourlet coefficients.

Easley, Labate, and Lim [2008] proposed a novel approach using the discrete shearless transform. Contrarily to the contourlet, the shearlet transform does not use filter banks. Image processing is in the Fourier space, and the IFFT processes the different decompositions levels back to the real domain.

The shearlet transform is obtained from a function ψ using a translation, a dilation operator $A = \begin{pmatrix} a & 0 \\ 0 & \sqrt{a} \end{pmatrix}$ as in a wavelet transform, and a shear operator described by a matrix $M = \begin{pmatrix} 1 & s \\ 0 & 1 \end{pmatrix}$ completes the transform. The shearlet has the

form $a^{-3/4} \psi(\begin{pmatrix} \frac{1}{a} & -\frac{s}{a} \\ 0 & \frac{1}{\sqrt{a}} \end{pmatrix}(x - t))$ with $\begin{pmatrix} \frac{1}{a} & -\frac{s}{a} \\ 0 & \frac{1}{\sqrt{a}} \end{pmatrix} = A^{-1}M^{-1}$ [Häuser and Steidl,

2012]. The shearlet transform uses different versions in the frequency domain (low-frequency range and the high-frequency range divided into two cones). Figure 1.18 shows the reconstructed image using the shearlets corresponding to horizontal and vertical bands and the low-frequency transform.

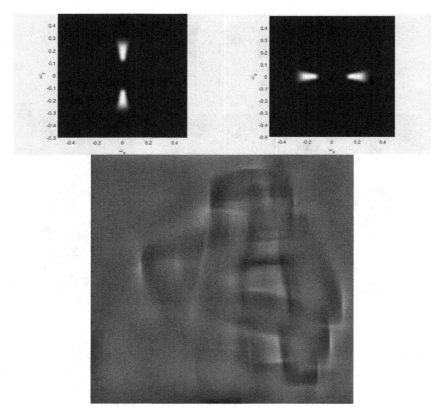

Fig. 1.18. Top: frequency band of directional filters (horizontal and vertical with no shearing); bottom: image reconstruction in Figure 1.17 using only no shearing bands.

Image fusion is one of the main applications of multiresolution analysis. The typical application consists of extracting the relevant information in multispectral images of the same object, satellite images in different spectra, or images obtained with varying techniques in medicine (X-ray, MRI,…). After realignments, image fusion typically uses mean, min, or max operators or more complex procedures. Shearlets and contourlets are preferred in image fusion [Miao *et al.*, 2011] over wavelets due to their superior capabilities to treat edges and curves [Tan *et al.*, 2020]. The quality of the fused image is better on shift-invariant transformed coefficients. Multiresolution schemes without downsampling are preferentially used in such applications [Da Cunha, Zhou, and Do, 2006]. Shearlet image fusion using neural networks furnishes excellent results [Geng *et al.*, 2012]. Shearlets and contourlets have found applications in most domains of wavelets applications, including denoising, texture analysis, and classification [Zhou *et al.*, 2013].

1.7.1. *Wavelet scattering technique*

Stephane Mallat [2012] introduced the wavelet scattering technique. Wavelet scattering has applications in classification [Singh and Kingsbury, 2017] as in palm vein recognition; a biometric technique successfully implemented as a method of access control [Elnasir, Shamsuddin, and Farokhi, 2015]. The method uses directional filters. Figure 1.19 shows images obtained with wavelet scattering at different angles at a given resolution scale. In a physics application, Eickenberg *et al.* [2018] simulate molecule properties. The scattering transform uses shift and rotation-invariant operators to separate the interactions at different scales and across scales, with cascaded wavelet transforms. According to the authors, 'scattering coefficients have the same invariance and stability properties as a quantum energy functional: they are invariant to rigid body motion and stable to deformations of the input density.'

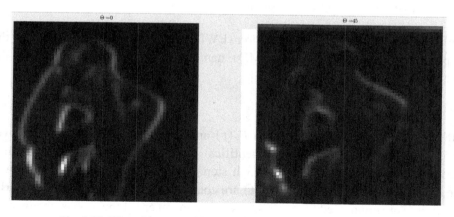

Fig. 1.19. Filtered images with wavelet scattering at 0 and 45° angles.

Wavelet Scattering (WS) is conceptually very interesting. The properties of WS are very similar to the ones found in convolutional neural networks but simpler to understand. Wavelet scattering networks did open the door to understanding how a convolutional neural network (CNN) works. Bruna and Mallat [2013] developed a new deep learning method based on their understanding of some of the central features of CNN. The network stacks several layers with a similar architecture. At the first level, the signal is filtered with a low-frequency scaling function:

$$S0 \, x[n] = x * \varphi [n] \qquad (1.44)$$

At the next level, the signal is convoluted with a wavelet function, and the result convoluted with the scaling function

$$S1 \, x[n] = | x * \psi (\lambda 1)| * \varphi J [n] \qquad (1.45)$$

with the function $\psi (\lambda 1)$ belonging to a wavelet dictionary. After subsampling, one repeats the above transformation at the next level

$$S2 \, x[n] = || x * \psi (\lambda 1)| * \psi (\lambda 2)| * \varphi [n] \qquad (1.46)$$

The low-pass filter is the equivalent of pooling in CNN, and wavelet filtering with fixed coefficients replaces the convolution. Instead of learning the convolution filters, the system chooses the most appropriate functions in a wavelet dictionary to describe the classification objective. The method reaches comparable results to some state-of-the-art deep learning algorithms in image processing.

1.8.   Empirical wavelet decomposition

The Empirical Wavelet Decomposition (EWD) follows the same purpose as the Empirical Mode Decomposition (EMD), namely, to decompose a signal into the sum of functions [Huang *et al.*, 1998].

$$f(t) = \sum_{k=0}^{N} f_k(t) \qquad (1.47)$$

with $f_k(t) = F_k(t) \cos(\varphi_k(t))$ with $F_k(t)$ and $\varphi'_k(t) > 0$ slowly varying over time. The method empirically identifies the oscillatory modes and then decomposes the data accordingly. Each step of the algorithm works as follows. The local maxima of the function $f(t)$ are connected by a cubic spline. Similarly, the minima are connected by cubic splines. The mean envelope m(t) is obtained by averaging the two functions. The first candidate is $r_1(t) = f(t) - m(t)$. If the function $r_1(t)$ does not fulfill the conditions on $f_k(t)$ then the process is iterated on $r_1(t)$ to obtain $r_2(t)$. One iterates then till the function $r_n(t) = f_1$ is so that $f_1(t) = F_1(t)\cos(\varphi_1(t))$ with $F_1(t)$ and $\varphi'_1(t) > 0$ slowly varying over time. The process is repeated on the residue $f(t) - f_1(t)$.

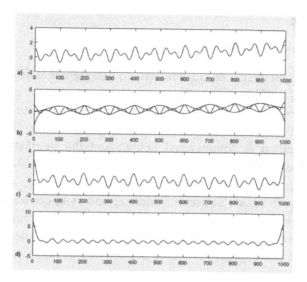

Fig. 1.20. Empirical mode decomposition of a function (a) is computed by relating the local maxima and minima by two cubic splines (b); (c) residue r_1; the function $f_1(t)$ after five iterations.

Figure 1.20 illustrates the different steps of the decomposition. First, a cubic spline connects the local maxima and minima of the function. The residue r_1 is represented in Figure 1.20c. The lower plot shows the first mode after five iterations. Gilles [2013] did extend the empirical mode decomposition to wavelets. The algorithm is quite different. It starts by identifying the N main frequencies ω_k (k=1,...,N) in the Fourier power spectrum. In a second step, one divides the spectrum into frequency bands centered at the medium position between two adjacent frequencies: $(\omega_k + \omega_{k+1})/2$. One associates wavelets and scaling to each band in the Fourier domain [Gilles, 2013]. The modes $f_k(t)$ correspond to the wavelet filtering of the signal on the bands associated with the main frequencies.

Bearing fault diagnosis is a classical application of wavelet applications. Gougam *et al.* [2019] combine feature extraction with the empirical wavelet transform to a fuzzy classifier separating the different issues into several classes of defaults, with a supplementary class for healthy bearings. In another approach to the same problem [Deng *et al.*, 2018], the fuzzy entropy values of the EWT serve as input to an SVM classifier. Zhao *et al.* [2017] describe the concept of fuzzy entropy for a time series. In other systems, bearing failures are classified by measuring the power contained in each band. Prediction is another application of empirical wavelet networks. One application predicts wind speed with a deep network supplied with the EWL components [Liu, Mi, and Li, 2018].

1.8.1. *Wavelet cross-correlation and coherence analysis*

Wavelet cross-correlation measures the similarity of two signals at different scales. Torrence and Compo [1998] have introduced to a large audience the cross-wavelet correlation. Given two time series following a white or red noise, they show that the power function of the cross-wavelet correlation has a similar distribution to a chi-square. The method is summarized below, and the interested reader is encouraged to read the original article. Software is publically available [Grinsted, Moore, and Jevrejeva, 2004].

White noise has zero mean, constant variance, and is uncorrelated in time. White noise has a power spectrum uniformly spread across all frequencies. Red noise also has zero mean constant variance but is serially correlated in time. A simple model for red noise generation uses the univariate lag-1 autoregressive process with

$$x_{n+1} = r\, x_n + z \qquad\qquad (1.48)$$

The lag-1 correlation coefficient of x(t+1) and x(t) is r with 0<r<1, z is Gaussian white noise. Red noise describes time series in meteorology or finance quite well. For instance, it describes the evolution of cloud cover [Eastman, Wood, and Bretherton, 2016] from a Lagrangian perspective (the observer follows a fluid parcel). Another example of a time series described as a red noise is the sea surface temperature during an El Niño event.

The continuous wavelet analysis allows the analysis of such phenomena in the time-frequency domain. The continuous wavelet transform of a discrete sequence x_n is defined as the convolution of x_n with a translated, scaled, and normalized wavelet:

$$W_n(s) = \sum_{n'=0}^{N-1} x_{n'} \psi^* \left(\frac{((n'-n)\delta t)}{s} \right) \qquad\qquad (1.49)$$

The wavelet function is normalized to unit energy to compare the above transform at different scales. After normalization, the wavelet power is $|W_n(s)|^2$. Following Gilman, Fuglister, and Mitchell Jr [1963], $\frac{|W_n(s)|^2}{\sigma^2}$ is distributed as $P_k \chi^2$ with P_k the discrete normalized Fourier power spectrum

$$P_k = \frac{(1-r^2)}{1+r^2-2r\cos(2\frac{\pi k}{N})}$$

(1.50)

with N, the number of data and k=0,..., N/2 the frequency index and σ^2 the variance of the time series. The distribution of the wavelet power follows a χ^2 distribution (Chi-square):

Given two time-series X and Y, the cross-wavelet spectrum is defined as

$$W_n^{XY}(s) = W_n^X(s)\, W_n^{Y*}(s)$$

(1.51)

and the cross-wavelet power is $|W_n^{XY}(s)|^2$. Confidence levels are derived from the chi-square distributions on X and Y [Jenkins, 1968]. The analysis of the data in a window (time and frequency) refines the analysis. After smoothing with a function S, Torrence and Webster (1998) define the wavelet coherence as

$$R(X,Y) = \frac{|S(W^{XY}/s)|^2}{S\left(\frac{[W^x]^2}{s}\right)S\left(\frac{[W^x]^2}{s}\right)}$$

(1.52)

Grinsted, Moore, and Jevrejeva [2004] show an inverse correlation between sea level pressure anomalies in the artic pole and the maximum ice level in the Baltic. The Baltic Sea is a transition zone between the North Atlantic region with an exchange of atmospheric mass with the Arctic, and therefore the correlation is plausible. The correlation between severe monsoon and El Niño episodes is also quite interesting. Maraun and Kurths [2005] found that 18 out of 28 strong winter monsoon years are before the development of an El Niño or during the decaying La Niña event. Vacha and Barunik [2012] analyze the price of heating oil, gasoline, and crude oil. They show that the three commodities strongly co-move, and natural gas is unrelated to all three for all investment horizons. A well-diversified energy portfolio may combine natural gas and oil. Bilgili [2015] shows that renewables' consumption has a significant positive impact on industrial production, hence, on economic growth, in lower and higher frequencies in the USA.

Mihanović, Orlić, and Pasarić [2009] generalize the wavelet coherence to the case of multiple time series. After removal of the effect of a single signal Z, the (squared) partial wavelet coherence is

$$RP^2(y, x, Z) = \frac{|1-R(x,y,Z)|^2|R(x,y)|^2}{|(1-R(y,Z)|^2\,|(1-R(x,Z)|^2}$$

(1.53)

Hu and Si (2021) extend the analysis to several variables and give the formula for multiple wavelet coherence together with a software code. The study of wavelet coherence is also valuable for finance analysts. Goodell and Goutte [2021] show a correlation between COVID-19 deaths and Bitcoin value. During hard COVID-19 episodes, bitcoin serves as a financial refuge. In medicine, the wavelet coherence of the signals of two electrodes measuring brain activity with EKG helps distinguish healthy patients from patients possibly developing Alzheimer's [Sankari, Adeli, and Adeli, 2012].

1.9.   Applications

It is not possible anymore to offer a complete review of wavelet applications, and many reviews cover some particular fields of applications. Let us mention [Unser, 2017] for biomedical applications. Kumar and Foufoula-Georgiou [1997] survey geophysical applications. Image compression and pattern recognition are in Szu, Telfer, and Garcia [1996]; Vetterli [1999]; Liu *et al.* [2000]. Applications to chemical analysis are in Leung, Chau, and Gao [1998].

In this first section dedicated to applications, only a few significant early applications are mentioned and furnish a rapid overview of the main domains of early applications. Recent applications and books on specialized topics are presented in section 1.10.

1.9.1.   *Data analysis*

Many applications, such as astronomy, medical imaging, or satellite imaging, benefit from wavelet analysis. The simple analysis of images at a well-chosen resolution permits extracting image features [Li, Manjunath, and Mitra, 1995]. Wavelets' good edge detecting properties are helpful in data fusion [Fonseca and Manjunath, 1996] of satellite images obtained from different satellites, and the images are fused using the more dominant high-frequency wavelet coefficients among images.

1.9.2.   *Data compression*

Multiresolution and subband coding are used in signal compression of images, videos, or sound. The old JPEG format was a compression method using discrete cosine transform. The discrete cosine transform (DCT) is defined as

$$X(k) = \sum_{n=0}^{N-1} x(n) \cdot cos(2\pi(2N+1) \cdot K/4n) \tag{1.54}$$

The JPEG 2000 replaced the old JPEG standard. The standard supports several decomposition schemes and most wavelets. In many applications, the blocky appearance of JPEG compressed images with DCT was not acceptable. Figure 1.21 shows superior image compression quality than images reconstructed at 0.125 bits per pixel.

JPEG at 0.125 bpp

JPEG2000 at 0.125 bpp

Fig. 1.21. An example comparing the quality of an image with JPEG and JPEG 2000. By courtesy of Christopoulos [1999].

One of the first 'real-world' applications of wavelets in data compression was the FBI fingerprint digitalization standard [Brislawn, 1995]. Fingerprint images are digitized at a resolution of 500 pixels per inch with 256 levels of gray. A single fingerprint needs about 0.6 Mbytes to store. The FBI has collected about 30 million fingerprints from the beginning of the century. Data compression is necessary. Compared to JPEG, the quality of the wavelet-based compressed image at a 15:1 compression factor is better. Roughly speaking, wavelet-based methods are superior to DCT to compress images when most of the information is in its contours (more on this in the section on contourlets and shearlets). The FBI compression standard combines wavelet packets and the best basis (see part 2). The idea consists of determining the best basis at each level of decomposition [Coifman and Wickerhauser, 1992]. The best basis is the function in a wavelet dictionary that minimizes the entropy. In other words, the method searches for decompositions requiring a small number of coefficients. Coifman suggests the following entropy:

$$S = \sum_{n,m} d_{m,n} \cdot \log_2 d_{m,n} \tag{1.55}$$

with $d_{m,n}$ the wavelets coefficients at level m.

1.9.3. *Denoising*

One of the most exciting applications of multiresolution analysis is in the domain of denoising [Donoho and Johnstone, 1994]. The main idea of the so-called thresholding methods is quite simple. Remove all the coefficients below a given threshold. This approach consists of approximating the signal with only the most significant coefficients. The problem is then to determine a threshold that is not too high to keep the essential signal features and not too low to reach efficient denoising. The approach works well on a signal corrupted with white noise. The wavelet transform of a white noise furnishes a distribution with normally distributed wavelet coefficients. Removing all the small coefficients at all levels of resolution is a way of filtering the signal in the whole frequency range.

One distinguishes between soft and hard thresholding. With hard thresholding, the coefficients are estimated with the expression

$$\hat{d}_{m,n} = \begin{cases} d_{m,n} & \text{if} \quad d_{m,n} > \lambda \\ 0 & \text{otherwise} \end{cases} \tag{1.56}$$

In the soft thresholding method, each coefficient is reduced by a small value. An example of soft thresholding is given below

$$\hat{d}_{m,n} = \begin{cases} \text{sgn}(d_{m,n}) \cdot (|d_{m,n}| - \lambda) & \text{if} \quad d_{m,n} > \lambda \\ 0 & \text{otherwise} \end{cases} \tag{1.57}$$

Opinions diverge strongly on which method is the best. Donoho and Johnstone [1994] have proposed several ways to choose the threshold value. An example of such a threshold is

$$\lambda = \sqrt{2 \cdot \sigma^2 \log n} \tag{1.58}$$

with σ^2 the variance from the original data set containing n values. (σ is also sometimes identified as the medium absolute deviation).

Another method to estimate the threshold λ is to minimize the Stein risk function:

$$S = n + a(\lambda) \cdot (\lambda^2 - 2) + \sum_{k=a(\lambda)+1}^{n} d_k^2 \tag{1.59}$$

with $a(\lambda)$ the number of coefficients less than equal to the threshold λ and d_k the wavelets coefficients rearrange into an increasing series.

Thresholding methods often rely on different assumptions about the signal and the noise distribution. A specific type of thresholding may prove to be almost optimal for a particular class of problems. In real-world applications, it is often difficult to compare the different results. The evaluation of denoising quality in images or videos often depends on the subjective judgment of the observer or the choice of some specific criteria. It is still difficult today to make a simple statement on the merits of the different thresholding methods.

Wavelet denoising is a standard approach still generating new approaches [Xing, Carbonetto, and Stephens, 2021]. Data are used to estimate wavelet coefficients' distribution and automatically select a proper amount of denoising at each level [Antoniadis, 1997]. A function f with some added noise gives the simplest model to discuss denoising. After decomposition, the coefficients d are also statistically distributed. Let us describe the main idea behind empirical Bayes shrinkage. Let us assume a noisy signal y and the wavelet coefficients d. Estimating θ with a Bayesian approach requires a prior distribution $p(\theta, \sigma2)$. The joint posterior distribution for $(\theta, \sigma2)$. given d is defined by

$$y = f + noise \tag{1.60}$$

$$d = \theta + noise$$

$$p(\theta, \sigma^2 | d) \propto f((d | \theta, \sigma^2) \, p(\theta, \sigma^2). \tag{1.61}$$

For denoising, the marginal posterior distribution is necessary

$$p(\theta|d) = \int_0^\infty p(\theta, \sigma^2|d)\, d\sigma^2 \tag{1.62}$$

The empirical Bayes filtering is quite efficient (see [Johnstone and Silverman, 2005]. Free public software packages are available [Nason, 2008]. The statistical distribution of the wavelet coefficients is estimated assuming some prior distribution, and the wavelet coefficients are shrunk depending on the distribution parameters.

1.9.4. *Super-resolution*

Image super-resolution refers to the process of recovering high-resolution images from low-resolution images. *Real-world applications* include medical imaging, surveillance, and security.

In medical applications, hardware or the maximal doses admitted for a patient limit image quality. Image super-resolution deep networks improve the image quality and its perception considerably. The integration of wavelet analysis reduces the model size and computational cost while maintaining competitive performance [Bae, Yoo, and Chul Ye, 2017]. The wavelet coefficients of the image form the input of the network that furnishes the corresponding residual of the high-resolution wavelet coefficients as output. The input and output coefficients are fused to create a high-resolution image. In Liu, Mi, and Li [2018], each wavelet subband is processed separately by a network adding a fusion layer to generate the super-resolution image. Huang *et al.* [2017] use three types of loss (or cost) functions for training: wavelet prediction loss, texture loss, and full-image loss.

Similarly, wavelet techniques enhance the quality of video super-resolution by integrating wavelet super-resolution and denoising in the network. The system exploits temporal relations to assemble frames [Zhu *et al.*, 2021].

Deeba *et al.* [2020] increase the quality of the super-resolution image by decomposing it without downsampling. The dyadic wavelet transform is not translation-invariant. Upon reconstruction with filtered wavelet coefficients, the image may present artifacts. The undecimated wavelet decomposition reduces the problem considerably. Thresholding with an undecimated transform rather than a decimated one improves the result by more than 2.5 dB in denoising applications [Starck, Murtagh, and Fadili, 2010]. The undecimated decomposition uses the same filters as the fast wavelet decomposition and reconstruction algorithms but skips downsampling between decomposition levels. It furnishes additional freedom for designing filters, for instance, to create nonnegative reconstruction filters that are very efficient against ringing [Starck, Fadili, and Murtagh, 2007]. The undecimated wavelet decomposition is superior to its decimated version to detect peaks. In Dimitriadis and Taubman [2020], a learning method based on single-image super-resolution predicts the detail coefficients from the approximation coefficients. The approach allows for higher compression rates in comparison to the JPEG2000 standard. Let us recall that the JPEG200 standard replaced the discrete cosine transform-based JPEG standard and was extended to video to become the standard in digital cinema. The accuracy of the prediction is highly dependent on the content of the test image, with specific features being highly predictable and others not predictable at all.

1.10. Recent applications of wavelet and multiresolution analysis

Reviewing the applications of wavelet and multiresolution is becoming increasingly difficult. Many edited books and monographs cover many specialized applications. In this book, we choose to spotlight particular applications in the context of specific chapters. To not overload this abridged book review, we only give their references. Many comments refer to articles that are quoted later in the book.

The book of Foufoula-Georgiou and Kumar [2014] focuses on geophysics. The analysis of seismic waves is an important application. Wavelet-based approaches are not only used to analyze earthquakes and seismic waves. The reflection of artificial seismic waves permits the localization of an oil layer. Applications in civil engineering [Chatterjee, 2015] are numerous, with many applications in structural analysis, particularly on large structures that may experience earthquakes. Intelligent buildings and bridges include damping elements [Adeli and Kim, 2009]. The dynamic response of a building with damping is a very challenging task that is notoriously difficult to solve with standard tools. Multiresolution approaches furnish improved tools for it.

Generally, time-series analysis is a central topic in wavelet analysis [Percival and Walden, 2000] and is essential in finance [Gallegati and Semmler, 2014]. The research does not limit predicting commodity or share prices. Correlations between the price of different commodities may depend on other factors such as the time of the year or meteorologic factors. Improved methods use wavelet cross-correlation and wavelet coherence.

Medicine greatly benefits from wavelet analysis. Applications include feature extractions, compression, and denoising in images or time series. Signal processing improves magnetic resonance imaging, electroencephalogram (EEG), and elec-trograms (EKG). Hramov *et al.* [2015] treat the topics of wavelet in neuroscience with contributions to brain-computer interactions and the analysis of neuronal spikes. The book by Addison [2017] contains further applications in medicine and biology. With the surge of deep networks, the research is shifting toward using convolutional neural networks in applications focusing on image processing (feature recognition, denoising, and many more). Part 7 below introduces the contributions of multiresolution analysis in deep learning.

Wavelets have broad applications in image and video compression. The classical 'A Wavelet Tour of Signal Processing: The Sparse Way' [Mallat, 2008] furnishes an excellent introductory text on many fields covering applications of wavelets in image processing, including texture or contour analysis. Prasad and Iyengar [2020] focus on image processing. Other books in image processing with wavelets specialize in pattern recognition [Liu *et al.*, 2000] or multimedia applications in security and surveillance. The latter includes the topics of watermarking, steganography (hiding a message in a potentially publically shared image), object detection, tracking, and motion [Singh *et al.*, 2020]. In access control, wavelet-based super-resolution is becoming an increasingly important application. The image of a camera is often of bad quality and has to be improved based on known prototypes, possibly with deep learning.

The fusion of multiple images or the combination of information from different sensors is an important application covered in several books [Stathaki, 2011]. Joshi and Upla [2019] discuss the topic of '*Multiresolution image fusion in remote sensing.*' Fuzzy logic or fuzzy neural systems are used either as an alternative or a complementary method to multiresolution analysis in sensor fusion. Escamilla-Ambrosio *et al.* [2017] address the medical context in which information on several signals or images is necessary for diagnostic purposes.

Wavelet applications in speech processing are in Farouk and Farouk [2014]. The book includes chapters on speech recognition, coding, transmission, enhance-ment, denoising, and some very actual topics, such as emotion and sentiment recognition and speech synthesis, which are today of central interest.

Wavelet analysis has a significant impact on engineering. Applications include engineering electromagnetics [Sarkar, Salazar-Palma and Wicks, 2002], adaptive and reconfigurable wireless systems based on wavelets [Nikookar, 2013], and analysis of transients in power systems [He, 2016] or design of inverters [Saleh and Rahman, 2011].

Process technique and controls have several dedicated specialized books. The main applications are chemical engineering [Motard and Joseph, 2013].

Wavelets are routinely used in manufacturing to test production quality based on wavelet computer vision [Kuzmanić and Vujović, 2015], for instance, in fabrics and tissues [Hinders, 2020]. Another widespread application is detecting abnormal noise in a gear train, preventing quality issues.

Applications of specialized topics such as wavelet networks are the subject of several books. Let us mention 'Wavelet neural networks: with applications in financial engineering, chaos, and classification' [Alexandridis and Zapranis, 2014]. The analysis of chaotic time series with multiresolution analysis identifies the unstable regions and focuses on a fine-scale analysis. In the controls field, active corrections stabilize the controller. In 'Foundations of wavelet networks and applications,' Iyengar and Phoha [2018] describe applications of wavelet networks as stock market trading advisors, classifiers in ECG-based drug detection, and predictors of chaotic time-series.

At the methodological level, excellent specialized books are available in statistics [Nason, 2008; Antoniadis and Oppenheim, 2012], functional data analysis [Morettin, Pinheiro and Vidakovic, 2017], noise reduction [Jansen, 2012], Bayesian inference [Müller and Vidakovic, 2012], numerical analysis [Cohen, 2003], solving differential equations [Ray and Gupta, 2018], spline and spline wavelet methods [Averbuch, Neittaanmäki, and Zheludev, 2014]. Sparsity is a central topic in modern signal processing. Dyadic wavelets are efficient signal compressors. An efficient representation of an image with a few wavelets is the main topic in signal processing. In recent years, sparsity has become a topic by itself. The book by Starck, Murtagh, and Fadili [2010], 'Sparse image and signal processing: wavelets, curvelets, morphological diversity,' focuses on sparsity and the concept of morphological signature. Morphological component analysis models an image as a sum of components. Each of its components has a given morphological signature. For a cartoon, the dictionary differs (i.e., curvelets for analyzing the sketch) from textures' analysis. Using dictionaries learned from data circumvents some difficulties faced by fixed dictionaries. This adaptivity is crucial to capturing complex texture patterns.

This short review furnishes a survey of the wealth of multiresolution and wavelet theory applications besides the most famous applications such as JPEG. It is beyond the scope of this book to include books with complete chapters on applications.

Each following chapter is completed whenever possible and meaningful by presenting a few applications, sometimes limiting the presentation to an exciting field. We hope that the discussed applications may trigger new applications in his domain of expertise.

1.10.1. *Applications of the Continuous Wavelet Transform (CWT)*

While it is true that the continuous wavelet transform is somewhat redundant compared to a dyadic transform, it has found many applications due to its translation invariance and good time-frequency resolution. Compared to the fast Fourier transform, the CWT often spreads lines in the frequency domain. Let us recall that the CWT is given by

$$W(a,b) = \int s(t)\, a^{-1/2}\, \psi^*\left(\frac{t-b}{a}\right) dt \qquad (1.63)$$

The Fourier transform of a cosine corresponds to a Dirac peak in the Fourier power spectrum and a ribbon for a CWT. Daubechies, Lu, and Wu [2011] introduced the synchrosqueezing wavelet transform (SWT) to improve the resolution power of the CWT. The time-frequency coefficients are 'relocated' on the frequency axis. One gets a concentrated image over the time-frequency plane, from which one may read the instantaneous frequencies. Starting from a cosine function, the SWT narrows the primary frequency component from a ribbon to a sharp line in the time-frequency plane. The time-axis stays unchanged; therefore, the transform is invertible. The relocation frequency corresponds to the complex instantaneous frequency

$$\omega_c = -\frac{i}{W(a,b)}\frac{\partial W(a,b)}{\partial b} \qquad (1.64)$$

The CWT coefficients W(a,b) within a band Δa are reassigned to the time-frequency plane $(b, \omega_r(a,b))$ with ω_r the real part of ω_c using the synchrosqueezing operator:

$$T(\omega,b) = \int \frac{W(a,b)}{a^{3/2}} \delta(\omega - \omega_r(a,b))\, da \qquad (1.65)$$

(The term $a^{-3/2}$ is necessary for inverting the transform). Daubechies and Maes [2017] initially tested the method on the problem of speaker identification. Using an improved synchrosqueezing approach, Hu *et al.* [2018] diagnose faults in planetary geartrain in a wind turbine. A great variety of machines use planetary gears. The great advantage of planetary over a standard gearbox is its compactness. Planetary gearboxes are tendentially less robust than traditional gearboxes. Fault detection with an acoustic method or a piezo-sensor is the conventional approach. Synchrosqueezing with a Gabor wavelet helps detect multiple faults like cog breaking or problems with bearings. Results indicate that the proposed method is a promising tool for the fault diagnosis and condition monitoring of a wind turbine planetary gearbox. Aeroengine vibration monitoring [Wang *et al.*, 2016] or seismic data analysis [Shang, Han, and Hu, 2013] are other applications of this technique.

Quite simple applications of the CWT include Running Wavelet Archetypes. Addison [2017] considers repetitive signals like the heart pulse rate measured with oximetry. Typically a tiny device is clamped on the finger, and it measures with a beam of light the amount of oxygen in the finger. Heartbeat is non-stationary and considerably varies over time. The averaging of the same points along each beat is a tricky task. The signal is repetitive with a period comparable to the CWT analysis's dilation 'a' of the best wavelet. The averaging is done using wavelets at different scales to guide the averaging process:

$$TRWA(a, b) = \alpha\, W(a, b) + (1 - \alpha)\, TRWA\, (a, b - P(a)) \qquad (1.66)$$

1.10.2. *Fluid dynamics applications of wavelets*

Wavelet analysis is part of the signal processing toolbox in many different fields. Meteorology and, more generally, fluid dynamics are still in the development phase with exciting new approaches. Let us discuss the specific aspects of wavelet analysis that make some applications especially interesting.

Kumar and Foufoula-Georgiou [1993] use two-dimensional wavelet analysis of precipitation forecasts. They postulate that the low-resolution component represents the mean rainfall while the rain intensity has a high-resolution self-similar structure. The range in which self-similarity holds depends on the storm structure. Verifying forecasts is challenging as predictions may be good at low scales but wrong locally. The prediction of rain has made significant progress in later years by integrating satellite and radar data combined with their visualization on a geographic map. The 2-dim decomposition of the predictions compared to the actual outcome permits defining mean squared error at different scales. With 2-dim orthogonal wavelets, the error is additive at different scales. The prediction error is scale-dependent both in time and scale, an attractive feature in guiding the development of new prediction tools. Weniger, Kapp and Friederichs, [2017] reviewed the topic. Wavelets are increasingly used in meteorology [Cabaneros, Calautit, and Hughes, 2020; Guo *et al.*, 2020]. Air pollution forecasts based on local meteorological conditions and wavelet networks are examples. Prediction and analysis of particular matter are increasingly essential topics in indoor and outdoor climates. Health issues related to particular matters (PM) at 2.5 μm and below are concerning. Air conditioning is a primary concern in predicting their appearance and palliating their effects through appropriate indoor filtering. Qiao *et al.* [2019] combine deep learning and wavelet analysis to improve the forecasting of PM2.5 levels in cities.

The analysis of turbulences benefits from wavelet techniques. Large-sized eddies contribute to particle concentrations in the surface-atmosphere boundary layer with turbulent aerosol fluxes in the second and minute scales [Conte, Contini, and Held, 2021]. The energy and particle fluxes are estimated by integrating the different parameters at different scales. For instance, pressure, air density, and airflow are integrated at different scales to compute the energy flows [Woods and Smith, 2010].

Airflows strongly influence the dynamics and thermal comfort of a house or a skyscraper, and therefore, their modelization is very important. Both small and large-scale dynamics affect energy transport. Near a wall, large-scale air motion modulates the small-scale dynamics. Baars *et al.* [2015] study the coupling using wavelet techniques.

Turbulence analysis is one of the early wavelet applications [Farge, 1992; Hudgins, Friehe, and Mayer, 1993]. The field includes wavelet modelization of fluid flow, statistical modeling multiscale models for computing Reynold numbers, and eddy-viscosity [Sagaut, Terracol, and Deck, 2013]. Numerical solutions of the Navier-Stokes equations are often too computing-demanding and replaced by simpler multiscale models. The most advanced solvers of the Navier-Stokes equations use multiscale approaches [Yu, 2021]. For problems for which numerical simulations are feasible, wavelet analysis also finds applications in analyzing the results. For example, Bassenne, Moin, and Urzay [2018] study particle-laden turbulence. Wavelet basis functions enable the analysis of turbulence at different scales as a function of the Stokes number, a dimensionless number characterizing the behavior of particles suspended in a fluid flow. Generally speaking, a large class of differential equations is efficiently solved using wavelet techniques [Beylkin, Coifman, and Rokhlin, 2009]. Wavelet-based methods are, for instance, used to solve heat equations [Yazdani and Nadjafikhah, 2020] numerically. As discussed in the following chapters, the combination of neural networks and wavelet analysis leads to new applications in predicting recurrent phenomena such as drought, flood, or the El Niño oscillation. Much research deals with the coupling of atmospheric and oceanographic phenomena. The approaches are either through modeling and simulations or time-series analysis with wavelet coherence approaches.

References

Addison, P.S. (2017) *The illustrated wavelet transform handbook: introductory theory and applications in science, engineering, medicine and finance* (CRC Press).

Adeli, H. and Kim, H. (2009) *Wavelet-based vibration control of smart buildings and bridges* (CRC Press Boca Raton, FL).

Alexandridis, A.K. and Zapranis, A.D. (2014) *Wavelet neural networks: with applications in financial engineering, chaos, and classification* (John Wiley & Sons).

Antoniadis, A. (1997). Wavelets in statistics: a review, *Journal of the Italian Statistical Society*, 6(2), pp. 97–130.

Antoniadis, A. and Oppenheim, G. (2012) *Wavelets and statistics* (Springer Science & Business Media).

Averbuch, A.Z., Neittaanmäki, P. and Zheludev, V.A. (2014) *Spline and spline wavelet methods with applications to signal and image processing* (Springer).

Baars, W. *et al.* (2015). Wavelet analysis of wall turbulence to study large-scale modulation of small scales, *Experiments in Fluids*, 56(10), pp. 1–15.

Bae, W., Yoo, J. and Chul Ye, J. (2017). Beyond deep residual learning for image restoration: Persistent homology-guided manifold simplification, *Proc. IEEE conference on computer vision and pattern recognition workshops*, pp. 145–153.

Bassenne, M., Moin, P. and Urzay, J. (2018). Wavelet multiresolution analysis of particle-laden turbulence, *Physical Review Fluids*, 3(8), p. 084304.

Berger, J., Coifman, R.R. and Goldberg, M.J. (1994). Removing noise from music using local trigonometric bases and wavelet packets, *Journal of the Audio Engineering Society*, 42(10), pp. 808–818.

Beylkin, G., Coifman, R. and Rokhlin, V. (2009) *Fast wavelet transforms and numerical algorithms, in Fundamental Papers in Wavelet Theory* (Princeton University Press), pp. 741–783.

Bilgili, F. (2015) Business cycle co-movements between renewables consumption and industrial production: A continuous wavelet coherence approach, *Renewable and sustainable energy reviews*, 52, pp. 325–332.

Brislawn, C.M. (1995). Fingerprints go digital, Notices of the AMS, 42(11), pp. 1278–1283.

Bruna, J. and Mallat, S. (2013). Invariant scattering convolution networks, *IEEE transactions on pattern analysis and machine intelligence*, 35(8), pp. 1872–1886.

Cabaneros, S.M., Calautit, J.K. and Hughes, B. (2020). Spatial estimation of outdoor NO2 levels in Central London using deep neural networks and a wavelet decomposition technique, Ecological Modelling, 424, p. 109017.

Candes, E.J. and Donoho, D.L. (2000). Curvelets: A surprisingly effective nonadaptive representation for objects with edges. (Stanford Univ Ca Dept of Statistics).

Chatterjee, P. (2015) Wavelet analysis in civil engineering. (CRC Press Boca Raton, FL, USA).

Chui, C.K. (1997) *Wavelets: a mathematical tool for signal analysis* (SIAM).

Cohen, A. (2003) *Numerical analysis of wavelet methods* (Elsevier).

Coifman, R.R. and Wickerhauser, M.V. (1992). Entropy-based algorithms for best basis selection, *IEEE Transactions on information theory*, 38(2), pp. 713–718.

Conte, M., Contini, D. and Held, A. (2021). Multiresolution decomposition and wavelet analysis of urban aerosol fluxes in Italy and Austria, *Atmospheric Research*, 248, p. 105267.

Croisier, A. (1976). Perfect channel splitting by use of interpolation/decimation/tree decomposition techniques, *Proc. Int. Symp. on Info., Circuits and Systems (Patras, Greece)*.

Da Cunha, A.L., Zhou, J. and Do, M.N. (2006). The nonsubsampled contourlet transform: theory, design, and applications, *IEEE transactions on image processing*, 15(10), pp. 3089–3101.

Daubechies, I. (1992) *Ten lectures on wavelets* (SIAM, Philadelphia, 1992).

Daubechies, I., Lu, J. and Wu, H.-T. (2011). Synchrosqueezed wavelet transforms: An empirical mode decomposition-like tool, *Applied and computational harmonic analysis*, 30(2), pp. 243–261.

Deeba, F. *et al.* (2020). Wavelet-based enhanced medical image super resolution, *IEEE Access*, 8, pp. 37035–37044.

Deng, W. *et al.* (2018). A novel fault diagnosis method based on integrating empirical wavelet transform and fuzzy entropy for motor bearing, *IEEE Access*, 6, pp. 35042–35056.

Dimitriadis, A. and Taubman, D. (2020). Augmenting JPEG2000 With Wavelet Coefficient Prediction, *Proc. 2020 IEEE International Conference on Image Processing (ICIP)*, (IEEE), pp. 1276–1280.

Do, M.N. and Vetterli, M. (2005). The contourlet transform: an efficient directional multiresolution image representation, *IEEE Transactions on image processing*, 14(12), pp. 2091–2106.

Donoho, D.L. and Johnstone, I.M. (1994). Ideal denoising in an orthonormal basis chosen from a library of bases, *Comptes rendus de l'Académie des sciences. Série I, Mathématique*, 319(12), pp. 1317–1322.

Easley, G., Labate, D. and Lim, W.-Q. (2008). Sparse directional image representations using the discrete shearlet transform, *Applied and Computational Harmonic Analysis*, 25(1), pp. 25–46.

Eastman, R., Wood, R. and Bretherton, C.S. (2016). Time scales of clouds and cloud-controlling variables in subtropical stratocumulus from a Lagrangian perspective, *Journal of the Atmospheric Sciences*, 73(8), pp. 3079–3091.

Elnasir, S., Shamsuddin, S.M. and Farokhi, S. (2015). Accurate palm vein recognition based on wavelet scattering and spectral regression kernel discriminant analysis, *Journal of Electronic Imaging*, 24(1), p. 013031.

Escamilla-Ambrosio, P.J. *et al.* (2017). Multi-Sensor Feature Extraction and Data Fusion Using ANFIS and 2D Wavelet Transform in *Structural Health Monitoring, Structural Health Monitoring: Measurement Methods and Practical Applications*, p. 109.

Farge, M. (1992). Wavelet transforms and their applications to turbulence, Annual review of fluid mechanics, 24(1), pp. 395–458.

Farouk, M.H. and Farouk (2014) *Application of wavelets in speech processing* (Springer).

Fonseca, L.M. and Manjunath, B. (1996). Registration techniques for multisensor remotely sensed imagery, *PE & RS- Photogrammetric Engineering & Remote Sensing*, 62(9), pp. 1049–1056.

Foufoula-Georgiou, E. and Kumar, P. (2014) Wavelets in geophysics. (Elsevier).

Gabor, D. (1946). Theory of communication. Part 1: The analysis of information, *Journal of the Institution of Electrical Engineers-Part III: Radio and Communication Engineering*, 93(26), pp. 429–441.

Gallegati, M. and Semmler, W. (2014) *Wavelet applications in economics and finance* (Springer).

Geng, P. *et al.* (2012). Image fusion by pulse couple neural network with shearlet, *Optical Engineering*, 51(6), p. 067005.

Gilles, J. (2013). Empirical wavelet transform, *IEEE transactions on signal processing*, 61(16), pp. 3999–4010.

Gilman, D.L., Fuglister, F.J. and Mitchell Jr, J.M. (1963). On the power spectrum of "red noise", *Journal of the Atmospheric Sciences*, 20(2), pp. 182–184.

Goodell, J.W. and Goutte, S. (2021). Co-movement of COVID-19 and Bitcoin: Evidence from wavelet coherence analysis, *Finance Research Letters*, 38, p. 101625.

Gougam, F. *et al.* (2019). Bearing fault diagnosis based on feature extraction of empirical wavelet transform (EWT) and fuzzy logic system (FLS) under variable operating conditions, *Journal of Vibroengineering*, 21(6), pp. 1636–1650.

Grinsted, A., Moore, J.C. and Jevrejeva, S. (2004). Application of the cross wavelet transform and wavelet coherence to geophysical time series, *Nonlinear processes in geophysics*, 11(5/6), pp. 561–566.

Grossmann, A. and Morlet, J. (1984). Decomposition of Hardy functions into square integrable wavelets of constant shape, *SIAM journal on mathematical analysis*, 15(4), pp. 723–736.

Guo, Q. *et al.* (2020). Air pollution forecasting using artificial and wavelet neural networks with meteorological conditions, *Aerosol and Air Quality Research*, 20(6), pp. 1429–1439.

Häuser, S. and Steidl, G. (2012). Fast finite shearlet transform, *arXiv preprint* arXiv:1202.1773 [Preprint].

He, Z. (2016) *Wavelet analysis and transient signal processing applications for power systems* (John Wiley & Sons).

Hinders, M.K. (2020) *Intelligent Feature Selection for Machine Learning Using the Dynamic Wavelet Fingerprint* (Springer Nature).

Hramov, A.E. *et al.* (2015) *Wavelets in neuroscience* (Springer).

Hu, W. and Si, B. (2021). Improved partial wavelet coherency for understanding scale-specific and localized bivariate relationships in geosciences, *Hydrology and Earth System Sciences*, 25(1), pp. 321–331.

Hu, Y. *et al.* (2018). Joint high-order synchrosqueezing transform and multi-taper empirical wavelet transform for fault diagnosis of wind turbine planetary gearbox under non-stationary conditions, *Sensors*, 18(1), p. 150.

Huang, H. *et al.* (2017).Wavelet-srnet: A wavelet-based cnn for multiscale face super resolution, *Proc. of the IEEE International Conference on Computer Vision*, pp. 1689–1697.

Huang, N.E. *et al.* (1998). The empirical mode decomposition and the Hilbert spectrum for nonlinear and non-stationary time series analysis, *Proc. of the Royal Society of London. Series A: mathematical, physical and engineering sciences*, 454(1971), pp. 903–995.

Hubbard, B.B. (1998) *The world according to wavelets: the story of a mathematical technique in the making* (AK Peters/CRC Press).

Hudgins, L., Friehe, C.A. and Mayer, M.E. (1993). Wavelet transforms and atmopsheric turbulence, *Physical Review Letters*, 71(20), p. 3279.

Iyengar, S.S. and Phoha, V.V. (2018) *Foundations of wavelet networks and applications* (Chapman and Hall/CRC).

Jansen, M. (2012) *Noise reduction by wavelet thresholding* (Springer Science & Business Media).

Jenkins, G.M. (1968) *Spectral analysis and its applications*, (Holden-Day, Inc., San Francisco, Card Nr. 67-13840).

Johnstone, I.M. and Silverman, B.W. (2005). EbayesThresh: R and S-Plus programs for Empirical Bayes thresholding, *J. Statist. Soft*, 12, pp. 1–38.

Joshi, M.V. and Upla, K.P. (2019) *Multi-resolution image fusion in remote sensing* (Cambridge University Press).

Kumar, P. and Foufoula-Georgiou, E. (1993). A multicomponent decomposition of spatial rainfall fields: 1. Segregation of large-and small-scale features using wavelet transforms, *Water Resources Research*, 29(8), pp. 2515–2532.

Kumar, P. and Foufoula-Georgiou, E. (1997). Wavelet analysis for geophysical applications, *Reviews of geophysics*, 35(4), pp. 385–412.

Kuzmanić, I. and Vujović, I. (2015). *Reliability and availability of quality control based on wavelet computer vision* (Springer).

Leung, A.K., Chau, F. and Gao, J. (1998). A review on applications of wavelet transform techniques in chemical analysis: 1989–1997, *Chemometrics and Intelligent Laboratory Systems*, 43(1–2), pp. 165–184.

Li, H., Manjunath, B. and Mitra, S.K. (1995). Multisensor image fusion using the wavelet transform, *Graphical models and image processing*, 57(3), pp. 235–245.

Liu, H., Mi, X. and Li, Y. (2018). Wind speed forecasting method based on deep learning strategy using empirical wavelet transform, long short term memory neural network and Elman neural network, *Energy conversion and management*, 156, pp. 498–514.

Liu, J. *et al.* (2000) *Wavelet theory and its application to pattern recognition* (World Scientific).

Magli, E., Olmo, G. and Presti, L.L. (1999). Pattern recognition by means of the Radon transform and the continuous wavelet transform, *Signal processing*, 73(3), pp. 277–289.

Mallat, S. (1999) *A wavelet tour of signal processing* (Elsevier).

Mallat, S. (2008) *A Wavelet Tour of Signal Processing: The Sparse Way* (Academic Press, Burlington, Mass).

Mallat, S. (2012). Group invariant scattering, *Communications on Pure and Applied Mathematics*, 65(10), pp. 1331–1398.

Maraun, D. and Kurths, J. (2005). Epochs of phase coherence between El Nino/Southern Oscillation and Indian monsoon, *Geophysical Research Letters*, 32(15).

Miao, Q. *et al.* (2011). A novel algorithm of image fusion using shearlets, *Optics Communications*, 284(6), pp. 1540–1547.

Mihanović, H., Orlić, M. and Pasarić, Z. (2009). Diurnal thermocline oscillations driven by tidal flow around an island in the Middle Adriatic, *Journal of Marine Systems*, 78, pp. S157–S168.

Morettin, P.A., Pinheiro, A. and Vidakovic, B. (2017) *Wavelets in functional data analysis* (Springer).

Motard, R.L. and Joseph, B. (2013) *Wavelet applications in chemical engineering* (Springer Science & Business Media).

Müller, P. and Vidakovic, B. (2012) *Bayesian inference in wavelet-based models* (Springer Science & Business Media).

Nason, G.P. (2008) *Wavelet methods in statistics with R* (Springer).

Nikookar, H. (2013). *Wavelet radio: adaptive and reconfigurable wireless systems based on wavelets* (Cambridge University Press).

Percival, D.B. and Walden, A.T. (2000) *Wavelet methods for time series analysis* (Cambridge University Press).

Pham, V. and Wong, K. (1999). Wavelet-transform-based algorithm for harmonic analysis of power system waveforms, *IEE Proceedings-Generation, Transmission and Distribution*, 146(3), pp. 249–254.

Qiao, W. *et al.* (2019). The forecasting of PM2. 5 using a hybrid model based on wavelet transform and an improved deep learning algorithm, *IEEE Access*, 7, pp. 142814–142825.

Ray, S.S. and Gupta, A.K. (2018). *Wavelet methods for solving partial differential equations and fractional differential equations* (CRC Press).

Sagaut, P., Terracol, M. and Deck, S. (2013). *Multiscale and multiresolution approaches in turbulence-LES, DES and Hybrid RANS/LES Methods: Applications and Guidelines* (World Scientific).

Saleh, S. and Rahman, M.A. (2011) *An introduction to wavelet modulated inverters* (John Wiley & Sons).

Sankari, Z., Adeli, H. and Adeli, A. (2012). Wavelet coherence model for diagnosis of Alzheimer disease, *Clinical EEG and neuroscience*, 43(4), pp. 268–278.

Sarkar, T.K., Salazar-Palma, M. and Wicks, M.C. (2002) *Wavelet applications in engineering electromagnetics* (Artech House).

Shang, S., Han, L. and Hu, W. (2013). Seismic data analysis using synchrosqueezing wavelet transform, in *SEG Technical Program Expanded Abstracts 2013. Society of Exploration Geophysicists*, pp. 4330–4334.

Simoncelli, E.P. and Freeman, W.T. (1995). The steerable pyramid: A flexible architecture for multiscale derivative computation, *Proc. International Conference on Image Processing*, (IEEE), pp. 444–447.

Singh, A. and Kingsbury, N. (2017).Multi-resolution dual-tree wavelet scattering network for signal classification, *arXiv preprint* arXiv:1702.03345 [Preprint].

Singh, R. *et al.* (2020) *Intelligent Wavelet Based Techniques for Advanced Multimedia Applications* (Springer Nature).

Starck, J.-L., Fadili, J. and Murtagh, F. (2007). The undecimated wavelet decomposition and its reconstruction, *IEEE transactions on image processing*, 16(2), pp. 297–309.

Starck, J.-L., Murtagh, F. and Fadili, J.M. (2010) *Sparse image and signal processing: wavelets, curvelets, morphological diversity* (Cambridge University Press).

Staszewski, W. (1997). Identification of damping in MDOF systems using time-scale decomposition, *Journal of sound and vibration*, 203(2), pp. 283–305.

Stathaki, T. (2011) *Image fusion: algorithms and applications* (Elsevier).

Szu, H., Telfer, B. and Garcia, J. (1996). Wavelet transforms and neural networks for compression and recognition, *Neural networks*, 9(4), pp. 695–708.

Tan, W. *et al.* (2020). Multimodal medical image fusion algorithm in the era of big data, *Neural Computing and Applications*, pp. 1–21.

Thonet, G. *et al.* (1998). Wavelet-based detection of ventricular ectopic beats in heart rate signals, *Applied Signal Processing*, 5(3), pp. 170–181.

Torrence, C. and Compo, G.P. (1998). A practical guide to wavelet analysis, *Bulletin of the American Meteorological society*, 79(1), pp. 61–78.

Torrence, C. and Webster, P.J. (1998). The annual cycle of persistence in the El Nño/Southern Oscillation, *Quarterly Journal of the Royal Meteorological Society*, 124(550), pp. 1985–2004.

Unser, M. (2017) Wavelets in medicine and biology. (Routledge).

Vacha, L. and Barunik, J. (2012). Co-movement of energy commodities revisited: Evidence from wavelet coherence analysis, *Energy Economics*, 34(1), pp. 241–247.

Vetterli, M. (1984). Multi-dimensional sub-band coding: Some theory and algorithms, *Signal processing*, 6(2), pp. 97–112.

Vetterli, M. (1999). Wavelets: approximation and compression--a review, in *Wavelet Applications VI*, (International Society for Optics and Photonics), pp. 28–31.

Vetterli, M. and Herley, C. (1992). Wavelets and filter banks: Theory and design, *IEEE transactions on signal processing*, 40, pp. 2207–2232.

Vetterli, M. and Kovacevic, J. (1995) *Wavelets and subband coding* (Prentice-hall).

Wang, S. *et al.* (2016). Matching synchrosqueezing wavelet transform and application to aeroengine vibration monitoring, *IEEE Transactions on Instrumentation and Measurement*, 66(2), pp. 360–372.

Weniger, M., Kapp, F. and Friederichs, P. (2017). Spatial verification using wavelet transforms: a review, *Quarterly Journal of the Royal Meteorological Society*, 143(702), pp. 120–136.

Woods, B.K. and Smith, R.B. (2010.) Energy flux and wavelet diagnostics of secondary mountain waves, *Journal of Atmospheric Sciences*, 67(11), pp. 3721–3738.

Xing, Z., Carbonetto, P. and Stephens, M. (2021). Flexible signal denoising via flexible empirical bayes shrinkage, *Journal of Machine Learning Research*, 22(93), pp. 1–28.

Yazdani, H.R. and Nadjafikhah, M. (2020). Solving differential equations by new wavelet transform method based on the quasi-wavelets and differential invariants, *Punjab University Journal of Mathematics*, 49(3).

Yu, K. (2021). *Multi-resolution Lattice Green's Function Method for High Reynolds Number External Flows* (Doctoral Dissertation Caltech).

Zhao, H. *et al.* (2017). A new feature extraction method based on EEMD and multiscale fuzzy entropy for motor bearing, *Entropy*, 19(1), p. 14.

Zhou, S. *et al.* (2013). Shearlet-based texture feature extraction for classification of breast tumor in ultrasound image, *Biomedical Signal Processing and Control*, 8(6), pp. 688–696.

Zhu, X. *et al.* (2021). Video super-resolution based on a spatio-temporal matching network, *Pattern Recognition*, 110, p. 107619.

Preprocessing: The Multiresolution Approach

Part 2

Chapter 2

Preprocessing: The Multiresolution Approach

Many applications combine wavelet analysis with another standard signal processing method for preprocessing. The goal is very often the reduction of a problem's dimensionality or complexity. This chapter takes the stand to identify some of the major issues in signal preprocessing and explain wavelet theory's contributions to them. The methodological aspects are privileged at the expense of an exhaustive presentation of the multitude of combinations between standard signal processing methods and multiresolution analysis.

It is challenging to define preprocessing, and the boundary between preprocessing and processing is often very fuzzy. Tentatively, preprocessing may be defined as transforming data into a form suitable for processing with a standard processing method. We focus primarily on two related topics that are not only central to signal preprocessing but are also at the very heart of soft computing:

- The curse of dimensionality:
  This expression refers to the fact that the sample size needed to estimate a function grows exponentially with the number of variables.
- The complexity issue:
  Some problems are intrinsically challenging to solve exactly. The necessary computing time to solve a complex problem increases very rapidly with the size of the problem (the number of inputs often characterizes the size of a problem). Science and art in signal processing consist of choosing the suitable method to find satisfactory solutions to hard problems with limited computing time.

Let us recall that soft computing solves computationally intensive problems with limited computing power and memory by giving up some precision. Soft computing covers a range of methods tolerant of imprecision, uncertainty, and partial truth. The necessary computing power to solve a problem depends on the problem's difficulty and the required accuracy of the solution. Also, the number of required data points in learning depends on these factors. In this chapter, we present several methods to determine or decrease the dimensionality of a problem through projection techniques, pursuits, and data transformation.

2.1. The double curse: dimensionality and complexity

A financial software company claimed that 90% of the development and computing time in financial problems is preprocessing. It is tough to argue against or confirm such a provocative statement as the concept of preprocessing cannot be defined generally. The boundary between preprocessing and processing is, in many problems, quite difficult to draw. Preprocessing corresponds to the preparation or the transformation of data into a form suitable for processing with a standard method. This definition reports the problem of defining what a common method is.

Some of the best tools in signal processing perform poorly at high dimensions. Therefore a significant part of preprocessing deals with the problem of dimension reduction. The general reasons involved for the failure of many classical signal processing methods at high dimensions are

- The curse of dimensionality
- The increasing complexity of many problems as the dimension increases.

In the first part of this chapter, we will discuss these two problems. Nevertheless, we should not hide the reality: the genuine reason for unsatisfactory modeling is not signal processing. In many cases, the failure to describe a problem correctly or find a solution is related to the human brain's difficulty dealing with more than three dimensions. For that reason, high-dimensional problems are often ill-posed, and the following challenges occur:

- Missing variables
- Inappropriate variables

Other common problems are
- Missing data
- Wrong data
- Noisy data

Publications on these problems are scarce. Understandably, one prefers to report on success than on failures. Also, it is difficult to learn from failures as the necessary know-how is often specific to a given and well-specified problem. This situation is nevertheless unsatisfactory and may lead to a broadening of the gap between applications and fundamental research.

Fortunately, one observes a new trend in many commercial signal processing tools. Many programs include diagnostics tools, often based on statistical methods, to diagnose outliers automatically, reject insignificant variables, or even suggest that some results are most likely not significant due to a lack of data.

In this chapter, we will discuss preprocessing from the multiresolution perspective. We have selected several preprocessing methods and show how multi-resolution may improve them. Among the multiresolution techniques, we focus here essentially on wavelet theory.

Wavelet preprocessing has become a standard tool for many problems. Feature extraction, classification, modeling, data compression, and denoising are the problems that have benefited most from multiresolution preprocessing. The preprocessing stage generally has more than one purpose. In image and speech processing, data reduction is very often the issue. Wavelet compression reduces the dimensionality of the image. Other applications are data filtering, denoising, or segmentation of the input space. Applications using wavelet preprocessing include fire detectors, filtering of satellite images, detection of emergency states in neurosurgical patients, quality control and inspection, denoising of magnetic resonance images, Chinese character recognition, face classification, image compression, classification of EEG signals, features extractions in seismic waves. Generally, wavelet preprocessing selects significant wavelet coefficients on which a standard processing method is applied (Figure 2.1).

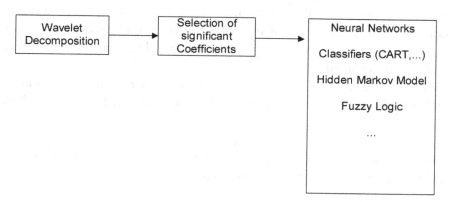

Fig. 2.1. Wavelet preprocessing is used in applications (image processing, pattern recognition, spectral analysis, controllers) combined with standard signal processing methods. The preprocessing stage generally selects significant wavelet coefficients for further processing with a standard method.

2.1.1. *Curse of dimensionality*

The curse of dimensionality is a term coined by Bellman [2015]. It refers to the fact that the sample size needed to estimate a function to a given accuracy grows exponentially with the number of variables in many problems. It is only in recent years that this expression has taken widespread significance. The implications of the curse of dimensionality became fully appreciated as more extensive computing power became available in the last years. The exponential growth of computing power has encouraged many industries and universities to address increasingly complex problems in which the curse of dimensionality did strike more often than expected. Beating the curse of dimensionality consists of finding an acceptable representation of the information with a reduced number of variables through diverse preprocessing techniques.

2.1.2. *Classification of problems' difficulty*

The complexity of a problem depends on the computing time, the number of steps, or the memory space required to solve it. A problem is easy or hard depending on how it scales with the number N of inputs.

An *easy* problem is a problem that is verifiable and solvable in polynomial time. An appropriate algorithm is guaranteed to terminate within a limited number of steps, which is a polynomial function of the size of the problem.

A very hard problem is a problem that is neither solvable nor verifiable in polynomial time. Many problems are an intermediate class, the so-called NP problems. A problem is NP if no polynomial function of the number of inputs N describes the increase correctly with N of the number of necessary steps to solve the problems with a deterministic Turing machine/algorithm, but a solution is verifiable in polynomial time.

Finally, a problem is NP-hard if solving it in polynomial time would make it possible to solve all problems in class NP in polynomial time [Garey and Johnson, 1979].

In soft computing, the determination of an optimal signal approximation using a redundant dictionary is NP-hard. It follows that

- the search for optimal decomposition of a signal using a redundant wavelet dictionary is an NP-hard problem.
- the search for an optimal fuzzy controller using a redundant dictionary of membership functions is NP-hard

Definition: dictionary/optimal approximation

Let H be a N-dimensional Hilbert. A dictionary D for H is a family of functions g_i of norm 1 in H, such that linear combinations of functions g_i in the dictionary are dense in H. The smallest possible dictionary is called a base of H, while the dictionary is redundant otherwise. We define an optimal approximation $\hat{f}$ of a function f, to be a linear combination of functions g_i in the dictionary such that $||\hat{f} - f||$ is minimum.

In reality, there are two main problems with increasing dimensions. On the one hand, the curse of dimensionality leads to the need for an exponentially growing dataset with increasing dimensions. On the other hand, many problems, such as decomposing a signal with a redundant dictionary optimally, are NP-hard, and the number of operations necessary to solve them also increases exponentially with the size of the dictionary.

A possible strategy to fight the double curse is to reduce the problem dimension and/or the requested solution's accuracy. We discuss these two approaches. In recent years, the incredible capabilities of deep networks to solve high-dimensional problems have puzzled many researchers. It became evident that the trick is that only a tiny portion of the space is populated.

2.2. Dimension reduction

The Karhunen-Loève transform is the classical linear method to reduce the dimension of a dataset with a projection technique. The Karhunen-Loève method corresponds to a change of basis, and the new basis is formed by a linear transform of the original orthogonal basis. The Karhunen-Loève method is ideal for reducing the dimension of a dataset of Gaussian random vectors. The dataset approximated on the most significant Karhunen-Loève basis minimizes the error compared to any other linear basis transform.

If the number of different bases is large, then the Karhunen-Loève method becomes intractable in many online problems. An Oja's neural network is preferable as it converges to the principal components.

We present an example (the problem of finding the best coordinates to represent data in a fuzzy system) for which wavelet preprocessing is necessary to implement the Karhunen-Loève transform efficiently.

In nonlinear problems, the Karhunen-Loève transform does not generally furnish good results. Alternatively, one uses nonlinear projection techniques such as projection pursuit regression and exploratory projection pursuit. The best basis and the matching pursuit algorithms are two good examples of wavelet-based versions. The *best basis* corresponds to searching within a redundant basis, an orthogonal basis that approximates best the Karhunen-Loève basis by minimizing an entropy function. The matching pursuit searches iteratively for the best matching between a basis contained in a dictionary and some portion of a signal. The algorithm is greedy because the contribution of the best matching basis is removed from the signal and the algorithm iterated on the residue.

2.3. Karhunen-Loève transform (principal components analysis)

The principal component analysis is the classical linear method to search for a low dimension space to embed data. A principal component analysis consists of a Karhunen-Loève transform corresponding to a change of basis. It furnishes an orthogonal basis of vectors representing the optimal direction of projections. The new basis corresponds to the eigenvectors of the covariance operator $R[n,m] = E\{Y[n]\, Y^*[m]\}$.

For random Gaussian vectors, Y of zero mean, the realizations of Y (sometimes called objects) define a cloud of points in $\mathfrak{R}^N$. The Karhunen-Loève transform furnishes an orthogonal basis of vectors g_n giving the directions of the principal axes of the cloud. The theorem below [Vetterli and Kovacevic, 1995] conveys the power and limitations of the Karhunen-Loève transform. The theorem states that provided the data points are randomly distributed, the Karhunen-Loève transform is the ideal tool to determine the optimal low-dimensional representation of data. A central condition in the theorem is that Y is a random vector. If this condition is not fulfilled, the process may be highly non-uniform, and the Karhunen-Loève may not provide good approximations of the process. In these cases, a nonlinear dimension compression method is generally necessary.

<u>Theorem:</u>
Let $\{g_m\}_{0\le m<N}$ be an orthogonal basis such as a gaussian random vector Y of zero mean can be decomposed as $Y = \sum_{m=0}^{N-1} <Y, g_m> g_m$. Define Y_M, as the first M coefficients $Y_M = \sum_{m=0}^{M-1} <Y, g_m> g_m$. For all $M\ge1$, the approximation error $\varepsilon(M)= E\{||Y-Y_M||^2\}$ is minimum if and only if $\{g_m\}_{0\le m<N}$ is a Karhunen-Loève basis ordered by increasing eigenvalues □.

Figure 2.2 shows the principal components analysis after learning with a network. Compared to the normal computation method, these networks have the advantage that they can be computed online without storing the covariance vector as in the matrix approach. Several types of neural networks solve the task of extracting the

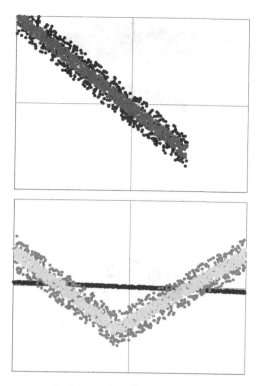

Fig. 2.2. Principal component analysis with Oja's networks. a) the principal component gives the main direction of the data. b) example showing the failure of the principal component analysis approach for nonlinear data (black line).

principal component of the signal. Let us mention the bottleneck networks [Baldi and Hornik, 1989] and Oja's networks [Oja, 1982]. The network searches for projections Ax of the data that maximize the correlation to x.

2.3.1. *Search for good data representation with multiresolution principal components analysis*

Many problems in soft computing correspond to finding out a good description of a control surface. The description of some knowledge can often be very simplified by choosing the right cartesian axis. For instance, the complexity of a fuzzy controller may sometimes be considerably reduced if the membership functions are chosen according to a preferred direction of the data. It is achieved by rotating the axis, such as the control surface is aligned according to the preferred direction.

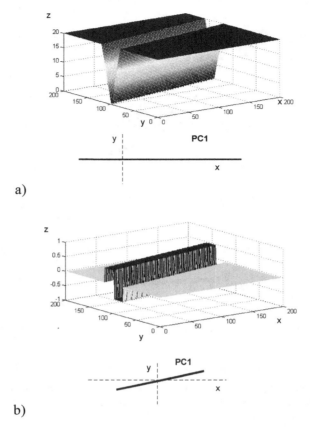

a)

b)

Fig. 2.3. Principal components analysis of the points defined on a square grid: a) Input data; the first principal component is along the x-axis; b) Wavelet coefficients; The first principal component gives the main direction of the triangular bump correctly.

Consider the surface in Figure 2.3a defined by the function's value $f(i,j)$ on a regular two-dimensional grid, indexed with its coordinates (i,j). The naive processing of the data points with a PCA of the input vectors $(i,j,f(i,j))$ gives a principal axis that is not well correlated to the direction of the triangular bump. It can be corrected by preprocessing the data first with a wavelet transform to obtain the wavelet coefficients d. In a second stage, the vectors $(i',j',d(i',j'))$ with an absolute value above a given threshold are processed with PCA. Figure 2.3b shows a one-level wavelet decomposition of the surface in Figure 2.3a with a one-dimensional Haar wavelet. The PCA of the wavelet coefficients gives the correct main direction.

Feng *et al.* [2000] show that face recognition based on PCA is improved if the principal component analysis is constrained to a midrange frequency subband.

Okimoto and Lemonds [1999] claim that principal component analysis in the wavelet domain provides powerful features for underwater object recognition. Bakshi [1999] reviews multiresolution principal analysis in process monitoring. Szu *et al.* [1998] apply wavelet preprocessing to independent component analysis.

In Li *et al.* [1999], images are analyzed with a PCA, and the k-principal components decomposed with wavelets. The high-resolution wavelet coefficients of the k-principal components enhance the low-resolution version of the image.

2.3.2. *Projection pursuit regression*

Parameter estimation often becomes unpractical in a high-dimensional space due to the sparseness of the data. Projection pursuit regression [Friedman and Stuetzle, 1981] aims to find simple approximations of a function f(**x**) from n observations. Let us consider a smooth function g, such as a spline or a polynomial. The algorithm searches for a vector $\mathbf{a} \in \mathfrak{R}^d$ that minimizes the residue r_1 with

$$r_1 = f(x) - g(\mathbf{a}^T \cdot \mathbf{x}) \tag{2.1}$$

The process is iterated, starting from the residue r_i ($i \geq 1$), till the residue is small enough. Dimension reduction is achieved by keeping the largest values of **a** and setting the others to zero.

2.3.3. *Exploratory projection pursuit*

Exploratory projection pursuits are methods that search for interesting low-dimension projections. Diaconis and Freedman [1984] furnish the basic motivation for the method. They observe that the projection of mixtures of gaussian distribution (typically d>10) to a low-dimensional space (typically d=2) is normal. Therefore, an interesting projection in a low-dimensional space differs strongly from a gaussian distribution. An index characterizes the projection. Exploratory projection pursuit searches for projections that maximize the projection index. We refer to Huber [1985] for a review paper; different indexes can be employed.

Strong connections do exist between exploratory projection pursuit and neural networks. Back-propagation in neural networks is a kind of projection pursuit, the mean-squares error taking the role of a projection index. The unsupervised BCM neuron is interpreted as a projection pursuit algorithm [Intrator,1992]. The above methods have been used in various speech or face classification problems and unsupervised feature extraction problems.

2.4. Dimension reduction through wavelet-based projection methods

2.4.1. *Best basis*

The wavelet matching pursuit algorithm [Davis *et al.*, 1994] and the best basis method are the main wavelet-based algorithms for dimension reduction. The best basis [Coifman and Wickerhauser, 1992] consists of choosing a redundant basis of orthogonal functions to compress the signal. The orthogonal redundant basis is chosen, such as the decomposition algorithm may be obtained from one set of filter coefficients.

The algorithm is best understood if one starts from the wavelet decomposition algorithm. A decomposition tree made of a cascade of filters computes the wavelet coefficients. The signal is decomposed into a low frequency and a high-frequency component at each decomposition level. At the next decomposition level, the low-frequency component of the signal is again processed after decimation (Figure 2.4b). Using the same two filters, a large number of different signal decompositions are possible by further processing the high-frequency components of the signal. The 2^J possible decompositions correspond to a full decomposition tree at level J with two orthogonal filters, and each basis function is orthogonal to the other bases.

Figure 2.4b shows the full decomposition tree for J=3. The nodes correspond to projections on a different function. The best basis algorithm furnishes a method to choose a good basis for data compression among the set defined by the full tree. The best basis method searches for a subtree (Figure 2.4c) with an optimal signal decomposition.

The search for the best basis among a dictionary of orthogonal bases consists of finding the basis that minimizes the approximation error:

$$\epsilon = \|f\|^2 - \sum_m |< f, g_m >|^2 \tag{2.2}$$

This search requires very often too much computing time. The problem can be simplified, to the cost of optimality, by searching to minimize a cost function $\gamma(x)$. The best basis corresponds to the partial tree with the minimum value of the cost function C.

$$C = \sum_m \gamma(|< f, g_m >|^2 / \|f\|^2) \tag{2.3}$$

For orthogonal wavelets, the function γ is the entropy function $S(x) = -x \log x$. is, and the cost function is

$$\sum_m S(|< f, g_m >|^2)/\|f\|^2) \tag{2.4}$$

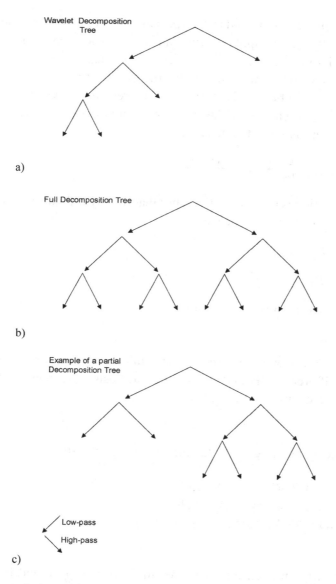

Fig. 2.4. Different decomposition trees: wavelet decomposition tree, full decomposition tree, partial decomposition tree. The best basis method determines the partial decom-position tree that minimizes the entropy of the decomposition coefficients.

This cost function is additive, and dynamic programming is, therefore, an appropriate search approach. The basis that minimizes the cost function in (2.4) corresponds to the Karhunen-Loève basis [Mallat, 1999]. Since the Karhunen-Loève basis is generally not part of the dictionary, the best basis method only finds a suboptimal solution. Compared to the Karhunen-Loève algorithm, the best basis is much more efficient computationally and furnishes a signal approximation of lower complexity in most cases. Sometimes, the best basis algorithm is described as a fast Karhunen-Loève transform [Wickerhauser, 1996].

Let us describe the best basis algorithm in more detail. Given a function or an indexed datafile f, the entropy of the energy distribution on the basis B={g_n}, with N basis function g_n, is according to (2.4)

$$S(f, B) = -\sum_{m=1}^{N} \frac{|<f, g_m>|^2}{\|f\|^2} \log_e \frac{|<f, g_m>|^2}{\|f\|^2} \tag{2.5a}$$

The entropy function is additive in the sense that for any orthonormal basis B_0 and B_1 of two orthogonal spaces, one has

$$S(f, B) = S(f, B_0 \cup B_1) \tag{2.5b}$$

with $B = B_0 \cup B_1$ $\hspace{6cm}$ (2.5c)

The best basis algorithm works as follows

Step 1:
Choose a mother wavelet ψ and construct a full decomposition tree till level J. Compute the different S(f,B(j,k,)) with B(j,k) the basis corresponding to the node (j,k) in the full decomposition tree. Set j=J-1.

Step 2:
Prune each tree by iterating the following operations till j=0

If S(j,k) ≤ S(j+1,2k)+S(j+1,2k+1) then
remove node (j+1,2k) and (j+1,2k+1) else
set S(j,k) equal to S(j+1,2 k)+S(j+1,2k+1)
j=j-1

The best tree is the pruned tree with the minimal entropy found by the above algorithm.

For non-orthogonal wavelets, the best basis uses a different cost function:

$$C = \sum_m S(|< f, g_m >|)/\|f\| \tag{2.6}$$

Figure 2.5 illustrates the algorithm with an example.

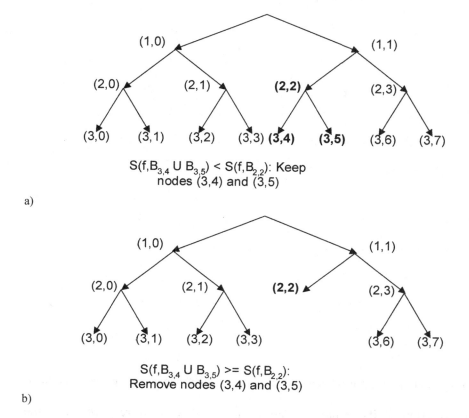

a)

$S(f, B_{3,4} \cup B_{3,5}) < S(f, B_{2,2})$: Keep
nodes (3,4) and (3,5)

b)

$S(f, B_{3,4} \cup B_{3,5}) \geq S(f, B_{2,2})$:
Remove nodes (3,4) and (3,5)

Fig. 2.5. Example showing the pruning algorithm of the best basis discriminant algorithm on the lowest level of decomposition for the two main cases: a) $S(f,B) \geq S(f, B1 \cup B2)$; b) $S(f,B) < S(f, B1 \cup B2)$.

2.4.2. *Matching pursuit*

A suitable signal decomposition as a weighted sum of a few wavelets decreases its dimension. While the best basis algorithm uses a dictionary that can be all constructed from a single set of filter coefficients, the matching pursuit uses a much larger wavelet dictionary. The best basis algorithm does not work for a general dictionary, and a different algorithm, for instance, the matching pursuit, must be implemented. The matching pursuit is a greedy algorithm. It searches at each iteration a function into the dictionary that matches some part of the signal (Figure 2.6).

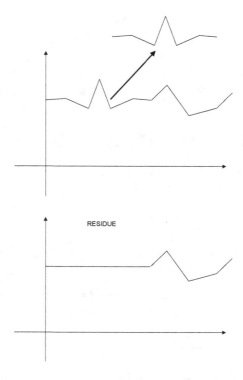

Fig. 2.6. Illustration of the matching pursuit. The matching pursuit is a greedy algorithm.

The contribution of its signal projection on this wavelet is removed, and the process is repeated with the residue. The search is terminated if the norm of the residue is below a given threshold. More formally, consider a function f approximated as a sum of functions in the dictionary. The first step in the algorithm consists of finding, with *brute force*, a basis function g_i such as

$$|< f, g_i >| \geq \beta \cdot sup_\gamma |< f, g_\gamma >| \tag{2.7}$$

with $0 < \beta \leq 1$ and γ indexing the different functions in the dictionary.

The function f is then

$$f = < f, g_i > \cdot g_i + Rf \tag{2.8}$$

With Rf, the residue. Since the residue is by definition orthogonal to g_0, one has:

$$\|f\|^2 = |< f, g_0 >|^2 + \|Rf\|^2 \tag{2.9}$$

It follows that the residue decreases at each iteration step. The convergence rate is related to β. The smaller it is, the slower the convergence rate is (For an exact computation of the convergence rate, see Mallat and Zhang [1993]).

2.5. Exploratory knowledge extraction

The search for good indicators and indexes in finance is a typical problem, and finding a suitable model may represent a substantial investment in effort and time toward a good dataset description. Also, the modeling of sensors may need some extensive basic research work. When modeling a complex unknown process from data, it is crucial to determine important variables and how much nonlinearity is necessary to obtain a satisfactory model. We will present two simple methods useful for data exploration at a very early stage.

2.5.1. *Detecting nonlinear variables' interactions with Haar wavelet trees*

The number of vanishing moments of a wavelet is related to the degree of the maximal order polynomial, such as its wavelet projection is zero- a wavelet has n vanishing moments if

$$\int_{-\infty}^{\infty} t^k \cdot \Psi(x) \cdot dx = 0, (k < n) \tag{2.10}$$

Any n-1 order polynomial projection on a wavelet with n vanishing moments is zero. This property is used in exploratory data analysis to detect low-order nonlinear interactions. Let us illustrate the method with a simple example using the Haar wavelet.

The Haar wavelet has one vanishing moment. Generally speaking, a wavelet filter with n vanishing moments acts like a differential operator and is equivalent to taking the nth derivative. The Haar wavelet has a unique vanishing moment. Therefore, the Haar transform is related to the first-order differential operator. The wavelet coefficients obtained from a one-level decomposition with Haar wavelets are proportional to the derivative of the surface along the considered direction. Similarly, the one-level wavelet coefficients of the derivative are linearly proportional to the second derivative. Let us use Haar wavelets to discover nonlinear interactions between variables. Consider the function $y_3(x_i, x_j) = x_i^2 x_j$ with ($0 < x_i, x_j < 65$, x_i, x_j integer). Figure 2.7 shows part of a decomposition tree. The first surface corresponds to the input data. After a wavelet decomposition on the x_i-axis, the surface defined by the wavelet coefficients is proportional to x_i-a wavelet decomposition on the x_i-axis results in a plane. Finally, a decomposition along the x_j-axis results in equal and non-zero coefficients. From the above decomposition, one deduces that the equation of the original surface contains an interaction term in $x_i^2 x_j$.

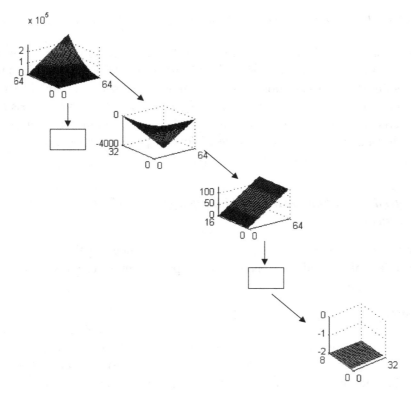

Fig. 2.7. The Haar decomposition of a surface with a wavelet tree decomposition facilitates the discovery of low-order interactions between data.

Generally speaking, identifying decomposition levels with large identical coefficients is a good indicator for low-order nonlinear interactions between variables.

Flehmig *et al.* [1998] took a slightly different approach to identify trends in process measurements. The data are fitted to a mth order polynomial through least-squares, and the residue quantifies the goodness of fit. The procedure is repeated till the low-order terms are identified. The method also relies on the fact that the number of vanishing moments is related to the degree of the maximal order polynomial, such as its projection is zero (eq. (2.10)). The residue corresponds to the energy contained in the low-resolution part of the signal. The method is also quite efficient when the signal is noisy. Flehming's approach is greatly simplified by taking m^{th} order splines. As m^{th} order cardinal B-splines form a basis for m^{th} order polynomials, wavelet decomposition of the data is sufficient to fit the data to an mth order polynomial. Although biorthogonal splines wavelets are non-orthogonal, the squared values of the low-order coefficients characterize well enough the goodness of fit. This approach is computationally much less demanding as no least-squares computation is necessary. The method's strength is detecting trends locally at many different resolutions and searching for nonlinear polynomial trends.

2.5.2. *Discovering non-significant variables with multiresolution techniques*

Assume a databank containing the output data y_k as a function of several input variables. For example, y_k may be the output of a sensor in volts, and the input variables may be temperature, time, humidity, or luminosity. In many cases, the databank may contain irrelevant data or noisy data. The problem is now identifying which variables are relevant before using standard modeling tools for learning or knowledge discovery. The multiresolution approach uses the following procedure. After having approximated the different data on a fine grid, data are preprocessed with a standard multiresolution analysis using one variable at a time. For instance, if there are two input variables, x_1 and x_2, then the output data y_k is given by a matrix. After a one-level wavelet decomposition of the rows, the columns are processed with a one-level decomposition. This process is repeated as many times as necessary to reach a very low-resolution level.

Let us define the projection indices $E_1(x_i)$, $E_2(x_i)$,...,$E_L(x_i)$,...$E_J(x_i)$ for a given variable x_i. The projection index E_L corresponds to the normalized energy in the wavelet coefficients at level L.

$$E_L(x_i) = \sum_{n=1,...,2^{L-1}} d^2{}_{L,n}(x_i) / \sum_{l=1,...,J} E_l(x_i) \tag{2.11}$$

Depending on the values of the projections indices, the variable may be assumed to be significant or not. If data are not noisy, variables with only low projection indices should be discarded. The interpretation of the indices is difficult in the case of very noisy data. As a guideline, very similar projection values indicate that the signal may be simply a white noise signal along the variable x_i. Let us show how to interpret the indices with two examples.

As a first example, consider the function $y_1=0.04\ x_i$ with $((0<x_i,x_j<65))$.

The output function y_1 is independent of the variable x_2 and only depends on x_1. All the wavelet coefficients corresponding to the decomposition along the x_2 axis are zero, while the wavelet coefficients along the second axis have non-zero values (Figure 2.8). It means that the variable x_2 can be discarded, and a low-resolution granularity description of the variable x_1 is sufficient (for instance, for modeling).

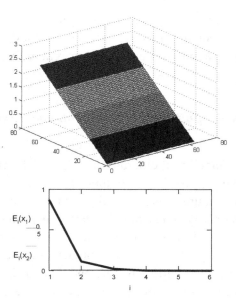

Fig. 2.8. a) Surface given by the equation y1=0.04 xi; Projection indices along the axis x1(−) and x2(--) for the curve in Figure 2.8a.

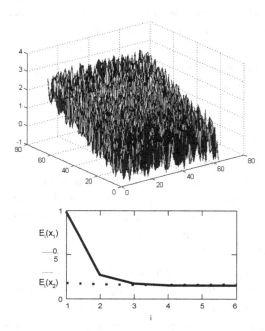

Fig. 2.9. a) Same function as in Figure 2.8 except for some additional noise. b) Projection indices along the axis x1 and x2.

The second example furnishes a somewhat more difficult case. This example is difficult because there is no unique interpretation of the projection indices. Consider the function $y_2=0.04$ x_i +N with $(0<x_i,x_j<65)$ and N a uniformly distributed random number between [-1,1]).

The coefficient $E_1(x_1)$ corresponding to the lowest resolution level has the highest value. It suggests preprocessing the signal to keep the low-frequency component along the x_1-axis. The coefficients $E_1(x_2)$ have similar values (Figure 2.9). The signal along the x_2-axis is characteristic of a white noise signal. In this case, one may try to discard the variable x_2. Let us point out that the above situation may also occur under different circumstances. The signal may be deterministic but contains many components at various frequencies, and low-resolution modeling of the process will give quite bad results.

2.6. Wavelets in classification

A multiresolution analysis is an essential tool for extracting important features in signals at different resolutions, which is necessary for many image classification problems. A multiresolution analysis also helps identify transients, edges, or spikes, essential in speech or image processing or stock market analysis.

The contribution to classification problems of multiresolution analysis is two-folded. In many classification problems, one applies multiresolution analysis to decrease the complexity of the data, such as a standard classification method becomes feasible.

Section 4.1.1 introduced the *best basis* algorithm. The basic idea behind the *best basis* is to find a function representation by using an orthogonal basis that minimizes the entropy. The algorithm searches for a low entropy signal representation with few coefficients. With slight modifications, the algorithm becomes a classification method. Instead of the entropy, the algorithm uses a different cost function: the relative entropy. The algorithm extracts features (wavelet coefficients) that characterize the dataset [Saito, 1994; Saito and Coifman, 1995]. In classification problems, the problem is not to find the best basis to compress a signal but to find a parsimonious signal representation that furnishes well-separated classes. In classification, the criterion for a good projection is a measure of class separability.

2.6.1. *Classification with local discriminant basis selection algorithms*

Linear Discriminant Analysis (LDA) is the standard linear classification method. LDA bisects the space with hyperplanes and finds the bisections that minimize the scatter of sample vectors within each class and maximize the scatter of mean vectors between classes.

Let Mc be the mean vector of class c and M the total mean vector:

$$Mc = 1/N \sum_1^N Xc_i \tag{2.12}$$

with x_c, the N points belonging to class c.

The sample covariance matrix of class c is given by

$$\Sigma_c = 1/N \sum_1^N (Xc_i - M_c) \cdot (Xc_i - M_c)^T \tag{2.13}$$

The within-class covariance is

$$\Sigma_w = \Sigma_c \Sigma_c \tag{2.14}$$

The between-class covariance is

$$\Sigma_b = \Sigma_c (M_c - M) \cdot (M_c - M)^T \tag{2.15}$$

LDA maximizes the class separability index J(s), which measures the separation between the different classes.

$$J(S) = tr[(S^T \Sigma_b S)^{-1} (S^T \Sigma_w S)] \tag{2.16}$$

The matrix S is a diagonal matrix containing the eigenvalues. The matrix S describes a map S^T x_i transforming the input space to maximize the class separability.

The linear discriminant basis method acts globally on the data, a drawback in many problems. A local approach is often necessary to separate the data correctly in different classes. The local discriminant basis selection algorithm [Saito, 1994] solves the issue. The best basis approach inspires the approach. The algorithm searches for a discriminate basis to separate the signal into different classes. Consider first a set of N_c one-dimensional training signals of the same length belonging to a given class. Its relative energy is

$$\Gamma_c(j, k, l) = \Sigma_c (\Sigma_1^{N_c} W c_{j,k,l}^2) / \Sigma_c (\Sigma_1^{N_c} X c_i^2) \tag{2.17}$$

with j giving the level of decomposition, k the branch in the tree at this level, l the position, Xc the original data, and Wc representing the wavelet decomposition coefficients.

The Kullback-Leibler distance $D_{c1,c2}$ between two classes (Kullback and Leibler, 1951) is a measure of the relative entropy of the energy in the different subbands: The Kullback-Leibler distance is:

$$D_{c1,c2}(j,k) = \sum_l \Gamma_{c1} \log \frac{\Gamma_{c1}(j,k,l)}{\Gamma_{c2}(j,k,l)} \tag{2.18}$$

The relative entropy is asymmetric. If an asymmetric quantity is preferred, one can use the expression:

$$D \equiv D_{c1,c2} + D_{c2,c1} = 1/2(\sum_l \Gamma_{c1} \log \frac{\Gamma_{c1}(j,k,l)}{\Gamma_{c2}(j,k,l)} + \Gamma_{c2} \log \frac{\Gamma_{c2}(j,k,l)}{\Gamma_{c1}(j,k,l)}) \tag{2.19}$$

The sum of all individual two-classes relative entropy for more than two classes measures the entropy. The local discriminant basis selection algorithm finds the best basis, like the best basis algorithm. The relative entropy function D is additive in the sense that for any orthonormal bases B_0 and B_1 of two orthogonal spaces, one has

$$D(f,B) = D(f, B_0 \cup B_1)$$

with $B = B_0 \cup B_1$

Dynamic programming can be applied to search for the best basis, and the best basis is the one that minimizes the relative entropy. The algorithm works as follows:

Step 1:
Choose a mother wavelet and construct a full decomposition tree till level J for the training data in each class. Compute the different relative entropies D(j,k) with j the decomposition level and k the node's position in the decomposition tree. Set j=J-1.

Step 2:
Prune the tree by iterating the following operations till j=0

If D(j,k) ≤ D(j+1,2 k)+D(j+1,2k+1) then
remove node (j+1,2k) and (j+1,2k+1) else
set D(j,k) equal to D(j+1,2 k)+D(j+1,2k+1)
j=j-1

Step 3:
Keep the k most discriminant basis functions to construct the classifier.

Figure 2.10 shows a single algorithm step on the lowest decomposition level for a given tree.

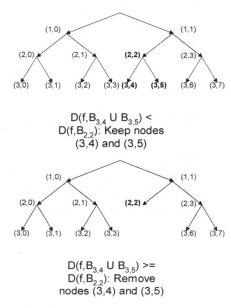

Fig. 2.10. Example showing the pruning algorithm of the best basis discriminant algorithm on the lowest level of decomposition for the two cases: a) D(f, B) ≥ D(f, B1 ∪ B2); b) D(f, B) ≤ D(f, B1 ∪ B2).

2.6.2. *Classification and regression trees (CART) with local discriminant basis selection algorithm preprocessing*

The combination of local discriminant analysis with CART (Classification And Regression Tree) offers new possibilities for classification. CART is a statistical model conceived at Stanford [Breiman *et al.*, 2017], and it belongs to the class of binary recursive partitioning methods.

The algorithm determines the next node to be processed, and it attaches two branches with end nodes to it. A so-called maximal tree is grown using a variable or a linear combination of variables to determine splits.

Figure 2.11 gives an example of a binary regression tree. Saito [1994) has shown that classifying seismic signals with a tree gives significantly better results if the data are preprocessed with a local discriminant basis selection algorithm. In this approach, the tree is grown on the signals represented in the local discriminant basis selection algorithm. The classification tree is carried out with a classification and regression tree (CART). Once complete, pruning reduces the complexity of the result.

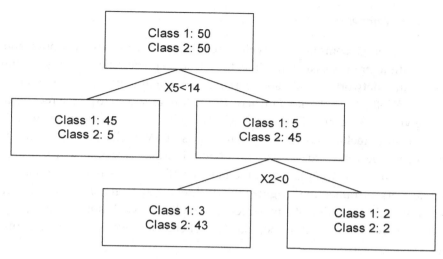

Fig 2.11. Example of classification with CART.

As mentioned earlier, wavelets are not shift-invariant. It is a major difficulty in some classification problems. Shift-invariant multiresolution representations are occasionally necessary, and using a redundant basis is a standard method of obtaining shift-invariancy. In Saito and Beylkin [1993], shift-invariant multi-resolution is based on the so-called auto-correlation shell, formed by dilations and translations of the auto-correlation functions of compactly supported wavelets. Auto-correlation shells have two attractive properties: i) with orthogonal wavelets, the auto-correlation is an interpolating function; ii) a fast algorithm computes the projection coefficients very efficiently.

2.7. Applications of multiresolution techniques for preprocessing in soft computing

This chapter briefly reviews the significant achievements of multiresolution preprocessing techniques in soft computing. The contribution of wavelets is substantial in many application areas. Liu *et al.* [2000] and Szu [1999] review wavelet transforms for pattern recognition. Wavelet methods are implemented in many intelligent systems, for instance, in power engineering [Ashenayi, 1997], for quality inspection of surface mounted devices [Brito *et al.*, 1997], condition monitoring, inspection [Serrano *et al.*, 1999], process monitoring in nuclear power plants [Schoonwelle *et al.*, 1996] image enhancement or registration in medical applications. Wavelet preprocessing has found an extensive range of applications in chemistry.

2.7.1. *Neural networks*

Many applications combining wavelet techniques and neural networks add a multiresolution preprocessing module to select characteristic features as input to the neural network. Applications range from automatic target recognition [Baras and Wolk, 1994; Park and Chao, 1997; Xun *et al.*, 1996], face recognition [Foltyniewicz, 1996], and Thai character recognition [de Vel *et al.*, 1995]. The success of these techniques is somewhat surprising. Wavelet decomposition is a priori, not the best method for pattern recognition due to the lack of translation invariance. An explanation is that if the number of examples is large enough, the neural network is trained to recognize the different statistical correlations patterns between wavelet coefficients at different levels of resolution. Kohonen-type Neural networks are also quite popular [Deschenes and Noonan, 1995; Tamayo and de Gyvez, 1996].

Many applications of wavelet preprocessing are in the medical domain. Medical images are well suited to wavelet processing as often the information is contained in sharp edges or localized contrasts. Also, detecting life-threatening situations in neurosurgical operations may benefit from multiresolution techniques. Wavelet processed intracranial pressure characterizes the patient's state [Swiercz *et al.*, 1998]. Many papers address the automatic classification of EEG signals [Hazarika *et al.*, 1997] with multiresolution techniques. Denoising medical images, for instance, magnetic resonance images [Sarty and Kendall, 1996], is also a classical application of wavelet preprocessing. Monitoring the depth of anesthesia for patients undergoing surgical operations is another application [Linkens *et al.*, 1997; Linkens and Abbod, 1998; Abbod and Linkens, 1998]. The system uses neuro-fuzzy and wavelet analysis to monitor and evaluate the depth of anesthesia based on the auditory evoked response signals, heart rate, and blood pressure. Depending on the evaluation of the depth of anesthesia, a rule-based fuzzy controller suggests a target concentration. This application is a good illustration of hybrid approaches' power to combine several signal processing methods.

Texture analysis significantly benefits from wavelet preprocessing. Wang *et al.* [1996, 1997] have followed such an approach to classify textures with a fuzzy ART model. Westra [2000] describes the application of wavelet and neuro-fuzzy classification techniques to identify defects in printed decorations. Wavelet preprocessing helps to classify clouds. Clouds' texture is extracted and fed into a neural network to determine the type of clouds [Shaikh *et al.*, 1996]. Face recognition and quality controls [Ko *et al.*, 1995] are two other domains. Interesting sensor applications combine wavelet preprocessing with neural networks. Pratt *et al.* [1995] use wavelet preprocessing on signals from electromagnetic sensors to diagnose the depth and nature of buried waste. The method is non-invasive, and its success rate is high. The condition of tools can be estimated using force, strain, or vibration sensors [Kamarthi and Pittner, 1997; Zhou *et al.*, 1995]. Another application is automatic sensor recalibration [Kunt *et al.*, 1998; Padgett *et al.*, 1998]. Gas sensors or electronic noses are known to drift over time and require a recalibration from time to time. Recalibration ensures the correct functioning of the sensors. The typical signature of sensors is a criterion for deciding on whether a recalibration is required.

Other examples are in the field of quality inspection and condition monitoring. The vibration signature measured from strain or force sensors in condition monitoring is compared to prototype vibrations. Samuel and Pines [1997] use piezoelectric strain sensors to identify the vibration signature from a planetary geartrain under fault conditions. In quality inspection, an image of an object is wavelet-transformed, and the algorithm identifies bad pieces by comparing some wavelet extracted features to a template image.

2.7.2. *Fuzzy logic*

Image processing is an important domain of application for multiresolution hybrid techniques. Besides the already mentioned neuro-fuzzy applications, different approaches combine fuzzy logic with multiresolution analysis. Tolias *et al.* [1999] propose an image queries software using a fuzzy similarity matching of the wavelet transformed color image. Hybrid methods combining fuzzy logic and multiresolution analysis are applied to contour extraction and segmentation. The system analyzes wavelet preprocessed images with a fuzzy system. Cheng and Cheng [1998] review early applications in computer tomography of the brain and digital mammography.

A multiresolution analysis is combined with fuzzy logic in automatic target recognition, tracking, and image registration. The multiresolution character of wavelet decomposition is advantageous when the distance to an object is unknown. Wang *et al.* [1997] describe a computer vision system for automatic target recognition and tracking.

Image segmentation is enhanced by including information on the image texture. Betti *et al.* [1997] improve the texture discrimination on synthetic aperture radar data by using a fractal representation of the texture derived from the wavelet coefficients.

Fuzzy systems also adaptively determine the thresholding method or parameters [Shark and Yu, 2000].

2.7.3. *Genetic algorithms*

Multiresolution methods and a genetic algorithm have taken much time to apply broadly. An important reason for that situation is that in many problems, the best basis or the matching pursuit algorithms are often superior to genetic algorithms [Lankhorst and van der Laan, 1995]. Matching pursuit or the best basis approach is the favored method to determine a good wavelet basis in a dictionary. Nevertheless, there are situations in which genetic algorithms may be preferred. For instance, genetic algorithms select wavelets from an extensive dictionary [Lee, 1999; Tagliarini *et al.*, 1996]. This approach has been used in texture classification [Naghdy and Turgut, 1997] and radio transients identification systems [Toonstra and Kinsner, 1996]. Also, some automatic target recognition [Wilson *et al.*, 1996] and image registration systems have been optimized with genetic algorithms. The image is first preprocessed, and well-discriminating wavelet coefficients are selected with the genetic search. Chalermwat and El-Ghazawi, [1999] use related approaches for image registration for texture classification. Recent works on multi-resolution techniques in genetic algorithms include research by Almutairi and Fieldsend [2019] and Yuan *et al.* [2021], showing in practical applications on voice separation with convolutional networks how to optimize the network with genetic algorithms at variable resolutions. In part 10, we show that multiresolution techniques are central to modern heuristics such as bee search or swarm search.

Genetic algorithms have also found applications in many other situations. Genetic algorithms are commonly used to optimize neural networks or systems of several neural networks in problems where gradient descent is not optimal. It is, therefore, not surprising that the optimization of wavelet networks with genetic algorithms has had some success [Yang *et al.*, 1997].

Hybrid methods combining genetic algorithms and multiresolution analysis have been tested in finance for trend analysis. Let us give here two examples. A fuzzy inference system for predicting stock trends has been designed by optimizing membership functions with a genetic algorithm [Kishikawa and Tokinaga, 2000]. The system predicts trends based on the multiresolution analysis of past data. The second application is on exchange rate forecasting. The method applies a neural network to predict future exchange rates. The efficiency of the network depends on the quality of the input data. Data are preprocessed by denoising them with a wavelet thresholding method (see 1.7.3). We have mentioned in the previous section that finding a good threshold method for wavelet denoising is a very important and difficult problem. The threshold value is selected through a genetic algorithm [Shin and Han, 2000].

Genetic algorithms will find many more applications connected to multi-resolution analysis, especially in multi-objective optimization and search problems or situations in which strong constraints are set on the space of possible solutions. As a final remark, we believe that part of the essence of genetic and evolutionary computing can often be expressed in the language of multiresolution. We refer to part 10 for more information.

References

Abbod, M. and Linkens, D. (1998). Anaesthesia monitoring and control using fuzzy logic fusion, *Yixué gongchéng. Applications, basis, communications*, 10(4), pp. 225–235.

Almutairi, A.T. and Fieldsend, J.E. (2019). Automated and surrogate multi-resolution approaches in genetic algorithms, *Proc. 2019 IEEE Symposium Series on Computational Intelligence (SSCI)*, IEEE, pp. 2066–2073.

Ashenayi, K. (1997). A Review of Applications of Intelligent Systems Technology in Power Engineering, *FRONTIERS OF POWER CONFERENCE*, A UNIVERSITY EXTENSION PROGRAM, p. XII–XII.

Bakshi, B.R. (1999). Multiscale analysis and modeling using wavelets, *Journal of Chemometrics: A Journal of the Chemometrics Society*, 13(3-4), pp. 415–434.

Baldi, P. and Hornik, K. (1989). Neural networks and principal component analysis: Learning from examples without local minima, *Neural networks*, 2(1), pp. 53–58.

Baras, J.S. and Wolk, S.I. (1994). Model-based automatic target recognition from high-range-resolution radar returns, *Automatic Object Recognition IV*, (International Society for Optics and Photonics), pp. 57–66.

Bellman, R.E. (2015). *Adaptive control processes*. Princeton university press.

Betti, A., Barni, M. and Mecocci, A. (1997). Using a wavelet-based fractal feature to improve texture discrimination on SAR images, *Proceedings of International Conference on Image Processing*, IEEE, pp. 251–254.

Breiman, L. *et al.* (2017). Classification and regression trees. Routledge.

Brito, A., Kosheleva, O. and Cabrera, S. (1997). Multi-resolution data processing is optimal: case study of detecting Surface Mounted Devices, *NIST special publication*, (918), pp. 157–161.

Chalermwat, P. and El-Ghazawi, T. (1999). Multi-resolution image registration using genetics, *Proc. 1999 International Conference on Image Processing (Cat. 99CH36348)*, IEEE, pp. 452–456.

Cheng, D.-C. and Cheng, K.-S. (1998). Multiresolution based fuzzy c-means clustering for brain hemorrhage analysis, *Proc. 2nd International Conference on Bioelectromagnetism (Cat. No. 98TH8269)*, IEEE, pp. 35–36.

Coifman, R.R. and Wickerhauser, M.V. (1992). Entropy-based algorithms for best basis selection, *IEEE Transactions on information theory*, 38(2), pp. 713–718.

Deschenes, C.J. and Noonan, J. (1995). Fuzzy Kohonen network for the classification of transients using the wavelet transform for feature extraction, *Information Sciences*, 87(4), pp. 247–266.

Diaconis, P. and Freedman, D. (1984). Asymptotics of graphical projection pursuit, *The annals of statistics*, pp. 793–815.

Feng, G.-C., Yuen, P.C. and Dai, D.-Q. (2000). Human face recognition using PCA on wavelet subband, *Journal of electronic imaging*, 9(2), pp. 226–233.

Flehmig, F., Watzdorf, R. and Marquardt, W. (1998). Identification of trends in process measurements using the wavelet transform, *Computers & chemical engineering*, 22, pp. S491–S496.

Foltyniewicz, R. (1996). Automatic face recognition via wavelets and mathematical morphology, *Proc. 13th International Conference on Pattern Recognition*, IEEE, pp. 13–17.

Garey, M.R. and Johnson, D.S. (1979) *Computers and intractability*. Freeman San Francisco.

Hazarika, N. *et al.* (1997). Classification of EEG signals using the wavelet transform, *Signal processing*, 59(1), pp. 61–72.

Huber, P.J. (1985). Projection pursuit, *The Annals of Statistics*, pp. 435–475.

Kamarthi, S. and Pittner, S. (1997). Fourier and wavelet transform for flank wear estimation—a comparison, *Mechanical Systems and Signal Processing*, 11(6), pp. 791–809.

Kishikawa, Y. and Tokinaga, S. (2000). Prediction of stock trends by using the wavelet transform and the multi-stage fuzzy inference system optimized by the GA, *IEICE transactions on fundamentals of electronics, communications and computer sciences*, 83(2), pp. 357–366.

Ko, H. *et al.* (1995). Image enhancements using wavelet preprocessing for printed circuit board classification, *Wavelet Applications II* (International Society for Optics and Photonics), pp. 473–480.

Kullback, S. and Leibler, R.A. (1951). On information and sufficiency, *The annals of mathematical statistics*, 22(1), pp. 79–86.

Kunt, T.A. *et al.* (1998). Optimization of temperature programmed sensing for gas identification using micro-hotplate sensors, *Sensors and Actuators B: Chemical*, 53(1–2), pp. 24–43.

Lankhorst, M.M. and van der Laan, M.D. (1995). Wavelet-Based Signal Approximation, *Evolutionary Programming IV: Proceedings of the Fourth Annual Conference on Evolutionary Programming*, MIT Press, p. 237.

Lee, D. (1999). An application of wavelet networks in condition monitoring, *IEEE Power Engineering Review*, 19(1), pp. 69–70.

Li, J., Zhou, Y. and Li, D. (1999). PCA and wavelet transform for fusing panchromatic and multispectral images, *Sensor Fusion: Architectures, Algorithms, and Applications III* (International Society for Optics and Photonics), pp. 369–377.

Linkens, D. and Abbod, M. (1998). Intelligent control of anaesthesia, IEE Colloquium on Intelligent Methods in Healthcare and Medical Applications (Digest No. 1998/514), IET, pp. 2–1.

Linkens, D., Abbod, M. and Backory, J. (1997). Closed-loop control of depth of anaesthesia: a simulation study using auditory evoked responses, *Control Engineering Practice*, 5(12), pp. 1717–1726.

Liu, J. *et al.* (2000). Wavelet theory and its application to pattern recognition. World scientific.

Mallat, S. (1999). A wavelet tour of signal processing. Elsevier.

Mallat, S.G. and Zhang, Z. (1993). Matching pursuits with time-frequency dictionaries, *IEEE Transactions on signal processing*, 41(12), pp. 3397–3415.

Naghdy, G. and Turgut, A. (1997). Evolutionary procedure for the optimisation of a generic texture classifier, *1997 IEEE International Conference on Intelligent Processing Systems (Cat. No. 97TH8335)*, IEEE, pp. 574–578.

Oja, E. (1982). Simplified neuron model as a principal component analyzer, *Journal of mathematical biology*, 15(3), pp. 267–273.

Okimoto, G.S. and Lemonds, D.W. (1999). Principal component analysis in the wavelet domain: New features for underwater object recognition, *Detection and Remediation Technologies for Mines and Minelike Targets IV* (International Society for Optics and Photonics), pp. 697–708.

Padgett, M.L., Roppel, T.A. and Johnson, J. (1998). Pulse coupled neural networks (PCNN), wavelets and radial basis functions: olfactory sensor applications, *1998 IEEE International Joint Conference on Neural Networks Proceedings. IEEE World Congress on Computational Intelligence (Cat. No. 98CH36227)*, IEEE, pp. 1784–1789.

Park, Y. and Chao, T.-H. (1997). Automatic target recognition processor using an optical wavelet preprocessor and an electronic neural classifier, *Optical Pattern Recognition VIII* (International Society for Optics and Photonics), pp. 299–306.

Pratt, L.Y. *et al.* (1995). Interpolation, wavelet compression, and neural network analysis for hazardous waste characterization, *Proc. 1995 IEEE International Conference on Systems, Man and Cybernetics. Intelligent Systems for the 21st Century* (IEEE), pp. 2058–2063.

Saito, N. (1994). Local feature extraction and its applications using a library of bases.

Saito, N. and Beylkin, G. (1993). Multiresolution representations using the autocorrelation functions of compactly supported wavelets, *IEEE Transactions on Signal Processing*, 41(12), pp. 3584–3590.

Saito, N. and Coifman, R.R. (1995). Local discriminant bases and their applications, *Journal of Mathematical Imaging and Vision*, 5(4), pp. 337–358.

Samuel, P.D. and Pines, D.J. (1997). Health monitoring and damage detection of a rotorcraft planetary geartrain system using piezoelectric sensors, *Smart Structures and Materials 1997: Smart Structures and Integrated Systems* (International Society for Optics and Photonics), pp. 44–53.

Sarty, G. and Kendall, E. (1996). Self-diffusion maps from wavelet de-noised NMR images, *Journal of Magnetic Resonance, Series B*, 111(1), pp. 50–60.

Schoonwelle, H., Van der Hagen, T. and Hoogenboom, J. (1996). Process monitoring by combining several signal-analysis results using fuzzy logic, in *Fuzzy Logic and Intelligent Technologies in Nuclear Science*.

Serrano, I., Lazaro, A. and Oria, J. (1999). Ultrasonic inspection of foundry pieces applying wavelet transform analysis, *Proc. 1999 IEEE International Symposium on Intelligent Control Intelligent Systems and Semiotics (Cat. No. 99CH37014)*, IEEE, pp. 375–380.

Shaikh, M.A. *et al.* (1996). Automatic neural network-based cloud detection/classification scheme using multispectral and textural features, *Algorithms for Multispectral and Hyperspectral Imagery II* (International Society for Optics and Photonics), pp. 51–61.

Shark, L.-K. and Yu, C. (2000). Denoising by optimal fuzzy thresholding in wavelet domain, *Electronics letters*, 36(6), pp. 581–582.

Shin, T. and Han, I. (2000). Optimal signal multi-resolution by genetic algorithms to support artificial neural networks for exchange-rate forecasting, *Expert Systems with Applications*, 18(4), pp. 257–269.

Swiercz, M. *et al.* (1998). Neural network technique for detecting emergency states in neurosurgical patients, *Medical and Biological Engineering and Computing*, 36(6), pp. 717–722.

Szu, H., Hsu, C. and Yamakawa, T. (1998). Image Independent Component Analysis via Wavelet Subbands, *5th Soft computing, Iizuka, Japan*, pp. 135–138.

Tagliarini, G.A. *et al.* (1996). Genetic algorithms for adaptive wavelet design, *Wavelet Applications III* (International Society for Optics and Photonics), pp. 82–93.

Tamayo, O.M. and de Gyvez, J.P. (1996). Preprocessing operators for image compression using cellular neural networks, *Proc. of International Conference on Neural Networks (ICNN'96)*, IEEE, pp. 1500–1505.

Tolias, Y., Panas, S. and Tsoukalas, L.H. (1999). FSMIQ: fuzzy similarity matching for image queries, *Proc. 1999 International Conference on Information Intelligence and Systems (Cat. No. PR00446)*, IEEE, pp. 249–254.

Toonstra, J. and Kinsner, W. (1996). A radio transmitter fingerprinting system ODO-1, *Proc. 1996 Canadian Conference on Electrical and Computer Engineering*, IEEE, pp. 60–63.

de Vel, O., Wangsuya, S. and Coomans, D. (1995). On Thai character recognition, *Proc. ICNN'95- International Conference on Neural Networks*, IEEE, pp. 2095–2098.

Vetterli, M. and Kovacevic, J. (1995). *Wavelets and subband coding*. Prentice-hall.

Wang, J., Naghdy, G. and Ogunbona, P. (1996). A new wavelet based ART network for texture classification, *1996 Australian New Zealand Conference on Intelligent Information Systems. Proceedings. ANZIIS 96* (IEEE), pp. 250–253.

Wang, S.X. *et al.* (1997). Development of gazing algorithms for tracking-oriented recognition, *Automatic Target Recognition VII* (International Society for Optics and Photonics), pp. 37–48.

Westra, R.L. (2000). Adaptive Control Using CCD-images: Towards a Template-invariant Approach. Mathematics, Maastricht University.

Wickerhauser, M.V. (1996). Adapted wavelet analysis: from theory to software. CRC Press.

Wilson, T.A. *et al.* (1996). Fusion of focus of attention alternatives for FLIR imagery, *Automatic Object Recognition VI*, International Society for Optics and Photonics, pp. 76–86.

Xun, Z., Ronghui, S. and Guirong, G. (1996). Automatic HRR target recognition based on Prony model wavelet and probability neural network, *Proc. International Radar Conference* (IEEE), pp. 143–146.

Yang, Z.-J., Sagara, S. and Tsuji, T. (1997). System impulse response identification using a multi-resolution neural network, *Automatica*, 33(7), pp. 1345–1350.

Yuan, W. *et al.* (2021). Evolving Multi-Resolution Pooling CNN for Monaural Singing Voice Separation, *IEEE/ACM transactions on audio, speech, and language processing*, 29, pp. 807–822.

Zhou, Q., Hong, G. and Rahman, M. (1995). A new tool life criterion for tool condition monitoring using a neural network, *Engineering Applications of Artificial Intelligence*, 8(5), pp. 579–588.

Spline-Based Wavelets Approximation and Compression Algorithms

Part 3

Chapter 3

Spline-Based Wavelets Approximation and Compression Algorithms

The first section furnishes a short introduction to cardinal B-spline. Cardinal B-splines are polynomial spline functions with equally spaced knots with the nice property to be defined recursively by integral functions. The following sections introduce three types of wavelet constructions based on B-splines (Biorthogonal, semi-orthogonal and orthogonal). Their choice is motivated by the fact that these wavelets can be used within a fuzzy logic framework. Each of these three spline-wavelets permits to cover well an important aspect of so-called fuzzy wavelet methods:

- Biorthogonal spline wavelets are typically implemented in fuzzy wavelet networks. These wavelets have the great advantage of compact supports, a valuable property for online learning.
- Semi-orthogonal spline wavelets are very useful in off-line learning since they are the closest spline wavelets to orthogonal.
- Orthogonal spline-based wavelets are good candidates for developing fuzzy rules in the frequency domain.

Multidimensional spline-based wavelets are easily constructed using cartesian products of univariate spline wavelets.

3.1. Spline-based wavelets

3.1.1. *Introduction to B-splines*

The theoretical foundations of spline decomposition lie in work by [Schoenberg, 1946]. The first significant applications of splines methods appeared quite later. Besides surface fitting, splines have been implemented in computer graphics [Bartels, Beatty, and Barsky, 1995; Dierckx, 1995] and broadly in sophisticated medical applications [Carr *et al.*, 1998]. Several signal processing software include spline analysis in their toolbox. Although the field has matured, new important works still appear in the literature. In particular, the integration of multiresolution into the scope of spline research [Cohen, Daubechies, and Feauveau, 1992; Sweldens, 1995] has opened up the field quite broadly. In this introduction, we limit the discussion to B-splines. One finds spline approximation in 3D animations and video games, and it would lead us beyond our topic to discuss advanced splines methods, such as the Non-Uniform Rational B-Spline (NURBS). See [Unser, 1999] for a review.

A B-spline function is a piecewise polynomial function defined on a lattice. The order of the spline function determines the properties of the spline. The most straightforward spline function is the characteristic function of the unit interval. The characteristic function N1(x) or Haar function [Haar, 1910] is

$$N^1(x) = \begin{matrix} 1 & 0 \le x < 1 \\ 0 & otherwise \end{matrix} \tag{3.1}$$

The characteristic function is a piecewise zero-order polynomial function (Figure 3.1).

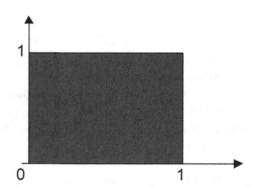

Fig. 3.1. The characteristic function.

Cardinal B-spline functions of higher orders can be defined iteratively by the integral equation:

$$N^k(x) = \int_0^1 N^{k-1}(x-t) \cdot dt \tag{3.2}$$

The second-order cardinal B-spline is the triangular function, a continuous function summing piecewise polynomials of order 1. In more general terms, a kth order cardinal B-spline is C^{k-2} continuous and composed of piecewise polynomials of degree k-1.

B-splines have helpful properties:

- The B-spline functions are the polynomial splines with the shortest support.
- All values are positive.
- Splines have a closed-form formula and piecewise polynomials. Spline-based wavelets are the only wavelets with such a property [Unser, 1999].
- Spline functions form a partition of unity: a superposition of translated B-splines fulfills the equation

$$\sum_{j=-\infty}^{\infty} N^k(x+j) \equiv 1. \qquad (3.3)$$

Figure 3.2 illustrates it on second-order splines. This property permits to give a simple fuzzy interpretation of a spline decomposition.

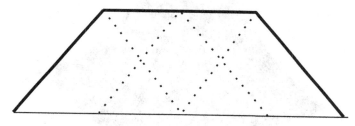

Fig. 3.2. Translated cardinal B-splines partition the unity.

- Suppose a function of the form $y = \sum_j a_j \cdot N_j^k$ with $N_j^k = N^k(x-j)$ with $k>1$. The derivative of y is $dy(x)/dx = \sum_j (k-1) \cdot (a_{j+1} - a_j) \cdot N_j^{k-1}$.

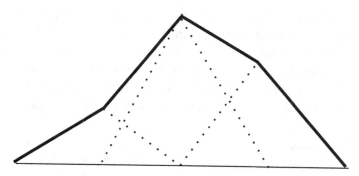

Fig. 3.3. Spline decomposition with second-order splines. The black curve is the sum of second-order splines.

Splines are central to function approximation theory and applications (Figure 3.3). Multivariate B-spline basis functions are generated by multiplying univariate basis functions (Figure 3.4). A basis function for an n-variables system is

$$N_j^k(x) = \prod_{i=1}^{n} N_{j,i}^k(x_i) \tag{3.4}$$

The good properties of univariate B-splines, such as bounded support and piecewise polynomial description, still hold in the multidimensional case.

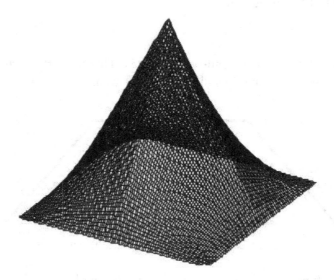

Fig. 3.4. Example of a two-variate B-splines based on the triangular function. Biorthogonal spline-wavelet.

Biorthogonal spline wavelets have useful properties in real applications. On the one hand, both the wavelet $\psi(x)$ and the dual wavelet $\tilde{\psi}(x)$ have a compact support; on the other hand, the scaling function $\varphi(x)$ is always positive. This permits to interpret the scaling functions as membership functions in a fuzzy framework. Biorthogonal spline wavelets are typically used in wavelet networks and also in online problems in which a simple method to process the boundaries is necessary.

Cohen, Daubechies, and Feauveau [1992] have shown how to construct biorthogonal spline wavelets based on compactly supported splines. Their method is quite general and offers great flexibility in the wavelets' design. For instance, the construction permits choosing the number of vanishing moments to a large extent. Let us recall that a wavelet has n vanishing moments if:

$$\int_{-\infty}^{\infty} t^k \cdot \psi(x) \cdot dx = 0 \, , (k < n) \tag{3.5}$$

When choosing a wavelet family for an application, the number of vanishing moments, the degree of the scaling function, and the support length must be considered.

Figure 3.5 shows biorthogonal spline wavelets indexed as (4,2). The scaling function is the second-order cardinal B-spline, and the function ψ has 4 vanishing moments. Biorthogonal wavelets fulfill the biorthogonality condition (Figure 3.6).

$$< \tilde{\psi}_{m,n}, \psi_{m',n'} >= \delta(m - m') \cdot \delta(n - n') \tag{3.6}$$

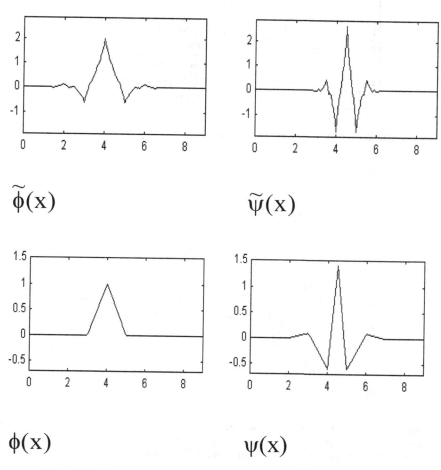

$\tilde{\phi}(x)$ $\tilde{\psi}(x)$

$\phi(x)$ $\psi(x)$

Fig. 3.5. Biorthogonal spline scaling and wavelet functions and their duals.

Table 3.1: The filter coefficients for the wavelet decomposition and reconstruction algorithms with (4,2) biorthogonal spline wavelets.

	k = 2	
J	p_j	q_j
1	0.994368911	0.707106781
2	0.419844651	0.353553905
3	0.176776695	
4	0.066291260	
5	0.033145630	

	k = 2	
J	g_j	h_j
1	0.707106781	0.994368911
2	0.353553905	0.419844651
3		0.176776695
4		0.066291260
5		0.033145630

The annex at the end explains the construction of spline wavelets.

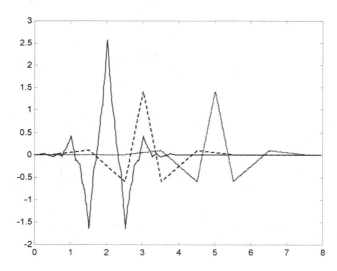

Fig. 3.6. The dual wavelet $\tilde{\psi}$ (solid line) is orthogonal to all wavelets $\psi_{m,n}$. The two wavelet functions in that example are orthogonal to the dual wavelet. The filter coefficients for the wavelet decomposition and reconstruction algorithms are in the table below.

3.1.2. *Semi-orthogonal B-wavelets*

Some of the most efficient algorithms in multiresolution analysis work best with orthogonal wavelets. The reason is that orthogonal wavelets fulfill the power complementarity condition. Denoising, compression, or approximation algorithms use this property. The squared value of the detail coefficients estimates the energy contained in the different projections. The total energy is the sum of the energy contained in detail and the lower-level approximation coefficients.

There are no orthogonal wavelet constructions with a spline as a scaling function. Only semi-orthogonal wavelet constructions are feasible. For semi-orthogonal wavelets, the power complementarity condition does not hold. Nevertheless, the squared values of the wavelet coefficients furnish an estimation of the signal energy contained at the different levels of resolution. This property is sufficient for many algorithms to work very well still.

Orthogonal wavelets with B-splines as scaling functions do not exist, except for the trivial case of the Haar wavelet. Semi-orthogonal B-wavelets are the wavelets that are the closest to an orthogonal wavelet. Semi-orthogonal B-wavelets are wavelets with B-splines as scaling functions. Semi-orthogonality means that wavelets of different resolutions are orthogonal to each other.

Definition: Semi-orthogonal wavelet:
A wavelet ψ is semi-orthogonal if the basis $\{\psi_{m,n}\}$ satisfies

$$< \psi_{m,n}, \psi_{m',n'} >= 0, m \neq m' \tag{3.7}$$

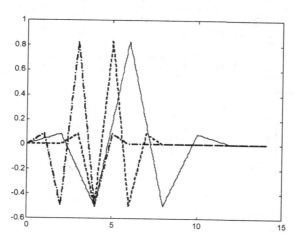

Fig. 3.7. Semi-orthogonal wavelets fulfill the condition $<\psi_{m,n}, \psi_{m',n'}> = 0$ for m $\neq$ m'. Illustration with second-order semi-orthogonal B-spline wavelets. The two-times dilated wavelets (solid line) are orthogonal to the two other wavelets.

Contrarily to orthogonal wavelets, translated versions of wavelets of a given resolution are not always orthogonal. Orthogonality is only between wavelets of different resolutions (Figure 3.7). Practically, one has different coefficients for the decomposition and reconstruction filters.

The filters associated with the semi-orthogonal B-spline constructions are not finite. Special procedures around endpoints are necessary, such as folding the data around the endpoints. The following table gives the first filter coefficients corresponding to the semi-orthogonal wavelets of order 2 and 4, associated with the linear B-spline and the cubic B-spline [Chui, Lemm, and Sedigh, 1992].

Table 3.2: The following table gives the first filter coefficients corresponding to the semi-orthogonal wavelets of order 2 and 4, associated with the linear B-spline and the cubic B-spline [Chui, 1992].

	Order 2		Order 4	
j	p_j	q_{j+1}	p_{j+1}	q_{j+4}
1	0.683012701	0.866025403	0.893162856	-1.475394519
2	0.316987298	-0.316987298	0.400680825	0.468422596
3	-0.116025403	-0.232050807	-0.282211870	0.742097698
4	-0.084936490	0.084936490	-0.232924626	-0.345770890
5	0.031088913	0.062177826	0.129083571	-0.389745580
6	0.022758664	-0.022758664	0.126457446	0.196794277
7	-0.008330249	-0.016660498	-0.066420837	0.207690838
8	-0.006098165	0.006098165	-0.067903608	-0.106775803
9	0.002232083	0.004464167	0.035226101	-0.111058440
10	0.001633998	-0.001633998	0.036373586	0.057330952
11	-0.000598084	-0.001196169	-0.018815686	0.059433388
12	-0.000437828	0.000437828	-0.019473269	-0.030709700
13	0.000160256	0.000320512	0.010066747	-0.031811811
14	0.000117315	-0.000117315	0.010424052	0.016440944

	Order 2		Order 4	
j	g_j	h_{j+1}	g_{j+1}	h_{j+4}
1	1	5/6	0.75	-24264/8!
2	0.5	-0.5	0.5	18482/8!
3		1/12	1/8	-7904/8!
4				1677/8!
5				-124/8!
6				1/8!

Depending on the order of the B-wavelets, the filters associated with the wavelet decomposition and reconstruction algorithms have different properties. At order zero, the B-wavelet corresponds to the Haar wavelet, while at high order, the wavelet almost matches the gaussian function. For odd-order and m≥3, the wavelet $\psi^m{}_b$ is approximated by sin(ω t) g(t-b) with g(t-b) the gaussian function. For even-order $\psi^m{}_b$ is almost of the form cos(ω t) g(t-b). The B-wavelet of increasing order approaches the limit set by Heisenberg to the product of a function's time and frequency resolution.

Heisenberg's uncertainty principle states that ($\Delta\omega$ $\Delta t \geq \frac{1}{2}$). The equality holds for a function f(t) of the form: $f(t) = a \cdot e^{i \cdot a \cdot t} \cdot e^{-b(t-u)^2}$. It follows that the time-frequency resolution of B-wavelets tends to ½ with increasing order.

3.1.3. *Battle-Lemarié wavelets*

We have mentioned the impossibility of constructing orthogonal B-wavelets with a B-spline scaling function. Nevertheless, orthogonal wavelets based on B-splines may be designed with an orthogonalization procedure. The resulting orthogonal wavelets are called Battle-Lemarié wavelets. The Battle-Lemarié wavelets [Battle, 1987; Lemarié, 1988] are piecewise polynomials. Their scaling function is not

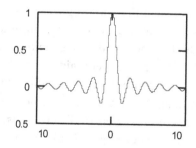

Sinc function

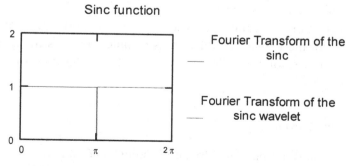

Fourier Transform of the sinc

Fourier Transform of the sinc wavelet

Fig. 3.8. The sinc wavelet is the equivalent of the Haar wavelet for the frequency domain.

positive everywhere; the main obstacle to a linguistic interpretation of the results of a decomposition. The properties of the Battle-Lemarié wavelets depend on the chosen order. The two extremes, N=0 and N→∞ correspond to two limit cases for filters. The scaling function of the first-order case corresponds to the characteristic function: a perfect spatial filter. The scaling function tends to the sinc function for large N, the perfect low-pass filter (Figure 3.8). By choosing the order of the Battle-Lemarié wavelet, one simultaneously chooses the type of filter. For this reason, Battle-Lemarié wavelets are good candidate functions for designing a fuzzy controller in the frequency domain (see part 2).

3.2. A selection of wavelet-based algorithms for spline approximation

One approximates a function f(x) as a weighted sum of wavelets

$$f(x) = \sum_{n,m} d'_{m,n} \cdot \psi_{m,n}(x) + \sum_{n,m_0} c'_{n,m_0} \cdot \varphi_{m_0,n}(x) \tag{3.8}$$

or equivalently as a weighted sum of scaling functions

$$\hat{f}(x) = \sum_{n,m} \hat{c}_{m,n} \cdot \varphi_{m,n}. \tag{3.9}$$

The two following sections present thresholding techniques, while the last section describes an adaptation of the matching pursuit algorithm to splines.

The thresholding method removes the coefficients with a squared value below a given threshold. The energy contained in the reconstructed signal compared to the total signal energy measures the quality of the approximation. The thresholding method is still applicable to semi-orthogonal wavelets, in which orthogonality holds only between wavelets of different resolutions and gives good results with biorthogonal splines. Biorthogonal spline wavelets are not orthogonal. Nevertheless, the orthogonality relation holds to a sufficient degree, and the thresholding method can also be applied.

For wavelet and scaling functions with compact support, each wavelet can be decomposed with the two-scales relation as a finite sum of scaling functions at one higher level of resolution. Therefore, thresholding algorithms on the scaling coefficients can be designed.

3.2.1. *Wavelet thresholding*

Part 1 gave a short introduction to thresholding, and we discuss some of its essential aspects here in more detail. Thresholding is a simple wavelet-based method to compress information furnishing an approximate description of a function f(x) with a limited number of terms. The filters corresponding to decomposition on an orthogonal basis fulfill the power complementarity condition. The power complementarity condition implies energy conservation. For a decomposition level, the energy conservation is expressed by the relation:

$$\Sigma_n \, c_{m,n}^2 = \Sigma_{n\prime} \, c_{m-1,n\prime}^2 + d_{m-1,n\prime}^2 \tag{3.10}$$

For a complete decomposition, the energy conservation becomes:

$$\Sigma_n \, f^2(x_n) = \Sigma_n \, d_{m,n}^2 = \Sigma_n \, d_{m-1,n}^2 + d_{m-2,n}^2 + \dots + d_{0,n}^2 + c_{0,n}^2 \tag{3.11}$$

The thresholding method sets to zero all coefficients below a given threshold (Figure 3.9). The function f(x) is reconstructable from the K coefficients among $d_{m,n}$, $c_{0,n}$ containing the most energy. The compression factor is the difference between the number of bits necessary to store the original signal and the memory capacity to store and address the K coefficients. The error $Er(\hat{f})$ on the reconstruction is the relative difference between the energy contained in the function f(x) and its estimate $\hat{f}(x)$ given by an expression of the form:

$$d_{m,n}^{\prime} = 0 \quad \text{if} \quad d_{m,n}^2 \leq T$$

$$d_{m,n}^{\prime} = 0 \quad \text{if} \quad d_{m,n}^2 > T$$

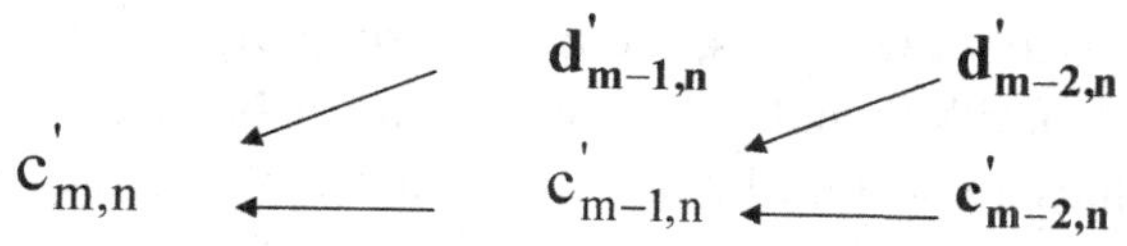

$$c_{m,n}^{\prime} \quad\longleftarrow\quad d_{m-1,n}^{\prime} \qquad\qquad d_{m-2,n}^{\prime}$$

$$c_{m,n}^{\prime} \quad\longleftarrow\quad c_{m-1,n}^{\prime} \quad\longleftarrow\quad c_{m-2,n}^{\prime}$$

Fig. 3.9. The thresholding method keeps the most significant coefficients among the wavelet coefficients and the approximation coefficients at the lowest level of resolution (i.e., bold coefficients) to compress the information—an illustration of the algorithm for a two-level decomposition tree. The coefficients $c\prime_{m,n}$ approximate the function f(x).

$$\hat{f}(x) = \Sigma_{n,m} \, d\prime_{m,n} \cdot \psi_{m,n}(x) + \Sigma_{n,m_0} \, c\prime_{m_0 \cdot n} \cdot \varphi_{m_0,n} \tag{3.12}$$

$$Er(\hat{f}) = \Sigma_n (f^2(x_n) - \hat{f}^2(x_n)) / \Sigma_n (f^2(x_n)) \tag{3.13}$$

This algorithm is optimal for orthogonal wavelets. For semi-orthogonal constructions, the algorithm is also generally applied. The energy is only partially conserved in a semi-orthogonal decomposition. To see this, let us express the norm of the function f as a function of the detail coefficients. To simplify the formalism, let us assume a complete decomposition of a function f of zero average.

$$< f, f > = < \Sigma_{m,n} d_{m,n} \cdot \psi_{m,n}, \Sigma_{m',n'} d_{m,n} \cdot \psi_{m',n'} > \qquad (3.14)$$

For semi-orthogonal wavelets, (3.12) can be put under the form:

$$< f, f > = \Sigma_m (\Sigma_n d_{m,n}^2 + \Sigma_{n \neq n'} d_{m,n} \cdot d_{m,n'} \cdot < \psi_{m,n}, \psi_{m,n'} >) \qquad (3.15)$$

Energy conservation is, in general, not fulfilled. There are two special cases in which energy conservation is fulfilled to a good degree. For the energy conservation to hold to a reasonable degree, the last term in (3.15) must be small. It is the case if

a) the function f(x) is reasonably described as a white noise signal. In this case, the coefficients $d_{m,n}$ are uncorrelated.

b) $< \psi_{m,n}, \psi_{m,n'} >$ is small for $n \neq n$ '.

In summary, for semi-orthogonal splines, the sum of the squared detail coefficients is generally not equal to the total energy contained in the signal. Nevertheless, the signal energy at the different levels of resolution equals the total energy. Therefore, keeping the largest coefficients is a good strategy that furnishes good results.

For some biorthogonal wavelets, the thresholding algorithm is also used. It is the case of several biorthogonal spline wavelets. In biorthogonal wavelets, the frame bounds' values indicate whether it is reasonable to use the thresholding algorithm. To see why let us introduce the notion of a frame.

Definition:
An ensemble of functions (or vectors) $\{\theta_n\}$ with n, an index is a frame of a Hilbert space H if there exist two constants A>0, B>0, such as for any f ∈ H:

$$A\|f\|^2 \leq \Sigma_n |< f, \theta >|^2 \leq B\|f\|^2 .$$

Biorthogonal wavelets are Riesz basis and form a frame (see part 1). The expression (B/A)-1 measures how far is a basis from being orthogonal. Orthogonal wavelets are tight frames meaning that A = B = 1.

Biorthogonal splines are, to a reasonable approximation, tight frames. In biorthogonal spline wavelets, the energy conservation holds in the first approximation.

3.2.2. *Thresholding in the spline-wavelet framework*

We will address the problem of finding a good representation of a function f(x) as a sum of scaling functions at different resolutions. More precisely, one searches for an approximation of f(x) in terms of the scaling functions associated with a dyadic wavelet decomposition: $f(x) = \sum_{m=0...J} \sum_n c'_{m,n} \cdot \varphi_{m,n}(x)$ with $\varphi_{m,n}(x) = 2^{m/2} \cdot \varphi(2^m \cdot x - n)$ (m, n integer).

The motivation behind this problem will become apparent in the following chapters, as we will use splines as scaling functions and interpret them as membership functions in a fuzzy framework. The least mean-squares (LMS) find the optimal decomposition as a sum of same-resolution scaling functions. The least mean-squares fitting is quite computer-intensive, and a neural network sometimes replaces the LMS approach. The complexity of the problem increases if one uses scaling functions of different resolutions. The least mean-square methods become rapidly practically intractable. Also, the linear dependence existing between scaling functions at different resolutions is computationally problematic. In those cases, one addresses the problem with a variant of the wavelet thresholding technique or a matching pursuit algorithm.

By definition of a multiresolution, any wavelet is a linear sum of the scaling function:

$$\psi(x) = \sum_k h_n \cdot \varphi(2 \cdot x - n) \tag{3.16}$$

Both the wavelet thresholding method and the matching pursuit may be used to search for a good decomposition in terms of scaling functions. For example, Figure 3.10 shows the second-order B-wavelet decomposition as a sum of scaling functions at one higher level of resolution. The function f(x) is first decomposed as a sum of wavelets: This equation, together with a similar relation for the scaling function, is called the two-scales relations.

$$f(x) = \sum_{m=0...M} \sum_n d'_{m,n} \cdot \psi_{m,n}(x) + c_{0,n} \cdot \varphi_{0,n} \tag{3.17}$$

In a second step, each wavelet is expressed as a sum of scaling functions using the two-scales relation:

$$f(x) = \sum_{m=0...M} \sum_n c'_{m,n} \cdot \varphi_{m,n}(x) \tag{3.18}$$

The necessary computing power to determine the coefficients $c'_{m,n}$ is generally much smaller than a least mean-squares approach that requires dealing with large matrices.

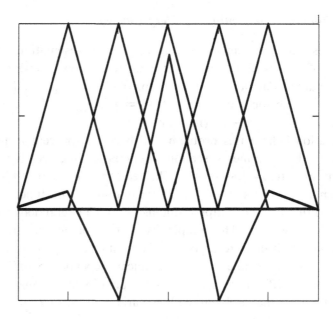

Fig. 3.10. Decomposition of a second-order spline wavelet into a sum of translated scaling functions. (coefficients are (1/12,-0.5,5/6,-0.5,1/12)).

An alternative and more efficient method is first to transform the detail coefficients with the reconstruction algorithm and keep the largest coefficients expressed in the scaling functions. First, the detail coefficients are expressed in terms of the scaling function using the reconstruction algorithm: $c_{m,n} = \sum_k g_{n-2k} \cdot c_{m-1,k} + h_{n-2k} \cdot d_{m-1,k}$. Rewriting the equation as the sum of a low-frequency $c_{ml,n}$ and a high-frequency contribution $c_{mh,n}$

$$c_{m,n} = c_{ml,h} + c_{mh,n} \tag{3.19}$$

one obtains

$$c_{mh,n} = \sum_k h_{n-2k} \cdot d_{m-1,k} \tag{3.20}$$

The problem of finding a good function description in terms of the scaling functions is by using the largest coefficients among the reconstructed coefficients $c_{mh,n}$ and the lowest level approximation coefficients. The coefficients $c_{mh,n}$ correspond to coefficients of the scaling function. Figure 3.11 illustrates this procedure.

$$c'_{mh,n} = 0 \quad \text{if} \quad c^2_{mh,n} < T$$

$$c'_{mh,n} = c_{mh,n} \quad \text{if} \quad c^2_{mh,n} \geq T$$

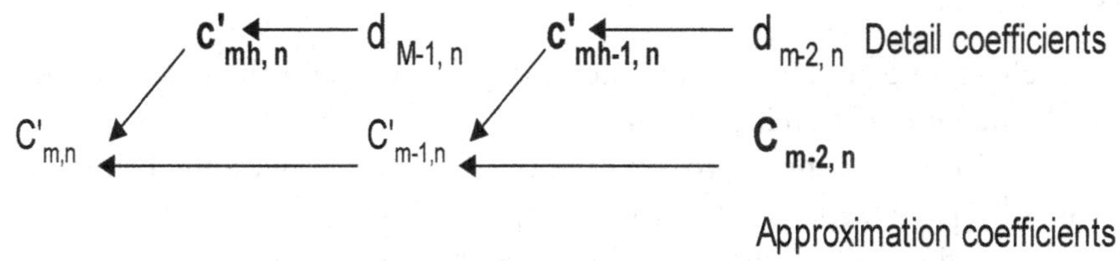

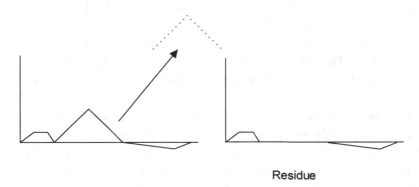

Fig. 3.11. The best fuzzy rules correspond to the largest coefficients among the wavelet coefficients expressed as scaling functions and the approximation coefficients at the lowest level of resolution (bold coefficients).

A level-dependent multiplicative factor can also be used in the spirit of regularization theory.

3.2.3. *Matching pursuit with scaling functions*

Mallat and Zhang [1993] designed the matching pursuit algorithm, an approach aiming at finding a wavelet decomposition with few coefficients. The algorithm also works with spline scaling functions [Shmilovici and Maimon, 1995, 1996, 1998; Thuillard, 1998] though a modified matching pursuit algorithm is preferable [Thuillard, 2000]. Figure 3.12 shows the basic idea of the modified matching pursuit algorithm described below.

Residue

Fig. 3.12. A matching pursuit algorithm determines the best membership functions and rules.

Algorithm:

Define a dictionary $\boldsymbol{D} = \{\varphi_{m,n}^k\}$ of scaling functions with $\varphi_{m,n}^k = 2^m \cdot \varphi(2^m \cdot x - n)$. The index k indexing the order of the scaling function, m the dilation, and n the translation (The normaliz ation factor is contrary to previous sections 2^m).

For each scaling function in the dictionary, decompose the data with the fast wavelet decomposition algorithm.

- Keep for each k, the approximation coefficient $c_{m,n}^k$ with the largest m such as $\left|c_{m,n}^k\right| > \beta \, sup_{m',n'}\left|c_{m',n'}^k\right|$ with 0<β≤1.
- Choose the coefficient that minimizes the residue (i.e. write f(x) = $c_{m,n}^k \cdot \varphi_{m,n}^k(x) + R(x)$ and choose the coefficient that minimizes <R(x),R(x)>).
- Take the residue as input.

Repeat the procedure till the residue is below a given value.

The algorithm is essentially the same as the wavelets' matching pursuit. The main idea behind this modification is the following. First, the condition $\left|c_{m,n}^k\right| > \beta \, sup_{m',n'}\left|c_{m',n'}^k\right|$ with 0<β≤1 ensures the convergence of the matching pursuit. Mallat and Zhang [1993] show that the convergence rate is related to the value β. Roughly, the smaller the β, the slower is the convergence rate. On the other hand, the additional step in the algorithm, requiring keeping the coefficient with the smaller resolution fulfilling the above condition, often discovers the most appropriate resolution to compress the signal. Figure 3.13 illustrates the algorithm with a simple example: the decomposition of a second-order spline function with a semi-orthogonal spline construction. Using a value of β=0.7 in $\left|c_{m,n}^k\right| > \beta \, sup_{m',n'}\left|c_{m',n'}^k\right|$ restricts the best matching coefficients to the bald coefficients. In Mallat's s algorithm, one could have chosen any of them. The second condition prescribes choosing the coefficient corresponding to the scaling function with the lowest resolution. The coefficient kept at this iteration is underlined.

If β is larger than 0.68, the algorithm furnishes the best matching function after a single iteration. The algorithm catches the last level of resolution. At lower resolutions, the approximation coefficients correspond to the decomposition of the unit impulse and rapidly decrease. A smaller β value would not have permitted to discover the proper resolution. On the other hand, a large value of β close to one is also not desirable as the slightest noise or some small deviation to the spline function may lead to choosing a suboptimal solution. For an a priori unknown function, we recommend a β value of about 0.9 for splines of order up to 3.

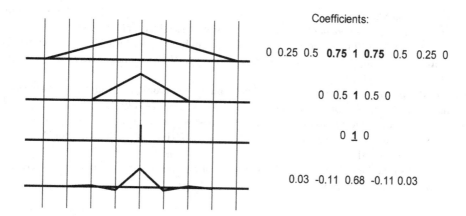

Coefficients:

0 0.25 0.5 **0.75** **1** **0.75** 0.5 0.25 0

0 0.5 1 0.5 0

0 **1** 0

0.03 -0.11 0.68 -0.11 0.03

Fig. 3.13. Illustration of the search algorithm with a modified matching pursuit algorithm. The algorithm discovers, in most cases, the best resolution to describe the dataset locally.

References

Bartels, R.H., Beatty, J.C. and Barsky, B.A. (1995). *An introduction to splines for use in computer graphics and geometric modeling* (Morgan Kaufmann).

Battle, G. (1987). A block spin construction of ondelettes. Part I: Lemarié functions, *Communications in Mathematical Physics*, 110(4), pp. 601–615.

Carr, J.C., Gee, A.H., Prager, R.W. and Dalton, K.J. (1998, February). Quantitative visualisation of surfaces from volumetric data, *Proc. 6th Int. Conf. Central Europe on Computer Graphics and Visualization* (WSCG'98) (pp. 9–13).

Chui, C.K., Lemm, J.M. and Sedigh, S. (1992). *An introduction to wavelets* (Academic Press).

Cohen, A., Daubechies, I. and Feauveau, J. (1992). Biorthogonal bases of compactly supported wavelets, *Communications on pure and applied mathematics*, 45(5), pp. 485–560.

Dierckx, P. (1995). *Curve and surface fitting with splines* (Oxford University Press).

Haar, A. (1910). Zur theorie der orthogonalen funktionensysteme, *Mathematische annalen*, 69(3), pp. 331–371 (in German).

Lemarié, P.-G. (1988). Ondelettes à localisation exponentielle, *J. Math. Pures Appl.*, 67, pp. 227–236 (in French).

Mallat, S.G. and Zhang, Z. (1993). Matching pursuits with time-frequency dictionaries, *IEEE Transactions on signal processing*, 41(12), pp. 3397–3415.

Schoenberg, I.J. (1946). Contributions to the problem of approximation of equidistant data by analytic functions. Part B. On the problem of osculatory interpolation. A second class of analytic approximation formulae, *Quarterly of Applied Mathematics*, 4(2), pp. 112–141.

Shmilovici, A. and Maimon, O. (1996). Best fuzzy rule selection with orthogonal matching pursuit, *Proc. Fourth European Congress on Intelligent Techniques and Soft Computing EUFIT*, pp. 592–96.

Shmilovici, A. and Maimon, O. (1998). On the solution of differential equations with fuzzy spline wavelets, *Fuzzy sets and systems*, 96(1), pp. 77–99.

Shmilovici, A. and Maimon, O.Z. (1995). Fuzzy systems approximation by frames-SISO case, *Proc. of 1995 IEEE International Conference on Fuzzy Systems* (IEEE), pp. 2057–2062.

Sweldens, W. (1995). Lifting scheme: a new philosophy in biorthogonal wavelet constructions, in *Wavelet applications in signal and image processing III* (International Society for Optics and Photonics), pp. 68–79.

Thuillard, M. (1998). Fuzzy-wavelets: theory and applications, Proc. Sixth European Congress on Intelligent Techniques and Soft Computing *(EUFIT'98)*, pp. 2–1149.

Thuillard, M. (2000). Applications of fuzzy wavelets and wavenets in soft computing illustrated with the example of fire detectors, in *Wavelet Applications VII* (International Society for Optics and Photonics), pp. 351–361.

Unser, M. (1999). Splines: A perfect fit for signal and image processing, *IEEE Signal processing magazine*, 16(6), pp. 22–38.

Automatic Generation of a Fuzzy System with Wavelet-Based Methods and Spline-Based Wavelets

Part 4

Chapter 4

Automatic Generation of a Fuzzy System with Wavelet-Based Methods Spline-Based Wavelets

Fuzzy rule-based systems have found numerous applications in many different fields. The two main fuzzy methods are Mamdani's min-max inference mechanism and the Takagi-Sugeno approach. Many variations of these two models have been proposed and applied with success. For instance, the product can be used as AND operator. Also, the defuzzification process can be done with many different methods. The center of gravity defuzzification and the fuzzy mean are the most popular.

Modeling a surface with the singleton Takagi-Sugeno model using splines as membership functions is equivalent to a functional decomposition with splines. It permits to relate multiresolution analysis to the problem of learning from data in fuzzy logic. The algorithms in the previous chapter describe how to choose the best scaling functions to describe a function. The chapter sketched the correspondence between splines and a fuzzy membership function. It shows how spline scaling functions are interpreted as membership functions in the fuzzy framework. The wavelet-based fuzzy approach uses the equivalence between the Takagi-Sugeno model and spline-wavelet modeling:

- A Takagi-Sugeno singleton model can be designed from a spline wavelet decomposition of the data.

Both representations are numerically equivalent, provided spline functions fuzzify the output space and one uses a center of gravity defuzzification method. The resulting spline decomposition consists of linguistically interpretable rules.

Combining it with the approaches in Part 3, we suggest that the fuzzy wavelet algorithm selects the most appropriate spline functions in a dictionary, comprising translated and dilated versions of so-called mother scaling functions.

Alternatively, the decomposition can be done in the spline wavelet space and expressed as a sum of higher resolution scaling functions.

4.1. Fuzzy rule-based systems

Fuzzy logic has found applications in basically all domains of science, from biology to particle physics. The majority of applications are clearly in control. What are the reasons for the success of fuzzy logic? The linguistic interpretation of fuzzy rules is undoubtedly one of the main reasons. The possibility of translating human expert knowledge formulated by an experienced practitioner without a solid mathematical background into a fuzzy system is the primary motivation behind fuzzy logic. Very often, the way around is at least as important. Fuzzy logic allows the development of transparent algorithms that can be explained to specialists, practitioners, or customers. Another strong point for fuzzy logic is that it represents a simple method for describing nonlinearities. Finally, fuzzy logic furnishes a theoretic framework to fuse information under different forms and qualities. The fusion of qualitative or even imprecise knowledge with information extracted from experimental data is quite challenging, especially when experts (human or machine) contradict each other. The process of reconciling the different experts is very often ad-hoc. Methods based on adaptive templates introduce transparency into the process.

The majority of applications use fuzzy rule-based systems expressed under the form of if-then rules:

$$R_i : if \ \pmb{x} \ is \ A_i \ then \ y \ is \ B \tag{4.1}$$

Here, A and B are linguistic terms, x is the input linguistic variable, and y is the output. The value of the input linguistic variable may be crisp or fuzzy. If the value of the input variable is a crisp number, then the variable x is called a singleton. For example, suppose that x is a linguistic variable for the temperature. The input linguistic variable may be crisp *'30 (°C)'* or fuzzy *'about 25'* in which *'about 25'* is a fuzzy set.

The Takagi-Sugeno and the Mamdani models are probably the most popular approaches to rule-based fuzzy systems. Alternatives to these models include, among others, the linguistic equation approach, a method that has proven to be successful in a broad range of applications [Juuso, 1996; Juuso and Järvensivu, 1998; Leiviskä and Juuso, 1996].

4.1.1. *Max-min method (Mamdani)*

An important definition in fuzzy logic is that of a membership function. The membership function $\mu(\hat{z})$ to a fuzzy set z is defined by the mapping $\mu(\hat{z}): Z \longrightarrow [0,1]$, in which Z represents the domain of definition of the fuzzy set z.

In the Mamdani approach, the fuzzy inference is processed in three steps:

<u>Step 1</u>: Determine a set of fuzzy rules and membership functions.
$$\mu_{A_i}(\hat{x}): X \longrightarrow [0,1]$$
$$\mu_{B_j}(\hat{y}): Y \longrightarrow [0,1]$$

<u>Step 2</u>: Compute the degree of fulfillment β_i of the inputs to the rule antecedents. The membership function corresponding to the fuzzy input I is defined as
$$\mu_I(\hat{x}): X \longrightarrow [0,1]$$
The expression gives the degree of fulfillment:

$$\beta_i = max_X[\mu_I(\hat{x}) \wedge \mu_{A_i}(\hat{x})] \text{ with } \wedge \text{ the minimum operator (or the product).}$$

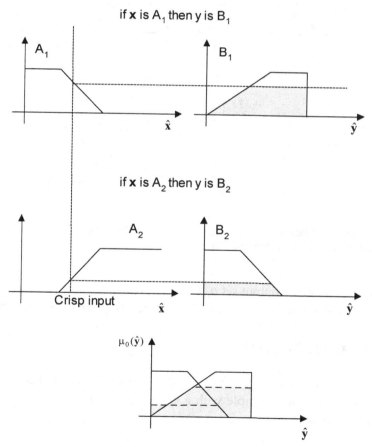

Fig. 4.1. Illustration of Mamdani inference mechanism.

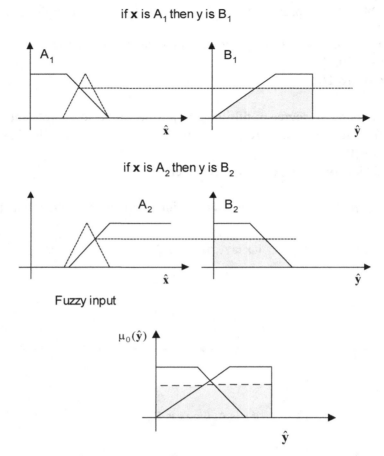

Fig. 4.2. Illustration of Mamdani inference mechanism when the input is a fuzzy set. In multivariate systems, the min operator is used for the conjunction AND.

Step 3: Derive the fuzzy output set $\mu_O(\hat{y})$.
The fuzzy output set $\mu_O(\hat{y})$ is obtained by aggregating the different output fuzzy sets:

$$\mu_O(\hat{y}) = max_{i,j}(\beta_i \wedge \mu_{B_j}(\hat{y}))$$

The Mamdani type of fuzzy system is illustrated with two examples.

Figure 4.1 shows an example with a crisp input, while Figure 4.2 shows the algorithm for a fuzzy input.

4.1.2. *Takagi-Sugeno model*

In the Takagi-Sugeno [1985] method [Takagi and Sugeno, 1985], the fuzzy rules are expressed differently:

$$R_i: if\ \textbf{\textit{x}}\ is\ A_i\ then\ y = f_i(\textbf{\textit{x}}) \tag{4.2}$$

Contrarily to Mamdani's s method, the output is a crisp number. The algorithm is slightly different (see Figure 4.3 for an example):

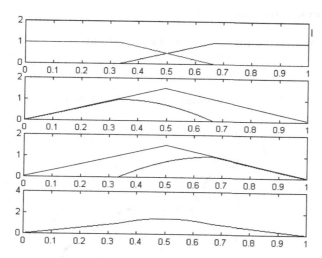

Fig. 4.3. Illustration of Takagi-Sugeno inference mechanism. From above: membership functions, triangular input function, and values of the first and second membership function. Last window: output.

Step 1: Determine a set of fuzzy rules and membership functions.

$$R_i: if\ \textbf{\textit{x}}\ is\ A_i\ then\ y = f_i(\textbf{\textit{x}})$$

$$\mu_{A_i}(\tilde{x}): X \longrightarrow [0,1]$$

Step 2: Compute the degree of fulfillment β_i of the inputs to the rule antecedents. The membership function corresponding to the fuzzy input I is defined as
$$\mu_I(\tilde{x}): X \longrightarrow [0,1]$$
The expression gives the degree of fulfillment:

$$\beta_i = max_X[\mu_I(\tilde{x}) \wedge \mu_{A_i}(\tilde{x})] \text{ with } \wedge \text{ the minimum or the product operator.}$$

<u>Step 3</u>: Derive the output.

$\hat{y} = \sum_i \beta_i \cdot f(\hat{x}) / \sum_i \beta_i$

$$f(\hat{x}) = \mathbf{a}^T_i \cdot \hat{x} + \mathbf{b}_i \tag{4.3}$$

This model is quite attractive as the coefficients $\mathbf{a}_i, \mathbf{b}_i$ is computed by a least-squares method.

4.1.3. *The singleton model*

In a singleton model, the fuzzy rule has a crisp output:

$$R_i : if\ x\ is\ A_i\ then\ y = b_i \tag{4.4}$$

Figure 4.4 illustrates, with an example, the singleton model.

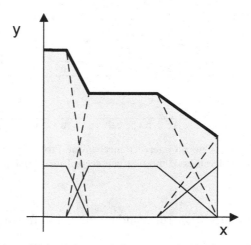

Fig. 4.4. Illustration of Takagi-Sugeno inference mechanism for a singleton model.

4.1.4. *Fuzzification of the output in a Takagi-Sugeno model*

In the setting of the singleton model, the Takagi-Sugeno model is equivalent to an ensemble of rules of the form:

$$R_i : if\ x\ is\ A_i\ then\ y\ is\ B \tag{4.5}$$

provided a center of gravity defuzzification is applied and

$$\mu_{Bj}(x) = N^k(x - n) \tag{4.6}$$

Let us consider a fuzzy system described by a set of rules of the form:

$$R_i : if \; \pmb{x} \; is \; A_i \; then \; y \; is \; B \; (C_{i,j})$$

where A_i and B_j are linguistic variables and $C_{i,j}$ the confidence level, let take the product as AND operator and the addition implementing the fuzzy union.

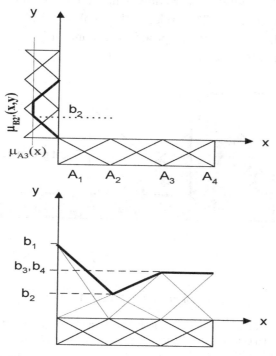

Fig. 4.5. The Takagi-Sugeno fuzzy system transforms into a fuzzy system with both fuzzified input and output.

A remarkable property of spline functions is used to compute the confidence levels starting from the weight b_i in a Takagi-Sugeno model. There exists an invertible relationship between the confidence levels $C_{i,j}$, and the spline coefficients b_i. Assume a confidence level $C_{i,j}$ for the rule $R_{i,j}$ given by the following expression:

$$C_{i,j} = N^k(b_i - j) \tag{4.7}$$

$N^k(b_i - j)$ is a kth order cardinal spline centered at j. In the fuzzy framework, N^k is interpreted as a membership function, and $N^k(b_i - j)$ corresponds to the degree of membership $\mu_{Bj}(b_i)$ to B_j (Figure 4.5).

The weight b_i can be computed from the different confidence levels $C_{i,j}$. The crisp output after defuzzification with a center of gravity defuzzification method gives precisely the value b_i.

$$b_i = \sum_j C_{i,j} \cdot y_j^c \tag{4.8}$$

with y_j^c the center of gravity of B_j or equivalently the position of the center knot of the B-spline function N^k. This relationship holds for all B-splines at any order. Figure 4.6 shows a graphical proof for second-order B-spline functions. A complete proof is in Brown and Harris [1994].

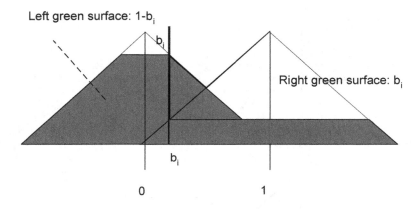

Center of gravity: $(0*(1-b_i)+1*b_i)/(b_i+1-b_i)=b_i$

Fig. 4.6. Graphical proof of the invertible relationship between the weight space and the confidence level space for the case of a center of gravity defuzzification and second-order splines.

4.2. Type-2 Fuzzy systems

Zadeh [1975] initially proposed Type-2 fuzzy logic to argue against the critics that no uncertainty is built into fuzzy membership functions. He proposed membership functions containing the possibility of including uncertainty directly in their definition per design. Type-2 fuzzy logic is often a necessity to compute with words. For instance, the term 'hot' is not the same for everybody. Type-2 membership function tries to capture it and makes the value of the membership function an interval instead of a real value. Figure 4.7 shows an example of a type-2 membership function:

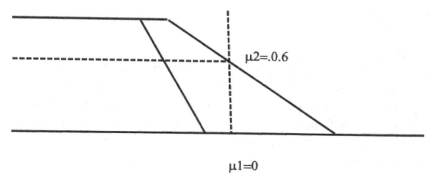

$$\mu 1=0$$

Fig. 4.7. A type-2 fuzzy membership function consists of an envelope describing the minimum and maximum value of the membership function, and these functions better describe uncertainty than type-1 fuzzy membership functions.

For each input x, two values give the membership functions maximum and minimum values. They define a range of possible values of the membership function. The largest one is $\overline{\mu}_j^n(x_i)$ and the lowest one $\underline{\mu}_j^n(x_i)$. The fuzzy rules are formulated in the 'if...then...' form as the classical approach (type-1). The inference result is also similarly computed using an operator on the lower values of the membership functions and then separately on the upper values. More specifically, a given rule n is

Rule n:

$$IF\ x_1\ is\ X_1^n\ and\ ...and\ x_j is\ X_j^n\ ..and\ x_I\ is\ X_I^n\ THEN\ y_1\ is\ Y^n \tag{4.9}$$

Given an input vector $x = (x_1, ..., x_I)$

For each x_i, two values of the membership functions on X_j^n $(1 \leq j \leq I)$ are defined as a lower one $\underline{\mu}_j^n(x_i)$ an upper one $\overline{\mu}_j^n(x_i)$.

The firing strength of the rule n is an interval $[\underline{f}_n, \overline{f}_n]$ with

$$[\underline{f}_n, \overline{f}_n] \equiv [\underline{\mu}_1^n(x_i) \times \underline{\mu}_2^n(x_i) \times ... \times \underline{\mu}_I^n(x_i), \overline{\mu}_j^n(x_i) \times \overline{\mu}_2^n(x_i) \times ... \times \overline{\mu}_I^n(x_i)]$$

$$\tag{4.10}$$

The difficulty of defining simple algorithms to compute the output of a fuzzy system has hindered the development of type-2 algorithms until Karnik and Mendel [2001a,b] proposed a straightforward method. Let us describe it succinctly. The so-called 'type reduction' computes the consequence of the rules as an interval $[y_d, y_u]$. The algorithm searches for the minimum y_l and the maximum y_r values of the expression

$$f = \sum_{j=1}^{N} f_j \, x_j / \sum_{j=1}^{n} f_j \tag{4.11}$$

with $f_j \in [\underline{f_j}, \overline{f_j}]$.

The main observation leading to their algorithm is the following. Consider the values x_j ordered in increasing values. The partial derivative $\partial f / \partial f_j = (1/\sum_{j=1}^{n} f_j)(y_j - f)$ describes how the firing strength changes with increasing or decreasing f. If $y_j > f$ then the derivative is positive while for $y_j < f$, it will become negative. The inequality is valid for any j, and therefore there exists a switch point k such as

$$\frac{\partial f}{\partial f_j} > 0 \; for \; y_j > k \; and \; \frac{\partial f}{\partial f_j} < 0 \; for \; y < k \tag{4.12}$$

and as illustrated in Figure 4.8, one chooses the lower values $\overline{f_j}$ below the switch point and the higher values $\underline{f_j}$ above it. The KM algorithm finds the switching point in generally a few iterations.

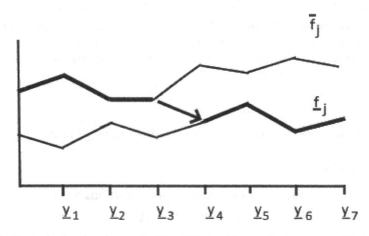

Fig. 4.8. Example showing the result of the KM algorithm on the two curves (thick line).

KM algorithm:

Init: set $f = (\underline{f_j} + \overline{f}_j)/2$ and set $\underline{f_j}$ resp. $\overline{f}_j$ in ascending order

Compute $f = \sum_{j=1}^{N} f_j \, \overline{y}_j / \sum_{j=1}^{n} f_j$

Find switch point k and set $f_j = \begin{cases} \underline{f_j} & j < k \\ \overline{f_j} & j > k \end{cases}$

and update f. Repeat till a termination criterium is reached. The function f converges to y_u □

A similar procedure is applied to determine y_d. As shown in Figure 4.8, one chooses

$$f_j = \begin{cases} f_j & j > k \\ \overline{f_j} & j < k \end{cases}) \text{ with k, the switch point}$$

Abiyev [2010] extended the structure to a type-2 neuro-fuzzy system. The development of Type-2 neuro-fuzzy systems leads to new applications, some of which achieve better results than classical fuzzy approaches. The neuro-fuzzy system uses a type-2 weight [Abiyev and Kaynak, 2010; Gaxiola *et al.*, 2014]. The main difference to a classical neuro-fuzzy system is that the weights are intervals:

$$\widetilde{w} = [\underline{w}, \overline{w}]$$

The type-2 fuzzy system may be of the Mamdani or Takagi-Sugeno type.

4.3. Interpolation, extrapolation, and approximation methods

Let us describe some applications of interpolation and extrapolation techniques with splines. For irregularly spaced data points, one may want to approximate their values on a regular grid. Once on a regular grid, a standard wavelet technique further processes the data. Another problem may be missing data or rules, and we will present a few methods adapted to those issues below.

Fuzzy wavelet methods are suitable for modeling problems with several variables. As the complexity of interpolation and approximation techniques increases rapidly with the number of variables, only the most straightforward methods are practicable in real problems. For this reason, we focus on strategies that work well in a multi-dimensional setting (at least at a low dimension!). The first possibility consists of using interpolation techniques. Let us remind that an interpolation function is a function ϕ for an ensemble of points (x_i, y_i) if:

$$\phi(x_i) = y_i \quad for\ all\ i \tag{4.13}$$

4.3.1. *Spline interpolants*

According to the Lagrange formula, it is possible to fit an interpolating polynomial of degree N-1 through any curve given by N points. In spline interpolation schemes, one tries to fit piecewise polynomials functions to N points (x_i,y_i). Each piecewise polynomial is of order k, and the interpolating function is requested to be in C^{k-1}, the set of functions with continuous $(k-1)^{th}$ derivative. The second-order spline interpolation corresponds to interpolating between the different points with a continuous function consisting of piecewise linear functions. The cubic spline interpolation is undoubtedly the most popular spline as it represents a good compromise between necessary computing power and smoothness. The following formula gives it for the interpolating function y:

$$y = A \cdot y_j + B \cdot y_{j+1} + C \cdot y_{j+1}''' + D \cdot y_{j+1}''' \tag{4.14}$$

with $A=(x_{j+1}-x_j)/(x_{j+1}-x_j)$, $B= 1-A$, $C=1/6\ (A^3-A)\ (x_{j+1}-x_j)^2$, $D=1/6\ (B^3-B)\ (x_{j+1}-x_j)^2$

The terms y" are computed through solving the equation:

$$1/6 \cdot (x_j - x_{j-1}) \cdot y_{-1}''' + 1/3 \cdot (x_{j+1} - x_{j-1}) \cdot y_j'''$$
$$+ 1/6 \cdot (x_{j+1} - x_j) \cdot y_{j+1}''' = (y_{j+1} - y_j)/(x_{j+1} - x_j)$$

$$- (y_j - y_{j-1})/(x_j - x_{j-1}) \tag{4.15}$$

The above equations show that computation of the cubic spline coefficients requires solving only a linear problem, which is why splines are so popular. The method works well in one dimension, but the complexity of the problem increases rapidly with the dimension.

B-splines are piecewise polynomial functions with a compact support. They are often used to interpolate data in empty regions [De Boor and De Boor, 1978]. Suppose N points (x_i, y_i) are known and one looks for an interpolation between these points with piecewise polynomial functions $\phi_k(x)$ with a compact support: $y(x) = \sum c_k\ \phi_k(x)$ and $y(x_i) = y_i$

Schoenberg and Whitney [1953] have shown that if a point x_i (N>i>1) is within the support of each function $\phi_k(x)$, then the problem has a unique solution obtained through a Gauss elimination method. The shape of the splines depends on the position of the knots. The resolution of this problem necessitates the knowledge and the storage of the N points. For a large number of data points, this is an inconvenience. Splines are easily adapted to higher dimensions by taking tensor products of splines of the same resolution.

4.3.2. *Multivariate approximation methods*

The Shannon sampling theorem shows that a band-limited function is recoverable from sample points on a regular grid, provided the sampling rate is large enough. Feichtinger [1990] proved that the reconstruction is still possible if the sampling points are not on a regular grid and the sampling density is high enough. Practically, the method is challenging for multivariable interpolations as it involves an inverse Fourier transform. From a practical point of view, interpolating in a high-dimensional space is complex, and one generally prefers using an approximation method. An exception is the Delauney interpolating scheme. We will present here the method in a 3-dimensional space. Figure 4.9 shows an example of the Delaunay interpolation scheme. Suppose one wants to interpolate the value of the function at a point Xg located on a regular grid.

Data points corresponding to the underlying function $y = f(x_1, x_2,..., x_d)$ are projected on the input space. First, one computes the Voronoi cell around the point on the grid one wants to estimate. The Voronoi cell corresponds to the ensemble of points closer or at the same distance to the chosen point than to any other point. After triangulation (See Okabe *et al.* [2009] for details on the triangulation method), each set of three (resp.d) connected nodes defines a plane P (or hyperplane at higher dimension) in $\Re^d$: $y = P(x_1, x_2,..., x_d)$. The value of the point on the grid $f(\mathbf{Xg})$ is computed from the equation of P.

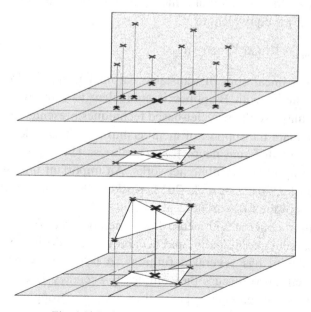

Fig. 4.9. Delaunay's triangulation method.

The Voronoi construction is quite general and works in any d-dimensional space. The Delaunay diagram can be constructed by connecting the points whose Voronoi cells share a (d-1) dimensional face.

The *neighbor-based* interpolation is another approach that works well at high dimensions. Each value on the grid is computed from its nearest neighbors with an averaging procedure. As an example, one may consider the simple estimation:

$$f(X_g) = \frac{1}{N}\Sigma_{i\,\in\,nearest-neighbors\;to\;X_g}\,y(x_i) \tag{4.16}$$

For non-uniformly distributed data points, a weighted averaging method improves the estimation.

4.4. Fuzzy wavelet

This section extends the equivalence between B-spline and fuzzy modeling to multiresolution fuzzy modeling. Wavelet-based fuzzy modeling is generally designed as a *fuzzy wavelet* [Thuillard, 1998]. Different authors have recognized the equivalency between fuzzy modeling and wavelet-spline modeling independently [Shmilovici and Maimon, 1998, 1996; Thuillard, 1998; Yu *et al.*, 1996; Yu and Tan, 1999].

If x is a singleton, $\mu_{A_i}(x) = N^k(2^{-m} \cdot x - n)$ with $N^k(2^{-m} \cdot x - n)$ a kth order cardinal B-spline function and the product operator for inference, then the system of Eq. (4.5) is equivalent to

$$y(x) = \Sigma_{m,n}\,b_{m,n} \cdot N^k(2^{-m} \cdot x - n) \tag{4.17}$$

The output y is a linear sum of translated cardinal B-splines in this case. The Takagi-Sugeno model with B-splines is equivalent to a multi-resolution spline model, and one may use the wavelet-based techniques presented in part 3.

The need to adapt the support of membership functions in learning has led to the development of different neuro-fuzzy methods. The support is adapted, for instance, by adding knots in spline networks. An important line of research uses clustering [Babuška, 2012; Bezdek, 2013; Kosko, 1992] with neural networks or different variants of the fuzzy c-mean algorithm.

Another central concern with neuro-fuzzy methods is to find the right balance between transparency, complexity, and accuracy of the designed fuzzy systems. Although complexity has several definitions, it is generally possible to agree on an explicit setting to discuss the complexity-accuracy issue. As soon as the notion of linguistic transparency appears, then opinions strongly diverge. A purely mathematical solution to that question is certainly not at hand, as linguistic transparency is a very human notion. *Keeping the man in the loop* is a central motivation for fuzzy logic, and therefore, a purely mathematical definition of linguistic transparency is not desirable. Linguistic transparency depends centrally on the level of education of the experts and their range of competence. Many neuro-fuzzy methods are declared transparent or linguistically interpretable without much justification. The transparency-complexity-accuracy issue is one of the most challenging fuzzy logic questions that plague modern neural networks research.

The fuzzy wavelet approach implements the following strategy. A dictionary of membership functions forming a multiresolution is first defined. Each membership function defines a 'small' or 'very small' term which is not modified during learning. The multiresolution character of the dictionary makes rules fusion and splitting quite simple (Figure 4.10).

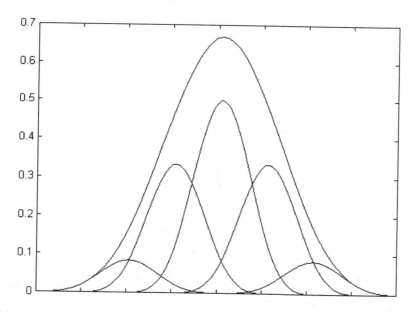

Fig. 4.10. Scaling functions at different resolutions in a dyadic multiresolution analysis. The cubic spline function is the sum of translated cubic splines at the next higher level of resolution (coefficients are (1/8; ½; ¾; ½; 1/8)). The same holds for the corresponding wavelet.

4.4.1. *General approach*

The fuzzy wavelet method takes advantage of the strong connection between a spline wavelet decomposition and a fuzzy system. Let us first recall how to make a fast wavelet decomposition. A very efficient recursive algorithm, called the fast wavelet transform, carries out the wavelet transform computation. The algorithm processes the data with a low-pass and a high-pass filter at each transform level. The high-pass filtered data $d_{m,n}$ are known as the detail wavelet coefficients.

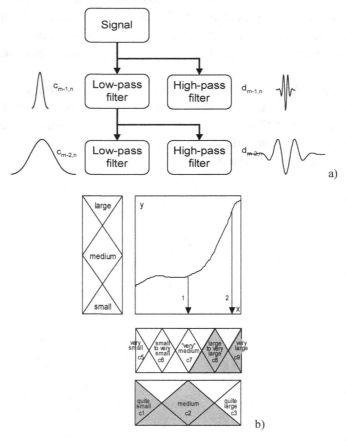

Fig. 4.11. a) Example of a fast wavelet decomposition using B-wavelets. The low-pass filter corresponds to the projection on dilated and translated spline functions; b) Example of fuzzy rules using spline membership functions at several resolutions.

The result of the low-pass transform, the coefficients $c_{m,n}$ are used as input data to compute the next level of detail wavelet coefficients. Figure 4.11 describes the algorithm symbolically. The connection between fuzzy logic and the fast wavelet algorithm is established through B-wavelets. The approximation coefficients $c_{m,n}$ of the B-wavelets represent the projections of the signal on spline functions. Spline functions are typical membership functions in fuzzy systems. The methods in part

3 determine appropriate membership functions and fuzzy rules. Let us recall what these methods are:

- Thresholding
- The matching pursuit for splines.

The algorithm is a modified version of the matching pursuit algorithm that works expressly well with splines. A modified matching pursuit determines appropriate membership functions and rules to approximate a function in terms of a small number of fuzzy rules. The resulting decomposition is linguistically formulated with the zero-order Takagi-Sugeno model with rules of the form: $R_i : if\ \boldsymbol{x}\ is\ A_i\ then\ y_i = b_i$ which can be put, if necessary, under the form

$R_i : if\ \boldsymbol{x}\ is\ A_i\ then\ y\ is\ B\ (C_{i,j})$ using the equivalency between the two formulations (Figure 4.12).

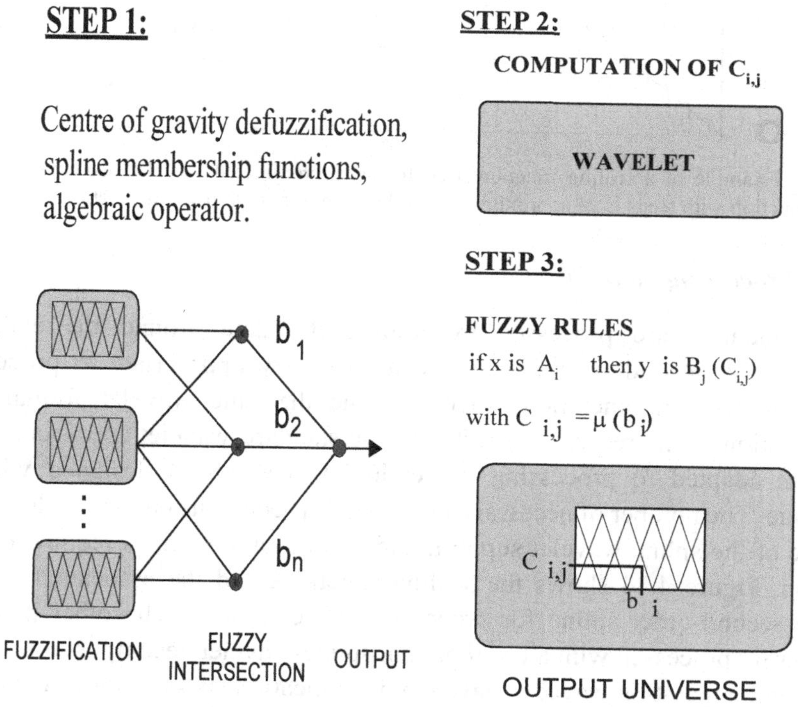

STEP 1:

Centre of gravity defuzzification, spline membership functions, algebraic operator.

STEP 2:

COMPUTATION OF $C_{i,j}$

WAVELET

STEP 3:

FUZZY RULES

if x is A_i then y is B_j $(C_{i,j})$

with $C_{i,j} = \mu\ (b_i)$

$C_{i,j}$ b_i

OUTPUT UNIVERSE

b_1

b_2

b_n

FUZZIFICATION   FUZZY INTERSECTION   OUTPUT

Fig. 4.12. The similarities between a fuzzy description and B-wavelets are used to determine fuzzy rules and confidence levels describing a data set.

4.5. Soft computing approach to fuzzy wavelet transform

For a large multivariable dataset, the memory and computing requirements of the wavelet analysis may be too large. Introducing a first approximation stage during the wavelet decomposition solves the problem. One uses the simple Haar wavelet in the first decomposition stages, corresponding to a simple averaging procedure. Spline wavelets are introduced only at resolution levels containing most of the signal energy, and the reconstruction algorithm uses spline wavelets at all levels. Figure 4.13 shows an example of an approximated scaling function for a triangular membership function. The method is very efficient in dealing with multivariable datasets, even if the data are noisy.

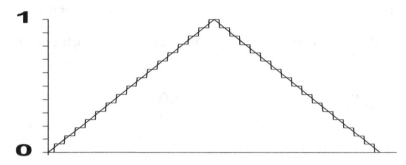

Fig. 4.13. Example of a scaling function used for an approximated wavelet decomposition. The scaling function with steps is an approximation of the triangular membership function.

4.5.1. *Processing boundaries*

The boundaries are processed by folding the data around the endpoints. Alternatively, second-generation wavelets are very appropriate to process the endpoints. Second-generation wavelets generalize the wavelet formalism to configurations that are not well suited to the standard wavelet approach. Spline-wavelets adapted to processing the endpoints have been designed with this technique. The number of necessary functions to process the endpoints depends on the size of the spline-wavelet support, and second-order splines require a unique function. Figure 4.14 shows the scaling functions and the associated wavelets for the second-order spline for processing the endpoints. The other points are customarily processed with a biorthogonal spline-wavelet decomposition.

Second-generation wavelets have many applications besides the one presented here. One uses them on an irregularly spaced grid or to construct multiresolution on a sphere. We will reencounter second generations wavelets as extensions of the fuzzy wavelet formalism will be discussed. One refers the reader to the annex for details on the construction of second-generation wavelets.

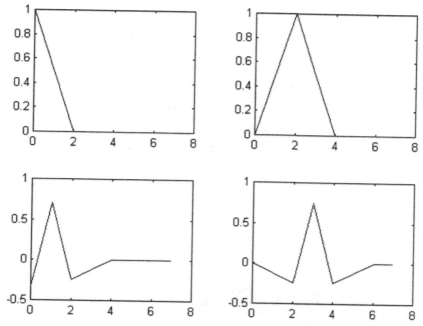

Fig. 4.14. Second-generation wavelet process the boundaries using the lifting scheme. Right: wavelet associated with the scaling function on the left side; left: scaling function for processing the last point with a second-order spline.

4.5.2. *Linguistic interpretation of the rules*

The adequacy of the linguistic formulation is critical, as one is dealing with human experts. If only translated versions of a single spline are used, then generally, through a simple rescaling, the rules can be put under a linguistic form that the human expert can process. For adaptive membership functions, the problem of interpretability becomes central. A significant problem is the lack of clear interpretability of many fuzzy systems generated with a neuro-fuzzy approach. The fuzzy wavelet approach overcomes this problem quite elegantly by using a multiresolution. Indeed, a scaling function at a given level of resolution is expressed as the sum of higher resolution scaling functions by using the two-scales relation, which is at the heart of the whole wavelet framework (Part 1):

$$\varphi(x) = \Sigma_k g_k \cdot \varphi(2 \cdot x - k) \tag{4.18}$$

Membership functions can be fused or split into membership functions at a higher resolution quite easily. We present a nontrivial example showing two approaches to make the results easily linguistically interpretable. Figure 4.15 illustrates the first approach.

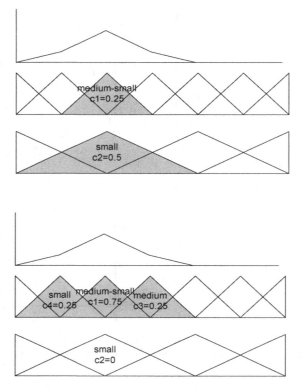

Fig. 4.15. The above curve can be expressed differently as a sum of scaling functions. The top decomposition is more compact for implementation, but the lower representation is linguistically better for a human expert.

The top representation in Figure 4.15 shows the superposition of two scaling functions corresponding to medium-small and small membership functions. In this example, the linguistic interpretation of the decomposition is not straightforward to a human expert. The degree of membership to *medium-small* is smaller than that of *small*, though the function has a peak within the medium-small range. For a human expert, such rules are counter-intuitive. In the present case, the fuzzy rules are of the type:

if x is medium-small then y is small;
if x is small then y is large.

The two rules contradict each other. So how can this problem be solved? A simple approach consists of splitting the scaling function corresponding to *small* into the sum of the scaling functions at the higher level of resolution.

After splitting the scaling function, one may express the results of the wavelet decomposition with linguistically coherent fuzzy rules. The degree of membership to medium-small is the largest, and the result is also understandable linguistically. The main disadvantage of this representation is that it may be too precise for the human expert. If this is the case, another approach transforms the description into a layered structure, as shown in Figure 4.16. This second approach is quite efficient if the number of levels of resolution is not too large.

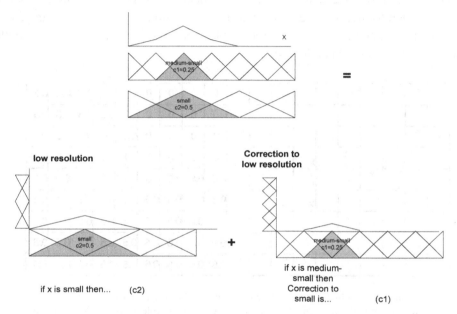

Fig. 4.16. The fuzzy rules are decomposed as the sum of a low-resolution description and its correction. This representation is a good compromise between the compactness of the representation and linguistic clarity.

4.5.3. *Fuzzy wavelet classifier*

Wavelet theory and fuzzy logic are complementary. It opens the possibility of developing a fuzzy wavelet classifier, a wavelet classifier with a linguistic interpretation of the classification. Wavelet-based classifiers have found applications in different fields, from crack detection to seismic analysis. The basic idea consists of first analyzing the signal with wavelet decomposition. The coefficients form the input vector to the classifier. The classifier learns to classify using many examples. The development of the classifier may use very different techniques going from look-up tables to Learning Vector Quantization (LVQ), Kohonen networks, decision trees, or genetic algorithms.

We present here an example of a fuzzy wavelet classifier. The classifier has been tested successfully on an industrial project: the development of algorithms integrated into a fire detector, capable of making automatically the distinction between a signal caused by deceiving phenomena and real fires.

The first stage of the algorithm consists of choosing a mesh size h for the observation data. The input space is divided into small hyperboxes H_l of volume h^3. The examples' database is slipped into two subsets, A and B. For a fire detector, the labels A and B correspond to '*deceiving phenomena*' and '*fire.*' One attributes a value to each hyperbox. (1/2 if no example lies within the hyperbox, 1 if all the examples have label A and 0 otherwise). One may reduce the mesh size if both elements (0 and 1) are in an hyperbox.

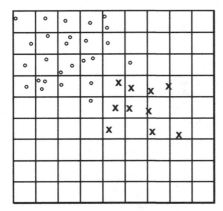

0	0	0	0	0	0.5	0.5	0.5	0.5
0	0	0	0	0	0.5	0.5	0.5	0.5
0	0	0	0	0.5	0	0.5	0.5	0.5
0	0	0	0	1	1	1	0.5	0.5
0.5	0.5	0.5	0	1	1	1	0.5	0.5
0.5	0.5	0.5	0.5	1	0.5	1	1	0.5
0.5	0.5	0.5	0.5	0.5	0.5	0.5	0.5	0.5
0.5	0.5	0.5	0.5	0.5	0.5	0.5	0.5	0.5
0.5	0.5	0.5	0.5	0.5	0.5	0.5	0.5	0.5

Fig. 4.17. The first stage of the classification corresponds to the coding of the examples after dividing the input space into hyperboxes—illustrations with two input variables. Right) The input matrix.

Figure 4.17 shows an example of the input matrix S after coding the input data database. The matrix S is processed using spline-wavelets. The matrix rows are processed first, and then the columns and one obtains three matrices. The first two matrices contain the detail coefficients as elements, while the third matrix corresponds to the result of the low-pass filtering. The detail coefficients corresponding to the high-frequency part of the signal characterize the boundaries between two domains (recall that the wavelet coefficients are good edge detectors!). The approximation coefficients $c_{m,n}$ furnish important information. The approximation coefficients $c_{m,n}$ correspond to the projection of the signal on the scaling function. The scaling functions can be interpreted as membership functions, and the coefficients used to compute the confidence levels of the rules are defined implicitly by $c_{m,n}$ [Thuillard, 1996]. An approximation coefficient $c_{m,n} = 1$, means that the hyperbox H_l, corresponding to the support of the bounded multivariate spline-wavelet used for the projection, contains only examples corresponding to the subset A. Undefined hyperboxes reduce the degree of membership.

4.5.4. *Offline learning from irregularly spaced data*

This section discusses the possibility of using fuzzy wavelet techniques after some nonlinear preprocessing of the input data. First, the data points are mapped bijectively onto a regular grid. Then the wavelet decomposition is carried out on the regular grid. Finally, one maps back the resulting approximation to the original grid. Let us examine how to carry out that program with an elementary example (Figure 4.18). The input space is two-dimensional and contains 16 points. The 16 data points are mapped bijectively onto a regular 4x4 matrix. The 4 points with the most significant values of x_2 are associated with the first row. After removing these 4 points, one repeats the procedure on the second row. The mapping does not preserve near-neighbors relationships. A mapping preserving near-neighbors relationships is generally computationally very demanding and is considered here.

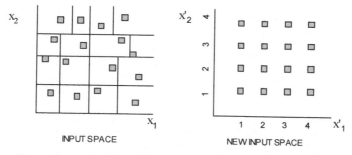

Fig. 4.18. Data points can be mapped bijectively on a regular grid. Once mapped on a regular grid, the fuzzy wavelet method applies.

After applying a fuzzy wavelet procedure on the regular grid, the approximating function becomes a weighted sum of 2-dim (or 1-dim) splines:

$$\hat{f}(x) = \Sigma \, c_{m,n} \cdot \varphi_{m,n}(x) \qquad (4.19)$$

with $\varphi_{m,n}(x) = 2^m \cdot \varphi(2^m \cdot x - n)$.

The inverse mapping does not change the weights; it modifies only the shape of the splines. The method is straightforward, and a fuzzy interpretation of the results is possible. At one level of resolution, all membership functions sum up to one and form a partition of unity. Also, the membership functions do not take negative values, as illustrated in Figure 4.19 with a one-dimensional example. The shape of the membership depends on the position and density of the data points in the input space. The dependence on the density of points is evident in Figure 4.19. In that sense, the method is highly adaptive. In general, the transparency of the fuzzy rules is smaller than in fuzzy systems using a dictionary of pre-defined fuzzy functions. The method's main drawback is that complexity reduction is much more difficult. The main point of the discussion is that those fuzzy wavelet methods are not limited to datasets on a regular grid. We come back in detail on this aspect later in the book.

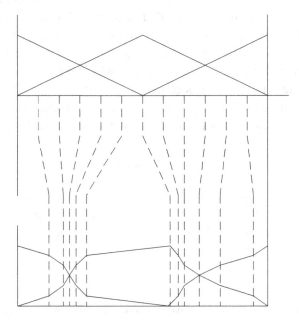

Fig. 4.19. The effect of nonlinear mapping is illustrated on second-order splines. The data points correspond to the lower end of the vertical dashed lines.

4.5.5. *Missing data*

In most applications, rules validation is probably the most important step in learning. The validation process is rarely fully automatic, as in most cases, some human intervention is necessary. Validation is often difficult as the input space is sparsely populated, especially at high dimensions with large regions free of any data. The human operator is confronted with a decision on what strategy to follow. There are essentially four alternatives:

- *Empty regions are ignored because they do not correspond to the range of the input space.*

It is an acceptable solution if the empty regions in the input space are irrelevant in real applications.

- *New data are explicitly collected within the empty regions.*

It is a typical approach during the development of new sensors.

- *Default rules are added to the system.*

Adding default rules is quite common in sensors or control applications. The default rules may have the function of guaranteeing an acceptable response of the system under very difficult conditions.

- *Rules within the empty regions are computed from neighboring areas.*

Generalization requires using interpolation and extrapolation techniques. It is the subject of the next section.

References

Abiyev, R.H. (2010). A type-2 fuzzy wavelet neural network for time series prediction, in *International Conference on Industrial, Engineering and Other Applications of Applied Intelligent Systems*, Springer, pp. 518–527.

Abiyev, R.H. and Kaynak, O. (2010). Type 2 fuzzy neural structure for identification and control of time-varying plants, *IEEE Transactions on Industrial Electronics*, 57(12), pp. 4147–4159.

Babuška, R. (2012) *Fuzzy modeling for control*. Springer Science & Business Media.

Bezdek, J.C. (2013) *Pattern recognition with fuzzy objective function algorithms*. Springer Science & Business Media.

Brown, M. and Harris, C.J. (1994). Neurofuzzy adaptive modelling and control.

De Boor, C. and De Boor, C. (1978) *A practical guide to splines*. springer-verlag New York.

Feichtinger, H.G. (1990). Coherent frames and irregular sampling, in *Recent Advances in Fourier Analysis and its applications*. Springer, pp. 427–440.

Gaxiola, F. *et al.* (2014). Interval type-2 fuzzy weight adjustment for backpropagation neural networks with application in time series prediction, *Information Sciences*, 260, pp. 1–14.

Juuso, E. (1996). Linguistic equations in system development for computational intelligence, *Proc. Fourth European Congress on Intelligent Techniques and Soft Computing-EUFIT*, pp. 2–5.

Juuso, E.K. and Järvensivu, M. (1998). Lime kiln process modelling with neural networks and linguistic equations, *Proc. 6th European Congress on Intelligent Techniques & Soft Computing-EUFIT*, pp. 7–10.

Karnik, Nilesh N and Mendel, J.M. (2001). Centroid of a type-2 fuzzy set, *Information sciences*, 132(1–4), pp. 195–220.

Karnik, Nilesh N. and Mendel, J.M. (2001). Operations on type-2 fuzzy sets, *Fuzzy sets and systems*, 122(2), pp. 327–348.

Kosko, B. (1992) *Neural networks and fuzzy systems: a dynamical approach to machine intelligence*. Prentice Hall.

Leiviskä, K. and Juuso, E. (1996). Modelling industrial processes using linguistic equations: Lime kiln as an example, *Proc. Fourth European Congress on Intelligent Techniques and Soft Computing-EUFIT*, pp. 2–5.

Okabe, A. *et al.* (2009) *Spatial tessellations: concepts and applications of Voronoi diagrams*. John Wiley & Sons.

Schoenberg, I.J. and Whitney, A. (1953). On Pólya frequence functions. III. The positivity of translation determinants with an application to the interpolation problem by spline curves, *Transactions of the American Mathematical Society*, 74(2), pp. 246–259.

Shmilovici, A. and Maimon, O. (1996). Best fuzzy rule selection with orthogonal matching pursuit, *Proc. Fourth European Congress on Intelligent Techniques and Soft Computing EUFIT*, pp. 592–96.

Shmilovici, A. and Maimon, O. (1998). On the solution of differential equations with fuzzy spline wavelets, *Fuzzy sets and systems*, 96(1), pp. 77–99.

Takagi, T. and Sugeno, M. (1985). Fuzzy identification of systems and its applications to modeling and control, *IEEE transactions on systems, man, and cybernetics*, (1), pp. 116–132.

Thuillard, M. (1996). The development of algorithms for a smoke detector with neuro-fuzzy logic, *Fuzzy sets and systems*, 77(2), pp. 117–124.

Thuillard, M. (1998). Fuzzy-wavelets: theory and applications, *Proc. Sixth European Congress on Intelligent Techniques and Soft Computing (EUFIT98)*, pp. 2–1149.

Yu, Y. *et al.* (1996). Near-optimal construction of wavelet networks for nonlinear system modeling, *Proc. 1996 IEEE International Symposium on Circuits and Systems (ISCAS)*, IEEE, pp. 48–51.

Yu, Y. and Tan, S. (1999). Complementarity and equivalence relationships between convex fuzzy systems with symmetry restrictions and wavelets, *Fuzzy sets and systems*, 101(3), pp. 423–438.

Zadeh, L.A. (1975). The concept of a linguistic variable and its application to approximate reasoning-I, *Information sciences*, 8(3), pp. 199–249.

Nonparametric Wavelet-Based Estimation and Regression Techniques

Part 5

Chapter 5

Nonparametric Wavelet-Based
Estimation and Regression Techniques

5.1. Introduction

The main goal of nonparametric regression techniques is to estimate a function
from the knowledge of a limited number of points $y_i = y(x_i)$. The data points are
obtained experimentally and corrupted with noise in many applications. Consider
the standard nonparametric regression problem: Let (X, Y) be a pair of random
variables with values in $x \in \Re^d$, $y \in \Re$. Assume that $y(x_i) = f(x_i) + \varepsilon_i$ where
ε_i is independent $N(0, \sigma)$ normally distributed copies of random variables. A
function y = f(x) is the regression function of Y on X if

$$E(Y \mid X = x) = f(x) \tag{5.1}$$

For the rest of the discussion, it is essential to consider the two typical sampling
designs, namely random and deterministic.

Random design: The input data x_i are copies of random variables X_i independent
and identically distributed on [0,1] with density g(x).
Deterministic design: The input variables X_i are non-random. The simplest case of
a deterministic design is the regular design, where x_i is on a regular grid.

We will limit the discussion to two basic methods: kernel estimators for regression
function and density estimation. Due to the particular role of splines in estimation,
a small section deals with smoothing splines techniques. A smoothing or
regression kernel is a positive, generally even, function with unit integral, and a
regression kernel is generally well localized. Spline functions are often used as
kernels. The uniform, gaussian, and quadratic kernels are also very popular
[Eubank, 1999].

Uniform kernel: $\phi(x) = 0.5,\ |x| \le 1,\ 0$ otherwise

Gaussian kernel: $\phi(x) = (2\pi)^{-1/2} \cdot \exp(-x^2/2)$

Quadratic: $\phi(x) = 0.75 \cdot (1 - x^2),\ |x| \le 1,\ 0$ otherwise

Nonparametric kernel estimators estimate a function f(x) from some data points (x_i, y_i). The estimate $\hat{f}(x)$ is expressed as a weighted sum of translated and dilated kernels:

$$\hat{f}(x) = \sum_{i=1}^{N} S_i(x) \cdot y_i \tag{5.2}$$

with S_i centered on x_i and N the number of points. The Watson-Nadaraya and the Müller-Gasser estimators are some of the most popular estimators. The Watson-Nadaraya estimator is given by

$$\hat{f}(x) = \frac{\sum_{i=1}^{N} \phi(\frac{x_i - x}{h}) \cdot y_i}{\sum_{i=1}^{N} \phi(\frac{x_i - x}{h})} \tag{5.3}$$

Watson-Nadaraya estimators have some interesting properties. In the case of a random design, they are Bayesian estimators of (x_i, y_i), in which (x_i, y_i) are i.i.d copies of a continuous random variable (X, Y). (To simplify the formalism without loss of generality, we consider 1-dimensional estimators.) The Watson-Nadaraya estimator minimizes the weighted mean squares error:

$$MSE = \sum_{i=1}^{N} \varphi(\tfrac{x_i - x}{h}) \cdot (y_i - c_i)^2 \tag{5.4}$$

It is seen by equating the derivative of (6.4) to zero:

$$\partial MSE / \partial c_i = 2 \cdot c_i \cdot \sum_{i=1}^{N} \varphi(\tfrac{x_i - x}{h}) - 2 \cdot \sum_{i=1}^{N} \varphi(\tfrac{x_i - x}{h}) \cdot y_i$$

from which one obtains that c_i is of the form of Eq. (5.3)

The Müller-Gasser estimator is defined by the expression:

$$\hat{f}(x) = h \cdot \sum_{i=1}^{N} \int_{\bar{x}_{j-1}}^{\bar{x}_j} \varphi(\tfrac{x_i - x}{h}) \cdot dx \cdot y_i \tag{5.5}$$

with $\bar{x}_j = (x_{j+1} - x_j)/2;;\ \bar{x}_{-1} = x_1;;\ \bar{x}_N = x_N.$

5.2. Smoothing splines

Smoothing splines accommodate constraints on the smoothness of the fitted function. A natural measure of the smoothness of a one-dimensional function f is an integral function of the mth derivative f(m) of f. Smoothing splines estimators search for a function $\hat{f}(x)$ minimizing the weighted sum of the smoothness measure $\int_0^1 (f^{(m)}(x))^2 \cdot dx$ and the average squared residual $1/N \cdot \sum_{i=1}^N (y_i - \hat{f}(t_i))^2$:

$$1/N \cdot \sum_{i=1}^N (y_i - f(t_i))^2 + \lambda \cdot \int_0^1 (f^{(m)}(x))^2 \cdot dx \tag{5.6}$$

When λ is large, the estimator rewards smoothness, and an estimator with large m^{th} derivatives is penalized. In the limiting case, $\lambda \to 0$, the optimized function $\hat{f}(x)$ is a least-squares estimator obtained by solving the equation:

$$(\Phi^T \cdot \Phi + n \cdot \lambda \cdot \Omega) \cdot b = \Phi^T \cdot y \tag{5.7}$$

$\Phi = \{\varphi_j(t_i)\}_{i,j=1\ldots n}$ a basis for the set of splines of order m+2 ((m ≥ 0).

$\Omega = \{\int_0^1 \varphi_i^{(m)} \cdot \varphi_j^{(m)} \cdot dt\}_{i,j=1\ldots,n}$

For a fixed λ, the estimator becomes parametric. The value is determined either through trial and error or preferably with cross-validation techniques.

Efficient computing methods exist for spline functions. For instance, the cubic smoothing spline minimizes the expression:

$$1/N \cdot \sum_{i=1}^N (y_i - f(t_i))^2 + \lambda \cdot \int_0^1 (f^{(2)}(x))^2 \cdot dx \tag{5.8}$$

Moreover, the method extends to functions of p variables by minimizing the expression:

$$1/N \cdot \sum_{i=1}^N \lambda \cdot \sum_{k_1+\cdots+k_p} \frac{m!}{k_1! \cdot \ldots k_p!} \cdot \left(\int_0^1 \cdots \int_0^1 (\partial^m f(t)/(\partial t_1^{k_1} \ldots \partial t_p^{k_p}) \cdot \right.$$

$$\begin{matrix}(y_i - f(t_i))^2 + \\ \\ \end{matrix}$$

$$dt_1 \ldots dt_p \tag{5.9}$$

The method is known as *thin-plate smoothing spline*. Smoothing-spline surface fitting techniques are described very thoroughly by Wahba [1979]. Smoothing splines estimators have found many applications for fitting a curve or a surface to a dataset. Applications to high-dimensional spaces are rare, as the number of points necessary to approximate the surface increases rapidly with the dimension (curse of dimensionality).

5.3. Wavelet estimators

At some time, the statistics community got very interested in wavelet theory. Several wavelet-based methods were created for nonparametric regression and density estimation and linear and nonlinear regression methods. The cross-fertilization between the classical wavelet specialists and the statisticians was significant, partly thanks to Donoho and Johnstone's work on denoising. This section first examines linear wavelet methods for curve estimation and then describes some of the methods for density estimation succinctly. Finally, we present some nonlinear techniques.

5.4. Wavelet methods for curve estimation

Most wavelet estimators are extensions of the Watson-Nadaraya and Müller-Gasser estimators. Wavelet estimators express the regression function $f_w(x)$ as a weighted sum of wavelets and scaling functions:

$$f_w(x) = \sum_n c_{M_0,n} \cdot \varphi_{J_0,n}(x) + \sum_{n,m \geq M_0} d_{m,n} \cdot \psi_{m,n}(x) \tag{5.10}$$

Different estimators are used to estimating the values of the coefficients. Antoniadis [1994, 1997] proposed a wavelet version of the Gasser-Müller estimator for the fixed design model.

$$\hat{f}_w(x) = \sum_{i=1}^{N} y_i \cdot \int_{A_i} E_m(x,s) \cdot ds \tag{5.11}$$

where $A_i = [s_{i-1}, s_i]$ are intervals that partition $[0,1]$ with $x_i \in A_i$. The kernel $E_m(x,s)$ is given by

$$E_m(x,s) = 2^m \cdot \sum_n \varphi(2^m \cdot x - n) \cdot \varphi(2^m \cdot s - n) \tag{5.12}$$

A computationally less demanding estimator is the wavelet version of the Watson-Nadaraya estimator given in the regular design by the expression:

$$\hat{f}_w(x) = c_{M_0,n} \cdot \varphi_{M_0,n}(x) + \sum_{m=M_0}^{M_{max}} \sum_n d_{m,n} \cdot \psi_{m,n}(x) \tag{5.13a}$$

with

$$c_{M_0,n} = \frac{1}{N} \cdot \sum_{i=1}^{N} y_i \cdot \varphi_{M_0,n}(x_i); \quad d_{m,n} = \frac{1}{N} \cdot \sum_{i=1}^{N} y_i \cdot \psi_{m,n}(x_i) \tag{5.13b}$$

and $2^{Mmax} = N$.

The choice of the low-resolution level M_0 determines the quality of the estimation very centrally. A high resolution may lead to a very noisy estimate, while some essential signal features may get lost, or even artifacts are created at too low resolution. For practical applications, cross-validation is often the preferred approach. Simple cross-validation consists of choosing the value M_0 as the minimizer of the error function CV(M) using the leave-one-out estimator $\hat{f}_{w,i}$:

$$CV(M) = 1/N \cdot \sum_{i=1}^{N}(y_i - \hat{f}_{w,i})^2 \tag{5.14}$$

More complicated cross-validation methods, such as Wahba's [1979] generalized cross-validation procedure, are also used.

5.4.1. *Biorthogonal wavelet estimators*

Wavelet estimators generally use orthogonal wavelets and do not belong to the class of kernel estimators. Therefore, interpreting orthogonal wavelet estimators within the kernel estimation framework is impossible. To create kernel wavelet estimators, wavelet estimators are generalized in the next section to biorthogonal wavelets. Biorthogonal wavelet estimators differ from the standard kernel estimators in the way that the coefficients $\hat{c}_{m,n}$ are obtained. The coefficients $\hat{c}_{m,n}$ are computed using the dual scaling functions. For instance, we will show that the coefficients can be calculated with a modified Watson-Nadaraya estimator using the dual spline scaling functions $\hat{\varphi}_{m,n}$. For the Müller-Gasser wavelet estimator, the kernel becomes:

$$E_m(x,s) = 2^m \cdot \sum_n \varphi(2^m \cdot x - n) \cdot \tilde{\varphi}(2^m \cdot s - n) \tag{5.15}$$

with $\tilde{\varphi}(2^m \cdot s - n)$ the dual function of $\varphi(2^m \cdot s - n)$.

The generalization for the wavelet equivalent Nadaraya-Watson estimator is given by

$$\hat{f}_w(x) = c_{M_0,n} \cdot \varphi_{M_0,n}(x) + \sum_{m=M_0}^{Mmax} \sum_n d_{m,n} \cdot \psi_{m,n}(x) \tag{5.16a}$$

with

$$c_{M_0,n} = \frac{1}{N} \cdot \sum_{i=1}^{N} y_i \cdot \tilde{\varphi}_{M_0,n}(x_i); \quad d_{m,n} = \frac{1}{N} \cdot \sum_{i=1}^{N} y_i \cdot \tilde{\psi}_{m,n}(x_i) \tag{5.16b}$$

For orthogonal wavelets, (5.16) is equivalent to (5.13).

5.4.2. *Density estimators*

Density functions estimation with the Parzen-Rosenblatt estimator is defined as

$$\hat{f}(x) = \frac{1}{N \cdot h^d} \cdot \sum_{i=1}^{N} K\left(\frac{x - x_i}{h}\right) \tag{5.17}$$

with d the dimension.

The naive density estimator is obtained by using the uniform kernel. At one dimension, this corresponds to forming the curve histogram. The same kernels as in regression may be used, for instance, splines, gaussian or quadratic kernels. Wavelet-based methods for density estimation are similar to wavelet-based regression methods. The density function f_{dw} is approximated as a weighted sum of scaling functions and wavelets:

$$\hat{f}_{dw}(x) = c_{M_0,n} \cdot \varphi_{M_0,n}(x) + \sum_{m=M_0}^{M_{max}} \sum_n d_{m,n} \cdot \psi_{m,n}(x) \tag{5.18}$$

The coefficients are approximated by using their empirical values:

$$c_{M_0} = \frac{1}{N} \cdot \sum_{i=1}^{N} \tilde{\varphi}_{M_0,n}(x_i) \tag{5.19a}$$

$$d_{m,n} = \frac{1}{N} \cdot \sum_{i=1}^{N} \tilde{\psi}_{m,n}(x_i) \tag{5.19b}$$

5.4.3. *Wavelet denoising methods*

Wavelet denoising methods belong to the standard signal processing toolbox and have many applications. One classifies them into two large categories, thresholding, and shrinkage. A wavelet coefficient is set to zero in thresholding if its value is below a given threshold value. Donoho and Johnstone [1994] proposed nonlinear denoising methods. All coefficients below a certain threshold are set to zero in the hard thresholding method. In the soft thresholding method, the wavelet coefficients are reduced by a factor α. The expression gives the coefficients after thresholding:

$$\hat{w}_{m,n} = sign(\hat{d}_{m,n}) \cdot max(0, |d_{m,n}| - \alpha) \tag{5.20}$$

Practically, shrinkage corresponds to multiplying some wavelet coefficients by a level-dependent positive factor smaller than one. Let us give an interpretation of linear shrinkage methods in spectral space. A wavelet decomposition uses perfect reconstruction filters, consisting of a low-pass filter T_{low} and a high-pass filter T_{high} fulfilling the power complementarity condition: $|T_{low}|^2 + |T_{high}|^2 = 1$. Linear shrinkage is equivalent to replacing the two filters with two new filters

T'_{high}, T'_{low} with $|T'_{low}|^2 = \alpha |T_{low}|^2$ and $\left|T'_{high}\right|^2 = \alpha(1-\varepsilon) \cdot \left|T_{high}\right|^2$. The coefficients are such that $\alpha < 1$ and ε is generally small and positive. Roughly, linear shrinkage results in damping the high-frequencies more than the low-frequency signal components. Antoniadis *et al.* [1994] suggested a linear shrinkage method extending smoothing splines to wavelets. The minimizer of the expression

$$\|f_w - f\|^2 + \lambda \cdot ((\Sigma_n(c_{m,n})^2)^{0.5} + (2^{j \cdot s} \cdot \Sigma_{m=J_0}^{\infty}(\Sigma_n(d_{m,n})^2))^{0.5} \tag{5.21}$$

is searched for on [0,1]. The solution to the variational problem is

$$\hat{f}_w(x) = c_{M_0} \cdot \varphi_{M_0,n}(x) + \Sigma_{m=M_0}^{Mmax} \Sigma_n \hat{\beta}_{m,n} \cdot \psi_{m,n}(x) \tag{5.22}$$

with $\hat{\beta}_{m,n} = \dfrac{d_{m,n}}{1+\lambda \cdot 2^{2sm}}$ \hfill (5.23)

Linear shrinkage reduces the wavelet coefficients by a factor proportional to the level m. Abramovich *et al.* [2000] describe nonlinear shrinkage methods.

5.5. Fuzzy wavelet estimators

5.5.1. *Fuzzy wavelet estimators within the framework of the singleton model*

Wavelet estimators based on orthogonal wavelets do not have a linguistic interpretation. A linguistic understanding of kernel estimation requires approximating the regression curve as a weighted sum of functions partitioning the unity and having only positive values. A solution to that problem consists of using biorthogonal wavelet estimators. Symmetric scaling functions, interpretable as membership functions, are taken as local functions. Except for the Haar wavelet, no orthogonal scaling function has positive values everywhere and is symmetric. So the solution consists of taking scaling functions associated with biorthogonal wavelets. The fuzzy wavelet estimator computes first the values $\hat{f}_m(x_n)$ on a regular grid with the dual function $\tilde{\phi}_{m,n}$ as kernel:

$$\hat{f}(x) = \Sigma_{i=1}^{N} \tilde{\varphi}(\tfrac{x_i-x}{h}) \cdot y_i / \Sigma_{i=1}^{N} \tilde{\varphi}(\tfrac{x_i-x}{h}) \tag{5.24}$$

For symmetric functions and regularly spaced points, the expression simplifies. In this case, one obtains

$$\hat{f}(k \cdot h) = \Sigma_{i=1}^{N} \tilde{\varphi}(\tfrac{x_i-k \cdot h}{h}) \cdot y_i / \Sigma_{i=1}^{N} \tilde{\varphi}(\tfrac{x_i-k \cdot h}{h}) \tag{5.25}$$

with k an integer (see Figure 5.1).

For uniformly distributed input data $(\sum_{i=1}^{N} \tilde{\varphi}_{m,n}(x_i) \cdot y_i)/\sum_{i=1}^{N} \tilde{\varphi}_{m,n}(x_i)$ is a good approximation of $< f(x), \varphi_{m,n} >$. Equation (5.26) furnishes, therefore, an estimation of $\hat{c}_{m,n}$ in $f_m(x) = \sum \hat{c}_{m,n} \cdot \varphi_{m,n}(x)$:

$$\hat{c}_{m,n} = (\sum_{i=1}^{N} \tilde{\varphi}_{m,n}(x_i) \cdot y_k)/\sum_{i=1}^{N} \tilde{\varphi}_{m,n}(x_i) \tag{5.26}$$

In the limit of infinitely many points, $\hat{c}_{m,n}$ equals $c_{m,n}$. If the function f(x) is regular enough. The second step of the algorithm is simple. The Watson-Nadaraya estimator interpolates between the points on the regular grid (Figure 5.1-5.2). The function $\varphi_{m,n}$ is used here as kernel.

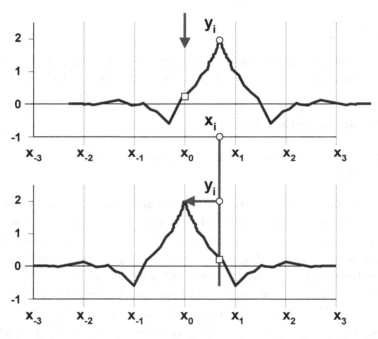

Fig. 5.1. Multiresolution spline estimators use dual spline estimators based on the functions $\tilde{\varphi}_{m,n}(x)$ to estimate the coefficients $\tilde{c}_{m,n}$ in $f_m(x) = \sum \hat{c}_{m,n} \cdot \varphi_{m,n}(x)$.

In summary, the fuzzy wavelet estimator is given by

$$\hat{f}_m(x) =$$
$$\sum_n (\sum_{i=1}^{N} \tilde{\varphi}(2^m x_i - x_n) \cdot y_i)/(\sum_{i=1}^{N} \tilde{\varphi}(2^m \cdot x_i - x_n)) \cdot \varphi_{m,n}(x) \tag{5.27}$$

with x_n on a regular grid.

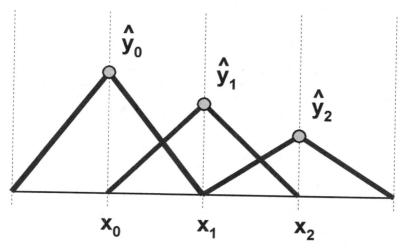

Fig. 5.2. The sum of spline functions: $f_m(x) = \sum \hat{c}_{m,n} \cdot \varphi_{m,n}(x)$ estimates a function f(x).

5.5.2. *Multiresolution fuzzy wavelet estimators: application to online learning*

The above method is easily generalized to a multiresolution (Figure 5.3) using an ensemble of estimators. Also, a fuzzy interpretation is possible for splines as scaling functions. In the multiresolution setting, appropriate rules are selected using a method quite similar to the one implemented in fuzzy wavenets. The estimation of the surface at one level of resolution is compared with the one at one lower level of resolution by decomposing the approximation coefficients with the low-pass filter associated with the fast wavelet decomposition algorithm. $\hat{c}_{m,n}$, Two validation conditions are necessary to validate the coefficient:

$$\left| \hat{c}_{m,n} - \sum_k p_{k-2n} \cdot \hat{c}_{m+1,k} \right| < \Delta \tag{5.28}$$

with the filter coefficients p corresponding to the low-pass decomposition coefficient for splines. Further, one requires also that

$$\left| \sum_{i=1}^N \tilde{\varphi}_{m,n}(x) \right| > T \tag{5.29}$$

to prevent divisions by a very small value.

The signal processor can make some computations in many online problems but has too little memory to store many data points. Most cross-validation methods are not implementable. The above method is very appropriate (For reviews on wavelet-based estimators, see Abramovich [2000] or Antoniadis [1997]).

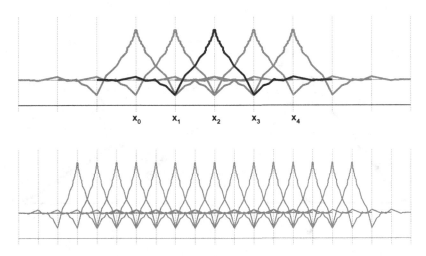

Fig. 5.3. Multiresolution fuzzy wavelet estimation using an ensemble of estimators.

The strength of the above approach is that the computation of a coefficient $\hat{c}_{m,n}$ requires only the storage of two values: the denominator and the nominator in (5.27).

As examples of the above methods, Loussifi *et al.* [2016] apply a kernel method to construct and initialize a fuzzy wavelet network. Yger and Rakotomamonjy [2011] use kernel methods to learn the wavelet shape and the appropriate scale and translation of the wavelets. The best kernel is chosen by setting constraints on the sparsity. They show the efficiency of the method on brain-computer interface and texture analysis.

References

Abramovich, F., Bailey, T.C., Sapatinas, T. (2000). Wavelet analysis and its statistical applications, *J. R. Stat. Soc. Ser. Stat.* 49, 1–29.

Antoniadis, A., Gregoire, G., McKeague, I.W. (1994). Wavelet methods for curve estimation, *J. Am. Stat. Assoc.* 89, 1340–1353.

Donoho, D.L., Johnstone, I.M. (1994). Ideal denoising in an orthonormal basis chosen from a library of bases, *Comptes Rendus Académie Sci. Sér. Mathématique* 319, 1317–1322.

Eubank, R.L. (1999). Nonparametric regression and spline smoothing. CRC press.

Loussifi, H., Nouri, K.; Braiek, N.B. (2016). A new efficient hybrid intelligent method for nonlinear dynamical systems identification: The Wavelet Kernel Fuzzy Neural Network, *Commun. Nonlinear Sci.*, 32, 10–30.

Wahba, G. (1979). Convergence rates of "thin plate" smoothing splines when the data are noisy, in *Smoothing Techniques for Curve Estimation* (Springer), pp. 233–245.

Yger, F. and Rakotomamonjy, A. (2011). Wavelet kernel learning, *Pattern Recognition*, 44(10-11), pp. 2614–2629.

Hybrid Neural Networks

Part 6

Chapter 6

Hybrid Neural Networks

6.1. Neuro-Fuzzy modeling

This section introduces the main learning techniques combining fuzzy logic and neural networks. Extensions to deep learning are treated separately in chapter 7.

6.1.1. *Adaptive Neuro-Fuzzy Adaptive Systems (ANFIS)*

A fuzzy learning approach is particularly interesting when prior knowledge exists of the system structure. Figure 6.1 presents a general scheme for a fuzzy neural system of the Takagi-Sugeno type.

Layer 1. The input layer transfers the input signal vector x = $\{x_1, x_2\}$ to the next layer.
Layer 2. Fuzzification layer with $A_{i,k}$ the membership functions.
Layer 3. Inference layer with output μ_{ik}.
Layer 4. In the normalization layer, the normalization factor for the output of the ith rule.

The first three layers are typical of fuzzy neural networks. They have the function of localizing interesting regions. The following layers correspond to the consequence of the antecedent fuzzy rules. In a Takagi-Sugeno fuzzy system, the consequent part reduces to a function $f(x_1, x_2, ..., x_n)$. The last layer normalizes the sum of the degrees of membership of the fuzzy rules to one.

The Adaptive Neuro-Fuzzy Inference System (ANFIS) has been widely used to learn fuzzy rules from data using the Takagi-Sugeno model. The architecture corresponds to the first layers in the fuzzy wavelet neural network in Figure 6.3.

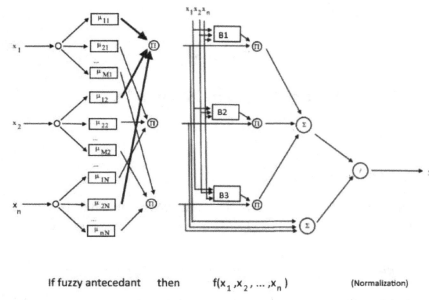

If fuzzy antecedant   then $f(x_1, x_2, \dots, x_n)$ (Normalization)

Fig. 6.1. The neuro-fuzzy system has an antecedent and a consequent part. The system learns the weight describing the output function in its simplest version. In the Takagi-Sugeno model, the function B_i is of the form $a_i x + b$.

6.1.2. *Neuro-fuzzy spline modeling*

In the zero-order Takagi-Sugeno model framework, B-splines and fuzzy networks are equivalent. Quoting Brown and Harris [1994], *..the main difference between these techniques is the level of abstraction at which there are interpreted. B-splines are viewed as numerical processing or computational systems, whereas fuzzy networks can be given a linguistic interpretation as a fuzzy algorithm using terms such as small or large to label the basis functions.* A B-spline network estimates a function $f(x)$ as a weighted sum of B-splines forming a partition of unity:

$$\hat{f}(x) = \sum_j c_j \cdot \varphi(x - x_j) \qquad\qquad (6.1)$$

The weights c_j are computed by either an instantaneous gradient descent rule, iterative conjugate gradient, or a least mean-squares method. Kalman filtering can be applied for state estimation and control (Gan and Harris, 1999). The coefficients are directly computed from a singular-valued decomposition in a batch operation. B-splines are particularly well suited to constrained problems. B-splines of order k are piecewise continuous polynomials with (k-2) continuous derivatives. The main constraint in moving systems (robots, ship docking, automatic guidance) is that both the velocity and the acceleration must be continuous—high order B-splines (k ≥ 4) fulfill these conditions. The cubic B-spline is the first spline to satisfy the acceleration condition.

Extensions of the model to first-order Takagi-Sugeno types of models have also been designed [Harris *et al.*, 1999a; 1999b]. Spline-based neuro-fuzzy methods have been implemented in a large number of research and development projects [Harris *et al.*, 1999a], in ship collision avoidance guidance [Harris *et al.*, 1999b], helicopter guidance [Doyle and Harris, 1996], autonomous underwater vehicle [Bossley, 1997], or an intelligent driver warning system [An and Harris, 1996].

6.2. Wavelet-based neural networks

6.2.1. *Wavelet networks*

The origin of wavelet networks can be traced back to Daugman [1988] work in which Gabor wavelets are applied to image classification. Wavelet networks became popular after Pati and Krishnaprasad [1993, 1991] and Szu *et al.* [1992]. They introduced wavelet networks as a special feedforward neural network. Zhang and Benveniste [1992] did apply wavelet networks to the problem of controlling a robot arm. As mother wavelet, they used the function

$$\psi(x) = (x^T \cdot x - dim(x)) \cdot e^{-1/2 \cdot x^T \cdot x} \tag{6.2}$$

Szu *et al.* [1992] take a different function, $\cos(1.75\ t)\exp(-t^2/2)$, as the mother wavelet for phonemes classification and speaker recognition. Simple combinations of sigmoids are alternatives chosen by Pati and Krishnaprasad [1991]. Marar *et al.* [1996] generalized the approach to polynomial functions of the sigmoid function.

Wavelet networks with a three layers perceptron structure are of the general form:

$$f(x) = \sum_{i=1}^{N} w_i \cdot det(D_i^{1/2}) \cdot \psi[D_i \cdot x - t_i] \tag{6.3}$$

with D the diagonal dilatation matrix and t the translation vector.

For classification, the output signal is often processed with a sigmoid function $\sigma(f(x))$ [Szu, Telfer, and Kadambe, 1992]. Wavelet networks are very successful in learning problems dealing with oscillating signals. The Mexican wavelet is the wavelet of choice in most wavelet networks, and its simple analytics expression and differentiability reduce the computational costs of learning. The function is nonzero on an infinite interval but approaches zero rapidly, and its symmetry makes it easy to generalize to higher dimensions.

$$\psi\left(\frac{x-\mu}{\sigma}\right) = (1 - \left(\frac{x-\mu}{\sigma}\right)^2)\exp\left(-\frac{\left(\frac{x-\mu}{\sigma}\right)^2}{2}\right) \tag{6.4}$$

Wavelet networks are universal function estimators that may represent a function to some precision very compactly [Hornik *et al.*, 1989; Kreinovich *et al.*, 1994]. Hornik has shown that an arbitrary continuous function on a compact set is approximated by a 3-layers neural network within a precision ε. More precisely, assume an arbitrary function f with p continuous derivatives on (0,1) and $|f^p(x)| \leq \Delta$, such that the function is equal to zero in some neighborhoods of the endpoints. The function f: $\Re \rightarrow \Re$ can be approximated by an expression of the type:

$$f(x) = \sum_{h=1}^{H} \beta_h \cdot s(w_h \cdot x + b_h) \tag{6.5}$$

with H the number of neurons in the hidden layer, w the weight between the input and the hidden layer, and β the weight between the hidden and the output layer.

The function s(x) is the transfer function, for instance, the sigmoid function. A wavelet network is a particular case of (6.5). Kreinovich, Sirisaengtaksin, and Cabrera [1994] proved that wavelet neural networks are asymptotically optimal approximators for the functions of one variable. Wavelet neural networks are optimal because they require the smallest possible number of bits to reconstruct a function within a precision ε.

From the practical point of view, determining the number of wavelets and their initialization represent two significant problems with wavelet networks. A good initialization of wavelet neural networks is extremely important for the fast convergence of the algorithm. Zhang and Benveniste [1992] initialize the coefficients with an orthogonal least-squares procedure. As an alternative, the dyadic wavelet decomposition initializes the network. Echauz [1998] applies a clustering method to position the wavelets. The distribution of points about a cluster furnishes information on the wavelet position and dilation of the wavelet. Echauz and Vachtsevanos also propose an elegant method using trigonometric wavelets, and he uses functions of the form:

$$cos\ trap(x) = cos(3\pi/2 \cdot x) \cdot min\{max\{3/2 \cdot (1 - |x|),0\},1\} \tag{6.6}$$

Polynomials can approximate trigonometric wavelets. Fitting the polynomial is a linear problem solved more efficiently than fitting trigonometric wavelets. The polynomial approximation serves for the initialization of the corresponding wavelets. In Boubez and Peskin [1993], the network is initialized by positioning and approximating low-resolution wavelets. New higher resolution wavelets are introduced and initialized subsequently to minimize the score. Rao and Kumthekar

[1994] use cascade correlation learning architecture to train the network. New wavelets are added one by one, and at each step, the network is trained till it converges. Yu *et al.* [1996] opt for the opposite approach; the wavelet network first uses many functions. Subsequently, the wavelet network is made as compact as possible using a shrinkage technique to delete non-essential nodes.

6.3. Extreme learning machines

Extreme Learning Machines (ELM) are simple and efficient in regression and pattern classification, and their structure is comparable to a single hidden feedforward neural network (Figure 6.2). There is a significant difference in that the parameters are not learned through a gradient technique but computed using a pseudo-inverse matrix. The method is also suited to online learning [Lan, Soh, and Huang, 2009].

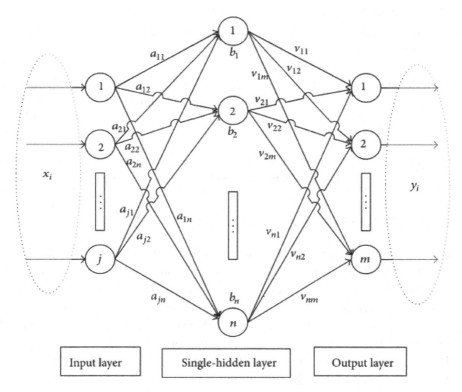

Fig. 6.2. Single Hidden Layer Feedforward Neural Network, (Ding *et al.*, 2015) Source: Shifei Ding under CC BY 3.0.

Backpropagation on the weights is a classical learning approach in a single hidden feedforward neural network. An Extreme Learning Machine (ELM) uses a different strategy, giving random values to the weights a_{ij} and bias b_i and learning $v_{j,k}$ using a pseudo-inverse of a matrix

$$y_i = \sum_{i=1}^{j} \sum_{j=1}^{n} \sum_{k=1}^{m} v_{j,k} \ g(a_{i,j}x_i + b_j) \tag{6.7}$$

or in matrix form

$$HV = Y \tag{6.8}$$

In its simplest form, learning in ELM proceeds in three steps [Deng *et al.*, 2010]:

Step 1. Randomly select numerical values between 0 and 1 to set input weights $a_{i,j}$ and the bias b_j.
Step 2. Calculate the output matrix H using the function g.
Step 3. Calculate the output weights $V = H^+Y$
with H^+ the pseudo-inverse matrix of H satisfying $H\,H^+H = H$ (see Penrose [1955] on Pseudo-inverse).

This simple approach is extremely fast in learning but not very robust, Ding *et al.* [2015] proposed an improved system minimizing the function:

$$\|V\|+C \ \|Y - HV\|$$

with a regularization constant C that weights the respective importance of accuracy versus the norm of V. The problem has a simple solution [Ding *et al.*, 2015].

6.3.1. *Wavelet kernel and Fuzzy wavelet ELM*

Despite its many successes, wavelet networks often face the difficulty of initializing the wavelet parameters (position and dilation) to achieve fast convergence. In order to remediate that problem, Huang [2014] suggested using ELM with wavelet kernels. The approach provided convincing results in EEG signal classification [Diker *et al.*, 2019] and electric price forecasting [Yang *et al.*, 2017]. The wavelet parameters and the numbers of hidden neurons play a significant role in the performance of ELM. Avci and Dogantekin [2016] use a genetic algorithm to search for the optimum values of these parameters and the numbers of hidden neurons of ELM in a diagnosis system to detect Alzheimer's disease. Alternatively, a fuzzy clustering approach can determine these parameters [Javed *et al.*, 2015]. Golestaneh *et al.* [2018] propose a fuzzy wavelet ELM architecture to reduce the complexity of the learning phase by reducing the number of learned parameters. Shrivastava and Panigrahi [2014] obtain remarkable results using that approach on an ensemble of wavelet networks to predict electricity prices. Hybrid networks combining several techniques often provide superior results. For example, Yahia, Said, and Zaied [2022] combine wavelet extreme learning machine and deep learning in classification with some success.

6.4. Dyadic wavelet networks or wavenets

Bakshi *et al.* [1994] first proposed wavelet networks. A wavenet corresponds to a feedforward neural network using wavelets as activation functions in its simplest version.

$$f(x) = \sum_{m,n} d_{m,n} \cdot \psi_{m,n}(x) + \bar{f} \qquad (6.9)$$

with $\bar{f}$ the average value of f, $d_{m,n}$ the coefficients of the neural network and ψ the wavelet.

Wavenets have been generalized to biorthogonal wavelets [Thuillard, 1999; 2000]. The principal difference between orthogonal wavelets is that the evolution equation depends on the dual wavelet. We have proposed the following evolution equation for biorthogonal wavelets.

$$\hat{d}_{m,n}(k) = \hat{d}_{m,n}(k-1) - LR \cdot (f(x) - y_k(x)) \cdot \tilde{\psi}_{m,n}(x) \qquad (6.10)$$

with LR the learning rate and $y_k(x)$ the kth input point. For data points that are independent, uniformly distributed copies of a random variable X, the estimated wavelet coefficients $\hat{d}_{m,n}(k)$ converge adiabatically to $d_{m,n}$ in the very low learning rate limit.

For orthogonal wavelets, (6.10) reduces to

$$\hat{d}_{m,n}(k) = \hat{d}_{m,n}(k-1) - LR \cdot (f(x) - y_k(x)) \cdot \psi_{m,n}(x) \qquad (6.11)$$

6.5. Wavelet-based fuzzy neural networks

Wavelet theory has a profound impact on signal processing as it offers a rigorous mathematical approach to the treatment of multiresolution. The combination of neural networks and wavelet theory has led to many new techniques: wavelet networks, wavenets, and fuzzy wavenets. In this section, we review wavelet-based neural networks. We distinguish two categories of methods. In the first one, the wavelet part is decoupled from learning. The wavelet coefficients are supplied to a neural network. The second category combines wavelet theory and neural networks into a single method. We limit the scope of this chapter to the second category, which covers wavelet networks, wavenets, and fuzzy wavenets. The wavelet network is an example successfully used in classification and identification problems. Wavelet networks are feedforward neural networks using wavelets as activation functions. The strength of wavelet networks lies in their capabilities to catch essential features in *frequency-rich* signals. In wavelet networks, both the position and the dilation of the wavelets are optimized besides the weights.

Originally, wavenets did refer to neural networks using dyadic wavelets. In wavenets, the position and dilation of the wavelets are fixed, and the network optimizes the weights. We propose to adopt this terminology. The theory of wavenets has been generalized to biorthogonal wavelets and the development of fuzzy wavenets [Thuillard, 2000]. Fuzzy wavenets extend wavelet-based learning techniques to online learning. A significant advantage of fuzzy wavenets techniques compared to most neuro-fuzzy methods is that the rules are validated online during learning using a simple algorithm based on the fast wavelet decomposition algorithm.

The similarities between the structure of a feedforward neural network and a wavelet decomposition are used in so-called wavelet networks. A wavelet network is a 3-layers feedforward neural network in which $\psi(a_i \cdot x + b_i)$ is a wavelet (Figure 6.3).

The output of the 3-layers neural network is

$$f(x) = \sum_{i=1}^{k} w_i \cdot \psi(a_i \cdot x + b_i) \tag{6.12}$$

with ψ the activation function and a_i, b_i, w_i the network parameters (weights) optimized during learning.

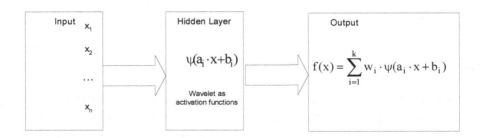

Fig. 6.3. The structure of a wavelet network is often a feedforward neural network.

If only the weights are optimized in (6.12), and the activation function is of the form $\psi_{m,n} = \psi(2^m x - n)$, with m,n integers, the network is referred to as a wavenet. A subset of wavelet networks is the so-called fuzzy wavelet networks or fuzzy wavenets. Using the two-scales relation [Mallat, 1999], a wavelet is decomposed into a sum of scaling functions $\psi(x) = \sum_r h_{n-2r}\varphi(2x - r)$. The wavelet network, given by (6.12), can be put under the form:

$$f(x) = \sum_{m,n,r} d_{m,n} \cdot h_{n-2r} \cdot \varphi_{m+1,n}(x) + \bar{f} \tag{6.13}$$

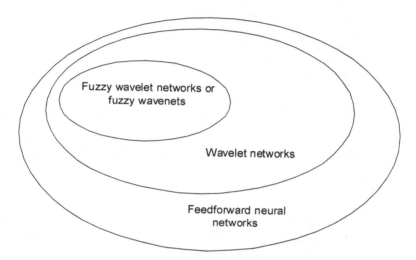

Fig. 6.4. The most popular wavelet networks are based on the perceptron structure. Fuzzy wavelet networks, also called fuzzy wavenets, can be regarded as a neuro-fuzzy model which belongs at the same time to the set of wavelet networks.

Fuzzy wavenets are wavelet networks with unique properties: the scaling function associated with these wavelets must be symmetric, everywhere positive, and with a single maximum. Under these conditions, the scaling functions are interpreted as fuzzy membership functions. Figure 6.4 summarizes the different wavelet-based neural networks using a feedforward type of network. Fuzzy wavenets are included within the category of wavelet networks.

6.5.1. *Fuzzy wavelet networks*

Adding a fuzzy layer to a wavelet network allows efficient learning if the output combines rapidly varying functions (Figure 6.5). Ho *et al.* [2001] describe the numerical output as a sum of wavelets. Each rule takes the form:

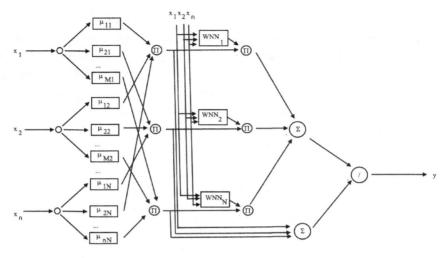

Fig. 6.5. The continuous fuzzy wavelet network has an antecedent and a consequent part. The system learns the weight describing the output function of WNNi of the form given by Eq. 6.14.

Rule k: If x_1 is A_{k1} and x_2 is A_{k2} and...and x_n is A_{kn} then y_k is

$$\sum_{i=1}^{m} w_{ik} \psi\left(\frac{x-b_{ik}}{a_{ik}}\right) \tag{6.14}$$

Learning with a gradient-descent is standard, but some authors use genetic algorithms or ICA to discover the best coefficients [Abiyev, 2011] to avoid staying at a local minimum. Particle swarm optimization is also used, for instance, by Cheng and Bai [2015].

Some other architectures are also quite successful in solving different problems. Adeli and Jiang [2006] combine a clustering fuzzy C-means and a wavelet network to model a dynamic system with unknown parameters. The output combines the wavelet functions to a linear dependency:

$$y(X_k) = \sum_{i=1}^{M} w_i \sum_{j=1}^{D} \psi\left(\frac{x_{k,j}-c_{ij}}{a_{ij}}\right) + \sum_{j=1}^{D} b_j X_{kj} + d \tag{6.15}$$

Abiyev [2010] proposed a type-2 fuzzy wavelet neural network (type-2 FWNN). It uses type-2 fuzzy membership functions in the antecedent and wavelet functions in the consequent parts. For structure identification, he implements a fuzzy clustering algorithm.

The dyadic fuzzy wavenet combines a neuro-fuzzy system with a fuzzy wavelet network limited to functions on a grid. It learns the best system description using dyadic scaling spline functions and wavelets.

The primary purpose of the continuous fuzzy wavelet approach is to describe rapidly varying signals sparsely. The system learns the best wavelet translation parameter resulting in applications such as EKG into sparse descriptions. The wavelet parameters (dilation and translation) are optimized so that a small number of them describe the signal well. Optimizing all parameters is not always the best strategy. Karatepe and Alcı [2005] obtained improved results by fixing the translation. Genetic algorithms or PSO are alternatives to gradient descent algorithms for learning. Tzeng [2010] applies an efficient genetic algorithm (GA) approach to adjust the dilation, translation, weights, and membership functions.

6.5.2. *Fuzzy wavenets*

Let us recall the framework we have worked in and the left situation in part 4. A significant challenge to fuzzy logic is translating the information contained implicitly in a collection of data points into linguistically interpretable fuzzy rules. A serious difficulty with many neuro-fuzzy methods is that they often furnish rules without a transparent interpretation; a rule is referred to as transparent if it has a clear and intuitive linguistic understanding. Multiresolution techniques provide a solution to this problem. The basic idea is to take a dictionary of membership functions forming a multiresolution and determine which membership functions are the most appropriate to describe the data points. The membership functions are chosen among the family of symmetric scaling functions, everywhere positive and with a single maximum. This family includes splines and some radial functions. The main advantage of using a dictionary of membership functions is that each term, *small* or *large*, is well defined beforehand and is not modified during learning. The multiresolution properties of the membership functions in the dictionary function permit the fusion and split of membership functions.

In the singleton model, the fuzzy rules are of the form:

$$R_i : \quad \text{if} \quad x \text{ is } A_i \text{ then } y = b_i.$$

Here A_i is a linguistic term, x is the input linguistic variable, while y is the output variable. The value of the input linguistic variable may be crisp or fuzzy. If spline functions N^k are taken, for instance, as membership function $\mu_{A_i}(\hat{x}) = N^k(2^m \cdot \hat{x} - n)$ then the system is equivalent to $y = \sum_j b_j \cdot N^k(2^m \cdot \hat{x} - n)$. In this particular case, the output y is a linear sum of translated and dilated splines. Under this form, the singleton Takagi-Sugeno model is equivalent to a multi-resolution spline model.

Rules validation is the main issue for online problems, especially if little memory is available. The previous chapters presented several multiresolution methods that suitably cannot tackle the validation problem. Ideally, one would like a system containing few rules as only a few points are available and refine the rules as it learns. The following sections will introduce several methods using a simple and efficient wavelet-based validation procedure. New rules are added to the systems as more information is collected. All presented approaches use the fast wavelet algorithm to validate the fuzzy rules, and the methods are referred to as fuzzy wavenets.

These fuzzy wavenet methods combine wavelet theory with fuzzy logic and neural networks. They permit the determination of appropriate fuzzy rules during online learning. The model is refined as more data are furnished to the system. The rule validation procedure is based on the fast wavelet decomposition and reconstruction algorithm. Learning is fully automated and does not require any external intervention, making these methods very useful in practical applications, for instance, during field testing of sensors and actuators. The detectors are installed in challenging test objects located all over the world. The sensor's signals are processed autonomously in the detector. The information is processed and stored in a compressed form. The compressed data can be transmitted to the laboratory, for instance, through simple communication means (mobile phone, ethernet). This approach permits carrying out large-scale field testing at moderate costs.

Spline wavenets have successfully modeled chaotic data [Billings and Coca, 1999]. The network's multiresolution structure captures both long and short-range correlations quite efficiently. The neural network uses a feedforward neural network with instantaneous gradient descent. As learning is off-line, their model completes the list of multiresolution neuro-fuzzy models presented in part 4 for off-line learning. The main difference between Billings' approach and the one shown below lies in small but essential details. In fuzzy wavenets, the evolution equation uses the dual scaling functions, not the scaling function itself. Using the dual permits to give an interpretation of the weights $\hat{c}_{m,n}$ in the expression $\hat{f}(x) = \sum_{m,n} \hat{c}_{m,n} \cdot \varphi_{m,n}(x)$. For locally uniformly distributed data and for small learning rates, the coefficients $\hat{c}_{m,n}$ tend, under some mild conditions on f($\mathbf{x}$), towards the approximation coefficient $c_{m,n}$ of the wavelet decomposition of f($\mathbf{x}$). The coefficients in both approaches are not the same. For orthogonal wavelets, this would hold, but not for biorthogonal wavelets.

6.5.3. *Learning with fuzzy wavenets*

Figure 6.6 shows the architecture of the learning algorithm. It consists of a series of neural networks, using both wavelets $\psi_{m,n}(x)$ and scaling functions $\varphi_{m,n}(x)$ as activation functions. Each neural network takes activation functions of a given resolution.

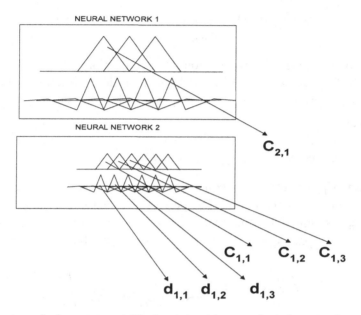

Fig. 6.6. Structure of a fuzzy wavenet. The input signal is approximated at several resolutions as a weighted sum of wavelets $\psi_{n,m,}$ and scaling functions $\varphi_{m,n}(x)$ at a given resolution.

The mth neural network optimizes the coefficients $\hat{c}_{m,n}$ and $\hat{d}_{m,n}$ with $f_m(x)$ the output of the mth neural network.

$$f_m(x) = \sum_n \hat{d}_{m,n} \cdot \psi_{m,n}(x) + \sum_n \hat{c}_{m,n} \cdot \varphi_{m,n}(x) \tag{6.16}$$

The evolution equation for the details $\hat{d}_{m,n}(k)$ and the approximation coefficients $\hat{c}_{m,n}(k)$ at step k are given by

$$\hat{d}_{m,n}(k) = \hat{d}_{m,n}(k-1) - LR \cdot (f_m(x) - y_k(x)) \cdot \tilde{\psi}_{m,n}(x) \tag{6.17}$$

$$\hat{c}_{m,n}(k) = \hat{c}_{m,n}(k-1) - LR \cdot (f_m(x) - y_k(x)) \cdot \tilde{\varphi}_{m,n}(x) \tag{6.18}$$

with $y_k(x)$, the kth input point, and LR, the learning rate, $\tilde{\varphi}_{m,n}(x)$, $\tilde{\psi}_{m,n}(x)$ the dual functions to $\varphi_{m,n}(x)$ and $\psi_{m,n}(x)$. The evolution equations (6.16-18) describe the evolution of $f_m(x)$. Assume datapoints $y_k = f(x_k)$, with x_k uniformly distributed copies of a random variable X. At each step, the coefficients $\hat{c}_{m,n}$, $\hat{d}_{m,n}$ are updated by a term which expectation is proportional to

$$E((\hat{f}_m(x) - y_k(x)) \cdot \tilde{\psi}_{m,n}(x)) = <\hat{f}_m(x) - f(x), \tilde{\psi}_{m,n}(x)>$$
$$= d_{m,n} - \hat{d}_{m,n} \tag{6.19a}$$

$$E((\hat{f}_m(x) - y_k(x)) \cdot \tilde{\varphi}_{m,n}(x)) = <\hat{f}_m(x) - f(x), \tilde{\varphi}_{m,n}(x)>$$
$$= c_{m,n} - \hat{c}_{m,n} \tag{6.19b}$$

In the adiabatic sense, the expectation of the function $f_m(x)$ converges to the projection of $f(x)$ on the space W_{m+1} under some mild conditions for the function $f(x)$. Since $\psi_{m,n}(x)$ and $\varphi_{m,n}(x)$ are independent, it follows that $\hat{c}_{m,n} \rightarrow c_{m,n}$ and $\hat{d}_{m,n} \rightarrow d_{m,n}$.

6.5.3.1. *Validation methods in fuzzy wavenets*

The validation procedure is explained starting from wavelet theory. For dyadic wavelets, a necessary condition for perfect reconstruction is that the space $V_{m-1} + W_{m-1}$ spanned by the scaling and wavelet functions at level m-1 is equivalent to the space $V_m : V_{m-1} + W_{m-1} \equiv V_m$, is symbolically expressed as

The approximation coefficients at level m are obtained from the wavelet and approximation coefficients at level m-1. A simple local validation criterion for an approximation coefficient $\hat{c}_{m,n}$ is to request that this coefficient can be approximated from the approximation and detail coefficients $\hat{c}_{m-1,n'}$, $\hat{d}_{m-1,n'}$ at one lower level of resolution. At each iteration step, the weights from the different networks are cross-validated using a central property of wavelets, namely that the approximation coefficients $c_{m,n}$ at level m can be computed from the approximation and wavelet coefficients at level m-1 using the reconstruction algorithm.

$$c_{m,n} = \Sigma_r\, g_{n-2r} \cdot c_{m-1,r} + h_{n-2r} \cdot d_{m-1,r} \tag{6.20}$$

with g_{n-2r} and h_{n-2r}, the filter coefficients for reconstruction (Beware the filter coefficients g, h are to a normalization factor $\sqrt{2}$ identical to the ones defined in part 1. The normalization is given here by the relation: $\varphi_{m,n}(x) = 2^m \cdot \varphi(2^m \cdot x - n)$.)

For a coefficient to be validated, the difference between the weight of the membership function (model m) and the weight computed from the approximation and wavelet coefficients at one level of resolution lower (model m-1) must be smaller than a given threshold (Figure 6.7).

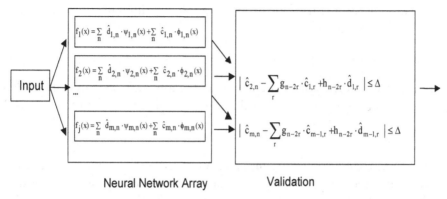

Fig. 6.7. The validation module compares the approximation coefficients $\hat{c}_{m,n}(k)$ to the approximation and wavelet coefficients at one level of resolution lower.

As validation criterion for the coefficient $\hat{c}_{m,n}$, we require

$$\left| \hat{c}_{m,n} - \sum_r g_{n-2r}\, \hat{c}_{m-1,r} + h_{n-2r} \hat{d}_{m-1,r} \right| \leq \Delta \tag{6.21}$$

The most appropriate membership functions and rules are chosen adaptively during learning. With only a few points, not much information is known, and the system is better described with a small number of rules. As the number of points increases, the system adds new rules if necessary. The method furnishes an automatic procedure to determine the best membership functions and rules adaptively. The *best* coefficients are chosen adaptively among the set of validated coefficients. The validated coefficients corresponding locally to the highest resolution are kept (default coefficient = average value).

6.5.4. *Learning with wavelet-based feedforward neural networks*

The convergence of the fuzzy wavenet method is not too fast, as the technique requires, for stability reasons, to use a small learning rate compared to a perceptron. Therefore, one may consider another approach using only scaling functions. The basic structure of the network is similar to the fuzzy wavenet, except that the mth neural network optimizes the coefficients $\hat{c}_{m,n}$, with $f_m(x)$ the output of the mth neural network (Figure 6.8).

$$f_m(x) = \sum_n \hat{c}_{m,n} \cdot \varphi_{m,n}(x) \tag{6.22}$$

The following expression gives the evolution equation

$$\hat{c}_{m,n}(k) = \hat{c}_{m,n}(k-1) - LR \cdot (f_m(x) - y_k(x)) \cdot \tilde{\varphi}_{m,n}(x) \tag{6.23}$$

The validation procedure uses the decomposition algorithm to compare the results at two levels of resolution.

$$c_{m,n} = \sum_k p_{k-2n} \cdot c_{m+1,k} \tag{6.24}$$

with g the filter's coefficients associated with the low-pass decomposition filter in the fast wavelet decomposition algorithm. The validation criterion for $\hat{c}_{m,n}$ is then

$$\left| c_{m,n} - \sum_k p_{k-2n} \cdot \hat{c}_{m+1,k} \right| \leq \Delta \tag{6.25}$$

What are good candidates for scaling and wavelet functions at high dimensions? Many problems require describing an n-dimensional surface with n larger than 2. From the theoretical point of view, there is no limit to the dimension of a wavelet [Kugarajah and Zhang, 1995; Kovacevic and Sweldens, 2000]. An evident approach to building wavelets in higher dimensions is through tensor products of one-dimensional wavelets (for instance, splines). This approach is versatile enough to describe with sufficient precision many n-dimensional surfaces.

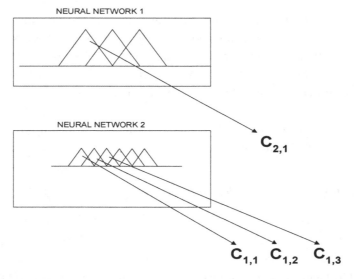

Fig. 6.8. Structure of a fuzzy wavenet. The input signal is approximated at several resolutions as a weighted sum of scaling functions $\varphi_{m,n}(x)$ at a given resolution.

The lifting scheme can also generate compactly supported biorthogonal wavelets on any lattice and any dimension. This approach becomes unpractical at high dimensions due to the increasing size of the filter. Radial functions are often very appropriate to deal with high-dimensional spaces, and the symmetry of radial functions permits a straightforward computation of their values. Micchelli *et al.* [1991] designed semi-orthogonal wavelets based on radial functions. Contrarily to other radial functions [Buhmann, 1994], the construction of Micchelli works at any dimension. The scaling functions are constructed from polyharmonic B-splines of the form:

$$f(x) = \|x\|^{2r-d} \cdot log\|x\|, d \ even \tag{6.26a}$$

$$f(x) = \|x\|^{2r-d}, d \ odd \tag{6.26b}$$

with r an integer and d the dimension. The integer must be such that $2r > d$.
    The Fourier transform of the scaling function is given by

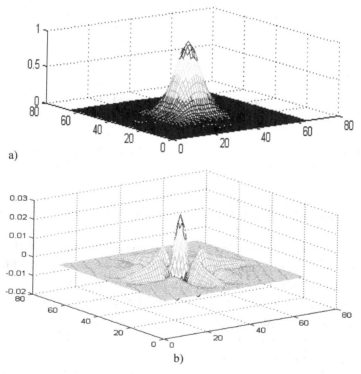

a)

b)

Fig. 6.9. Radial scaling functions may be used for multidimensional wavenets as an alternative to tensor products of univariate functions. a) Scaling function in two dimensions, b) associated wavelet.

$$\hat{\varphi}(\omega) = (\Sigma_{j=1}^{d} \sin^2(\omega_j/2) / \| \omega/2 \|^2)^r \tag{6.27}$$

with $\omega = (\omega_1, \ldots, \omega_d)$.

Figure 6.9 shows the 2-dimensional scaling function for $r = 2$ and $d = 2$. The associated wavelet is shown below (Figure 6.9b). The wavelet and scaling functions are obtained by the inverse Fourier transform of the function:

$$\psi(\omega/2) = 2^{-d} \cdot \| \omega/2 \|^{2r} |\varphi(-\omega/2)|^2 / \Sigma_{k \in Z^d} \hat{\varphi}(-\omega/2 + 2 \cdot \pi \cdot k) \tag{6.28}$$

Table 6.1 presents the different approaches combining fuzzy logic and wavelets presented in this chapter.

Table 6.1: Three different Fuzzy wavelet schemes.

Method	Input membership function	Output
(Dyadic)		
Fuzzy wavenet:	Spline	$\Sigma_{k1} w_{k1} \varphi_{a_{k1}, c_{k2}} (x_1, x_2, \ldots, x_n) +$ $\Sigma_{k2} w_{k2} \psi_{a_{k2}, c_{k2}} (x_1, x_2, \ldots, x_n$
(Continuous)		
Fuzzy wavelet network:	Type-1 Fuzzy	$\Sigma_k w_k \psi_{a_k, c_k} (x_1, x_2, \ldots, x_n)$
Type-2 Fuzzy wavelet network:	Type-2 Fuzzy	$\Sigma_k \tilde{w}_k \psi_{a_k, c_k} (x_1, x_2, \ldots, x_n)$

6.6. Applications of wavelet, fuzzy wavelet networks, and wavenets

Figure 6.10 summarizes the different fuzzy wavelet techniques introduced in the last chapters. Part 7 completes this presentation by discussing the application of fuzzy logic and multiresolution analysis in deep networks.

For off-line learning with data on a regular grid, appropriate membership functions and rules are determined with fuzzy wavelet techniques. The most appropriate rules are chosen based on the decomposition coefficients or a matching pursuit algorithm. If some data are missing, the values on a grid are estimated with standard regression and approximation techniques. Approximation techniques can also be chosen for a random design, though an alternative solution consists of mapping the input space onto a regular grid. In that latter case, the position and shape of the membership functions depend on the location and density of points in the input space.

The chosen methods for online learning are wavelet-based neural methods (fuzzy wavenets and fuzzy wavelet networks) or multiresolution estimation (fuzzy wavelet estimators).

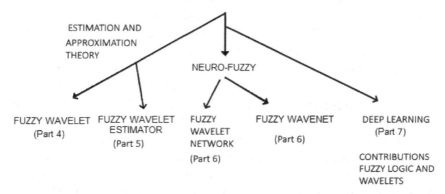

Fig. 6.10. Summary of the different methods to develop fuzzy rules from data with wavelet-based approaches.

Finally, a current approach used in numerous applications ranging from finance [Popoola, 2006] to medicine consists of combining a Fuzzy Neural Network with wavelet processing (Figure 6.11).

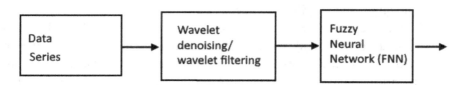

Fig. 6.11. Wavelet preprocessing and prediction with a fuzzy neural network.

Most fuzzy wavelet network applications relate to analyzing and classifying time series with multiple variables input and a single output. More advanced systems in control [Al-khazraji *et al.*, 2011] deal with MIMO (Multiple inputs, multiple outputs). The short review of applications below furnishes a survey of possible (fuzzy) wavelet network applications.

Finance/business

Wavelets and wavelet networks are used in finance to model market fluctuations [Becerra *et al.*, 2005]. The analysts exploit the filtering properties of wavelets to extract features correlated with the market price. Predictions based on time series analysis of data are the principal application of fuzzy wavelet neural networks (FWNN).

Medicine

Image processing and classification are essential in medicine, and wavelet-based methods are ubiquitous [Aldroubi and Unser, 1996]. Classification of oscillating signals (ECG, EMG, EEG) with wavelet-based methods is standard practice [Cheng and Liu, 2008; Turkoglu et al., 2003; Übeyli, 2009]. The subject is discussed briefly in the section on deep learning.

Feature extraction and pattern classification are the two fundamental steps in signal classification. Existing wavelet-based classification methods use either some indicators representing globally the wavelet coefficients (energy, cluster position) or treat the coefficients as features. Li et al. [2005] developed an efficient fuzzy wavelet packet-based feature extraction method to classify high-dimensional biomedical data (magnetic resonance spectra). In wavelet-packet-based classification, an algorithm searches for the minimum entropy basis among all the bases in the specified basis dictionary [Wickerhauser, 1993]. Another approach selects the best basis using a measure of their discriminatory power [Saito and Coifman, 1995] to distinguish different classes. Li, Pedrycz, and Pizzi [2005] describe a fuzzy set approach to finding the best discriminatory basis. A fuzzy c-means algorithm classifies the values in each subband, and the algorithm chooses the wavelet basis with the best discriminatory power.

Energy optimization and building science

Abiyev [2009] uses a fuzzy wavelet neural network to predict electricity consumption in the energy field. The stability of electric networks is a central issue as energy production reaches its limit at a particular time in the day or some seasons. The price of electricity in the USA varies significantly during the day, with hefty penalties at peak energy to incite companies or private persons to limit their energy consumption at peak hours. Load forecasting implies direct financial return and information for electricity providers or users. In a building, load prediction permits developing a demand-control strategy by breaking the peaks through different approaches, including energy storage or delayed reaction. Prediction of electric consumption is becoming a central issue in energy management. Ribeiro, Mariani, and dos Santos Coelho [2019] have demonstrated the effectiveness of wavelet networks for short-term load forecasting.

The energy needed in a building to achieve comfort at low energy depends critically on the cooling water optimization [Henze et al., 2013; Thuillard et al., 2014]. Fouling the heat exchanger is detrimental to the energy transfer, and it results in significant energy loss (The cooling fluid circulates into the pipes without properly delivering its energy). Sun *et al.* [2008] implement a wavelet network to predict fouling of the heat exchanger.

Let us discuss here some applications of intelligent control in buildings. With the ongoing energy transition out of oil, photovoltaics (PV) increasingly supplies energy to the building with PV cells mounted on the roof or the facade. Photovoltaic systems are non-linear, and their optimization under different weather conditions is complex. Hassan *et al.* [2017] developed a high-performance fuzzy wavelet neuro-controller to find the optimal working point. Zhang and Wang [2012] use a similar model to predict annual electricity consumption in cities. Kodogiannis *et al.* [2013] validate the approach to the short-term electric load forecasting of the Power System of the Greek Island of Crete.

Estimating the energy performance of a building is becoming a requirement for building increasingly. Abiyev and Abizada [2021] use a type-2 fuzzy wavelet neural network to integrate the uncertainties in the process. Such a line of research is crucial as too many buildings fail to fulfill the promised energy performances, and including uncertainty in the model is an essential step in the right direction.

Let us finally mention that FWNN has found applications in predicting the behavior of a building during an earthquake and testing the robustness of highrise structures [Jiang and Adeli, 2005]. Smart structures, such as magnetorheological (MR) dampers, equip bridges or highrises. Salajegheh *et al.* [2007] show the robustness and high performance of the wavelet networks for structural optimization. Improved genetic algorithms and neural networks find the optimal weight of structures subject to multiple natural frequency constraints. Mitchell *et al.* [2012] model the non-linear behavior of the damper systems with an adaptive wavelet-based adaptive neuro-fuzzy inference system. This approach effectively models the non-linear behavior of the structure–MR damper system subjected to a variety of disturbances using shorter training times than an adaptive neuro-fuzzy inference system model.

Fault diagnosis
Power transformers and energy distribution benefit from FWNN for quality assessment [Morsi and El-Hawary, 2009], fault detection [Dong *et al.*, 2008; Mufti and Vachtsevanos, 1995], and power stabilization [Tofighi *et al.*, 2015].

Hydrology
Fuzzy logic and wavelet are combined in a neural network by either developing a neural network with antecedent fuzzy rules and adding wavelet layers as output or processing the data with a fuzzy c-means algorithm. Huang *et al.* [2017] use the latter approach for water quality prediction in rivers. Prediction of the lake [Noury

et al., 2014] or river level [Adamowski and Sun, 2010; Okkan, 2012; Shafaei *et al.*, 2014; Wei *et al.*, 2013] and drought forecasting [Younesi *et al.*, 2018] are standard applications of (fuzzy) wavelet networks. Dixit *et al.* [2015] have used a wavelet network to improve wave forecasting. The system can predict high waves in the ocean up to 36 hours in advance, significantly improving previous systems using standard neural networks.

Modeling and control

A combination of fuzzy logic and wavelet analysis helps control dynamic systems like robots [Abiyev *et al.*, 2013; Han and Lee, 2012; Karimi *et al.*, 2006; Lin, 2006; Yen *et al.*, 2019] capable of compensating for nonsmooth nonlinearities, like friction, dead zone, and uncertainty in a dynamic system. Fuzzy wavelet networks have impressive generalization capabilities. Various applications, for instance, identification and control of dynamic systems [Abiyev and Kaynak, 2010; Sheikholeslam and Zekri, 2013; Yilmaz and Oysal, 2015], manipulators [El-Sousy and Abuhasel, 2016], or robots, have been developed over the years. Figure 6.12 shows a fuzzy wavelet network integrated into a control loop (After Zekri *et al.* [2008]. FWNN are also parts of some recurrent networks [Hsu, 2011; Wang *et al.*, 2014]. Hsu [2011] uses an adaptive fuzzy wavelet neural synchronization controller (AFWNSC) to synchronize two non-linear identical chaotic gyros by combining a fuzzy wavelet neural network to approximate an ideal controller online and a fuzzy compensator to guarantee stability.

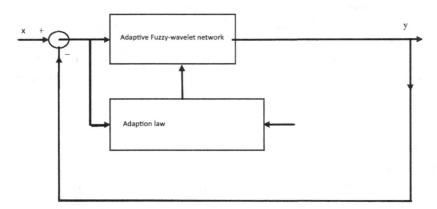

Fig. 6.12. An adaptive fuzzy wavelet (gain) controller with a feedback loop.

Fuzzy wavelet neural methods have been applied to robotics [Yen *et al.*, 2017, 2019], the control of electro-hydraulic servo systems [Chen *et al.*, 2018], and fault detection [Shahriari-kahkeshi and Sheikholeslam, 2014].

References

Abiyev, R. and Abizada, S. (2021). Type-2 fuzzy wavelet neural network for estimation energy performance of residential buildings, *Soft Computing*, 25(16), pp. 11175–11190.

Abiyev, R.H. (2009). Fuzzy wavelet neural network for prediction of electricity consumption, *AI EDAM*, 23(2), pp. 109–118.

Abiyev, R.H. (2010). A type-2 fuzzy wavelet neural network for time series prediction, *Proc. International Conference on Industrial, Engineering and Other Applications of Applied Intelligent Systems*, Springer, pp. 518–527.

Abiyev, R.H. (2011). Fuzzy wavelet neural network based on fuzzy clustering and gradient techniques for time series prediction, *Neural Computing and Applications*, 20(2), pp. 249–259.

Abiyev, R.H. and Kaynak, O. (2010). Type 2 fuzzy neural structure for identification and control of time-varying plants, *IEEE Transactions on Industrial Electronics*, 57(12), pp. 4147–4159.

Abiyev, R.H., Kaynak, O. and Kayacan, E. (2013). A type-2 fuzzy wavelet neural network for system identification and control, *Journal of the Franklin Institute*, 350(7), pp. 1658–1685.

Adamowski, J. and Sun, K. (2010). Development of a coupled wavelet transform and neural network method for flow forecasting of non-perennial rivers in semi-arid watersheds, *Journal of Hydrology*, 390(1–2), pp. 85–91.

Adeli, H. and Jiang, X. (2006). Dynamic fuzzy wavelet neural network model for structural system identification, *Journal of Structural Engineering*, 132(1), pp. 102–111.

Aldroubi, A. and Unser, M. (1996). *Wavelets in Medicine and Biology*. CRC press Boca Raton, FL.

Al-khazraji, A., Essounbouli, N. and Hamzaoui, A. (2011). A robust adaptive fuzzy wavelet network based controller for a class of non-linear systems, *International Journal of Modelling, Identification and Control*, 12(3), pp. 290–303.

An, P.E. and Harris, C.J. (1996). An intelligent driver warning system for vehicle collision avoidance, *IEEE Transactions on Systems, Man, and Cybernetics-Part A: Systems and Humans*, 26(2), pp. 254–261.

Avci, D. and Dogantekin, A. (2016). An expert diagnosis system for Parkinson disease based on genetic algorithm-wavelet kernel-extreme learning machine *Parkinson's Disease*. Online.

Bakshi, B.R., Koulouris, A. and Stephanopoulos, G. (1994). Wave-Nets: novel learning techniques, and the induction of physically interpretable models, in *Wavelet Applications*, International Society for Optics and Photonics, pp. 637–648.

Becerra, V.M., Galvão, R.K. and Abou-Seada, M. (2005). Neural and wavelet network models for financial distress classification, *Data Mining and Knowledge Discovery*, 11(1), pp. 35–55.

Billings, S. and Coca, D. (1999). Discrete wavelet models for identification and qualitative analysis of chaotic systems, *International Journal of Bifurcation and Chaos*, 9(07), pp. 1263–1284.

Bossley, K.M. (1997). Neurofuzzy modelling approaches in system identification.

Boubez, T.I. and Peskin, R.L. (1993). Wavelet neural networks and receptive field partitioning, *Proc. IEEE International Conference on Neural Networks*, IEEE, pp. 1544–1549.

Brown, M. and Harris, C.J. (1994). Neurofuzzy adaptive modelling and control'.

Buhmann, M.D. (1994). Pre-wavelets on scattered knots and from radial function spaces: A review, in *Research Report/Seminar für Angewandte Mathematik*, Eidgenössische Technische Hochschule, Seminar für Angewandte Mathematik.

Chen, X. *et al.* (2018). Identification recurrent type 2 fuzzy wavelet neural network and L2-gain adaptive variable sliding mode robust control of electro-hydraulic servo system (EHSS), *Asian Journal of Control*, 20(4), pp. 1480–1490.

Cheng, B. and Liu, G. (2008). Emotion recognition from surface EMG signal using wavelet transform and neural network, *Proc. 2nd International Conference on Bioinformatics and Biomedical Engineering (ICBBE)*, pp. 1363–1366.

Cheng, R. and Bai, Y. (2015). A novel approach to fuzzy wavelet neural network modeling and optimization, *International Journal of Electrical Power & Energy Systems*, 64, pp. 671–678.

Daugman, J.G. (1988). Complete discrete 2-D Gabor transforms by neural networks for image analysis and compression, *IEEE Transactions on Acoustics, Speech, and Signal Processing*, 36(7), pp. 1169–1179.

Deng, W.Y., Zheng, Q.H., Chen, L. and Xu, X.B. (2010). Research on extreme learning of neural networks, *Chinese Journal of Computers*, 33(2), pp. 279–287.

Diker, A., Avci, D., Avci, E. and Gedikpinar, M. (2019). A new technique for ECG signal classification genetic algorithm Wavelet Kernel extreme learning machine, *Optik*, 180, pp. 46–55.

Ding, S., Zhang, N., Xu, X., Guo, L. and Zhang, J. (2015). Deep extreme learning machine and its application in EEG classification, *Mathematical Problems in Engineering*, 2015.

Dixit, P., Londhe, S. and Dandawate, Y. (2015). Removing prediction lag in wave height forecasting using Neuro-Wavelet modeling technique, *Ocean Engineering*, 93, pp. 74–83.

Dong, L. *et al.* (2008). Rough set and fuzzy wavelet neural network integrated with least square weighted fusion algorithm based fault diagnosis research for power transformers, *Electric Power Systems Research*, 78(1), pp. 129–136.

Doyle, R. and Harris, C. (1996). Multi-sensor data fusion for helicopter guidance using neuro-fuzzy estimation algorithms, *The Aeronautical Journal*, 100(996), pp. 241–251.

Echauz, J. (1998). Strategies for fast training of wavelet neural networks, in 2nd International Symposium on Soft Computing for Industry, 3rd World Automation Congress, Anchorage, Alaska, May, pp. 10–14.

Echauz, J. and Vachtsevanos, G. (1996). Elliptic and radial wavelet neural networks, *Proc. 2nd World Automation Congress*, pp. 27–30.

El-Sousy, F.F. and Abuhasel, K.A. (2016). Self-Organizing Recurrent Fuzzy Wavelet Neural Network-Based Mixed $H_2 H_\infty$ Adaptive Tracking Control for Uncertain Two-Axis Motion Control System, *IEEE Transactions on Industry Applications*, 52(6), pp. 5139–5155.

Gan, Q. and Harris, C.J. (1999). Fuzzy local linearization and local basis function expansion in non-linear system modeling, *IEEE Transactions on Systems, Man, and Cybernetics, Part B (Cybernetics)*, 29(4), pp. 559–565.

Golestaneh, P., Zekri, M. and Sheikholeslam, F. (2018). Fuzzy wavelet extreme learning machine, Fuzzy Sets and Systems, 342, pp. 90–108.

Han, S.I. and Lee, J.M. (2012). Precise positioning of nonsmooth dynamic systems using fuzzy wavelet echo state networks and dynamic surface sliding mode control, *IEEE Transactions on Industrial Electronics*, 60(11), pp. 5124–5136.

Harris, C., Hong, X. and Wilson, P. (1999). An intelligent guidance and control system for ship obstacle avoidance, *Proceedings of the Institution of Mechanical Engineers, Part I: Journal of Systems and Control Engineering*, 213(4), pp. 311–320.

Harris, C.J., Wu, Z.Q. and Gan, Q. (1999). Neurofuzzy state estimators and their applications, *Annual Reviews in Control*, 23, pp. 149–158.

Hassan, S.Z. *et al.* (2017). Neuro-Fuzzy wavelet based adaptive MPPT algorithm for photovoltaic systems, *Energies*, 10(3), p. 394.

Henze, G.P., Henry, W. and Thuillard, M. (2013). Improving campus chilled water systems with intelligent control valves: a field study, in *AEI 2013: Building Solutions for Architectural Engineering*, pp. 103–112.

Ho, D.W., Zhang, P.-A. and Xu, J. (2001). Fuzzy wavelet networks for function learning, *IEEE Transactions on Fuzzy Systems*, 9(1), pp. 200–211.

Hornik, K., Stinchcombe, M. and White, H. (1989). Multilayer feedforward networks are universal approximators, *Neural Networks*, 2(5), pp. 359–366.

Hsu, C.-F. (2011). Adaptive fuzzy wavelet neural controller design for chaos synchronization, *Expert Systems with Applications*, 38(8), pp. 10475–10483.

Huang, G. (2014). An insight into extreme learning machines: random neurons, random features and kernels, *Cognitive Computation*, 6(3), pp. 376-390.

Huang, M. *et al.* (2017). A new efficient hybrid intelligent model for biodegradation process of DMP with fuzzy wavelet neural networks, *Scientific reports*, 7(1), pp. 1–9.

Javed, K., Gouriveau, R. and Zerhouni, N. (2015). A new multivariate approach for prognostics based on extreme learning machine and fuzzy clustering, *IEEE Transactions on Cybernetics*, 45(12), pp. 2626–2639.

Jiang, X. and Adeli, H. (2005). Dynamic wavelet neural network for non-linear identification of highrise buildings, *Computer-Aided Civil and Infrastructure Engineering*, 20(5), pp. 316–330.

Karatepe, E. and Alcı, M. (2005). A new approach to fuzzy wavelet system modeling, *International Journal of Approximate Reasoning*, 40(3), pp. 302–322.

Karimi, H.R. *et al.* (2006). Wavelet-based identification and control design for a class of non-linear systems, *International Journal of Wavelets, Multiresolution and Information Processing*, 4(01), pp. 213–226.

Kodogiannis, V.S., Amina, M. and Petrounias, I. (2013). A clustering-based fuzzy wavelet neural network model for short-term load forecasting, *International Journal of Neural Systems*, 23(05), p. 1350024.

Kovacevic, J. and Sweldens, W. (2000). Wavelet families of increasing order in arbitrary dimensions, *IEEE Transactions on Image Processing*, 9(3), pp. 480–496.

Kreinovich, V., Sirisaengtaksin, O. and Cabrera, S. (1994). Wavelet neural networks are asymptotically optimal approximators for functions of one variable, *Proc-1994 IEEE International Conference on Neural Networks (ICNN'94)*, IEEE, pp. 299–304.

Kugarajah, T. and Zhang, Q. (1995). Multidimensional wavelet frames, *IEEE Transactions on Neural Networks*, 6(6), pp. 1552–1556.

Lan, Y., Soh, Y.C. and Huang, G.B. (2009). Ensemble of online sequential extreme learning machine, *Neurocomputing*, 72(13-15), pp. 3391–3395.

Li, D., Pedrycz, W. and Pizzi, N.J. (2005). Fuzzy wavelet packet based feature extraction method and its application to biomedical signal classification, *IEEE Transactions on Biomedical Engineering*, 52(6), pp. 1132–1139.

Lin, C.-K. (2006). Nonsingular terminal sliding mode control of robot manipulators using fuzzy wavelet networks, *IEEE Transactions on Fuzzy Systems*, 14(6), pp. 849–859.

Mallat, S. (1999) A wavelet tour of signal processing. Elsevier.

Marar, J.F., Carvalho Filho, E.C. and Vasconcelos, G.C. (1996). Function approximation by polynomial wavelets generated from powers of sigmoids, in *Wavelet Applications III*, International Society for Optics and Photonics, pp. 365–374.

Micchelli, C.A., Rabut, C. and Utreras, F.I. (1991). Using the refinement equation for the construction of pre-wavelets III: Elliptic splines, *Numerical Algorithms*, 1(3), pp. 331–351.

Mitchell, R., Kim, Y. and El-Korchi, T. (2012). System identification of smart structures using a wavelet neuro-fuzzy model, *Smart Materials and Structures*, 21(11), p. 115009.

Morsi, W.G. and El-Hawary, M. (2009). Fuzzy-wavelet-based electric power quality assessment of distribution systems under stationary and nonstationary disturbances, *IEEE Transactions on Power Delivery*, 24(4), pp. 2099–2106.

Mufti, M. and Vachtsevanos, G. (1995). Automated fault detection and identification using a fuzzy-wavelet analysis technique, *Conference Record AUTOTESTCON '95. Systems Readiness: Test Technology for the 21st Century,* IEEE, pp. 169–175.

Noury, M. *et al.* (2014). Urmia lake water level fluctuation hydro informatics modeling using support vector machine and conjunction of wavelet and neural network, *Water Resources*, 41(3), pp. 261–269.

Okkan, U. (2012). Wavelet neural network model for reservoir inflow prediction, *Scientia Iranica*, 19(6), pp. 1445–1455.

Pati, Y.C. and Krishnaprasad, P.S. (1991). Discrete Affine Wavelet Transforms For Anaylsis And Synthesis Of Feedfoward Neural Networks, *Advances in Neural Information Processing Systems*, pp. 743–749.

Pati, Y.C. and Krishnaprasad, P.S. (1993). Analysis and synthesis of feedforward neural networks using discrete affine wavelet transformations, *IEEE Transactions on Neural Networks*, 4(1), pp. 73–85.

Penrose, R. (1955). A generalized inverse for matrices, *Mathematical Proceedings of the Cambridge Philosophical Society* (Vol. 51, No. 3, pp. 406–413) (Cambridge University Press).

Popoola, A.O. (2006) *Fuzzy-wavelet Method for Time Series Analysis.* University of Surrey (United Kingdom).

Rao, S.S. and Kumthekar, B. (1994). Recurrent wavelet networks, *Proc. 1994 IEEE International Conference on Neural Networks (ICNN'94)*, IEEE, pp. 3143–3147.

Ribeiro, G.T., Mariani, V.C. and dos Santos Coelho, L. (2019). Enhanced ensemble structures using wavelet neural networks applied to short-term load forecasting, *Engineering Applications of Artificial Intelligence*, 82, pp. 272–281.

Saito, N. and Coifman, R.R. (1995). Local discriminant bases and their applications, *Journal of Mathematical Imaging and Vision*, 5(4), pp. 337–358.

Salajegheh, E., Gholizadeh, S. and Torkzadeh, P. (2007). Optimal desigin of structures with frequency constraints using wavelet back propagation neural.

Shafaei, M. *et al.* (2014). Predicrion Daily Flow of Vanyar Station Using ANN and Wavelet Hybrid Procedure, *Irrigation and Water Engineering*, 4(2), pp. 113–128.

Shahriari-kahkeshi, M. and Sheikholeslam, F. (2014). Adaptive fuzzy wavelet network for robust fault detection and diagnosis in non-linear systems, *IET Control Theory & Applications*, 8(15), pp. 1487–1498.

Sheikholeslam, F. and Zekri, M. (2013). Design of adaptive fuzzy wavelet neural sliding mode controller for uncertain non-linear systems, *ISA Transactions*, 52(3), pp. 342–350.

Shrivastava, N.A. and Panigrahi, B.K. (2014). A hybrid wavelet-ELM based short term price forecasting for electricity markets, *International Journal of Electrical Power & Energy Systems*, 55, pp. 41–50.

Sun, L. *et al.* (2008). Research on the fouling prediction of heat exchanger based on wavelet neural network, in. *2008 IEEE Conference on Cybernetics and Intelligent Systems*, IEEE, pp. 961–964.

Szu, H.H., Telfer, B.A. and Kadambe, S.L. (1992). Neural network adaptive wavelets for signal representation and classification, *Optical Engineering*, 31(9), pp. 1907–1916.

Thuillard, M. (2000). Applications of fuzzy wavelets and wavenets in soft computing illustrated with the example of fire detectors, in *Wavelet Applications VII*, International Society for Optics and Photonics, pp. 351–361.

Thuillard, M., Reider, F. and Henze, G.P. (2014). Energy efficiency strategies for hydronic systems through intelligent actuators, *ASHRAE Trans*, 120(1), pp. 1–8.

Tofighi, M. *et al.* (2015). Direct adaptive power system stabilizer design using fuzzy wavelet neural network with self-recurrent consequent part, *Applied Soft Computing*, 28, pp. 514–526.

Turkoglu, I., Arslan, A. and Ilkay, E. (2003). A wavelet neural network for the detection of heart valve diseases, *Expert Systems*, 20(1), pp. 1–7.

Tzeng, S.-T. (2010). Design of fuzzy wavelet neural networks using the GA approach for function approximation and system identification, *Fuzzy Sets and Systems*, 161(19), pp. 2585–2596.

Übeyli, E.D. (2009). Combined neural network model employing wavelet coefficients for EEG signals classification, *Digital Signal Processing*, 19(2), pp. 297–308.

Wang, Y., Mai, T. and Mao, J. (2014). Adaptive motion/force control strategy for non-holonomic mobile manipulator robot using recurrent fuzzy wavelet neural networks, *Engineering Applications of Artificial Intelligence*, 34, pp. 137–153.

Wei, S. *et al.* (2013). A wavelet-neural network hybrid modelling approach for estimating and predicting river monthly flows, *Hydrological Sciences Journal*, 58(2), pp. 374–389.

Wickerhauser, M.V. (1993). Acoustic signal compression with wavelet packets, in *Wavelets: A Tutorial in Theory and Applications*, pp. 679–700.

Yahia, S., Said, S. and Zaied, M. (2020). A novel classification approach based on Extreme Learning Machine and Wavelet Neural Networks, *Multimedia Tools and Applications*, 79(19), pp. 13869–13890.

Yahia, S., Said, S. and Zaied, M.. (2022). Wavelet extreme learning machine and deep learning for data classification, *Neurocomputing*, 470, pp. 280–289.

Yang, Z., Ce, L. and Lian, L. (2017). Electricity price forecasting by a hybrid model, combining wavelet transform, ARMA, and kernel-based extreme learning machine methods, *Applied Energy*, 190, pp. 291–305.

Yen, V.T. *et al.* (2017). Robust adaptive sliding mode control for industrial robot manipulator using fuzzy wavelet neural networks, *International Journal of Control, Automation and Systems*, 15(6), pp. 2930–2941.

Yen, V.T., Nan, W.Y. and Van Cuong, P. (2019). Recurrent fuzzy wavelet neural networks based on robust adaptive sliding mode control for industrial robot manipulators, *Neural Computing and Applications*, 31(11), pp. 6945–6958.

Yilmaz, S. and Oysal, Y. (2015). Non-linear system modeling and control with dynamic fuzzy wavelet neural network, in *2015 International Symposium on Innovations in Intelligent SysTems and Applications (INISTA)*, IEEE, pp. 1–7.

Younesi, M. *et al.* (2018). Drought forecasting using artificial wavelet neural network integrated model (WA-ANN) and time series model (ARIMA), *Irrigation Sciences and Engineering*, 41(2), pp. 167–181.

Yu, Y. *et al.* (1996). Near-optimal construction of wavelet networks for non-linear system modeling, *Proc. 1996 IEEE International Symposium on Circuits and Systems (ISCAS)*, IEEE, pp. 48–51.

Zekri, M., Sadri, S. and Sheikholeslam, F. (2008). Adaptive fuzzy wavelet network control design for non-linear systems, *Fuzzy Sets and Systems*, 159(20), pp. 2668–2695.

Zhang, P. and Wang, H. (2012). Fuzzy wavelet neural networks for city electric energy consumption forecasting, *Energy Procedia*, 17, pp. 1332–1338.

Zhang, Q. and Benveniste, A. (1992). Wavelet networks, *IEEE Transactions on Neural Networks*, 3(6), pp. 889–898.

Multiresolution and Deep Neural Networks

Part 7

Chapter 7

Multiresolution and Deep Neural Networks

7.1. Introduction

New achievements in Machine Learning (ML), such as deep learning, regularly make the headlines, with deep learning finding many commercial applications. Deep learning is a subfield of Machine Learning (ML) using multilayered neural networks to learn from a vast amount of data. As the field progresses at incredible speeds, we will also report on new developments and applications connected to multiresolution analysis. This chapter introduces some of the main techniques succinctly to discuss some of the contributions of multi-resolution research to deep learning and machine learning in the following chapters. In 2019, the three pioneers [Yann Le Cun, Yoshua Bengio, and Geoffrey Hinton] were awarded the Turing price, the most prestigious price in computer sciences. These three researchers and their team revolutionized the field of artificial intelligence by creating neural network architectures with impressive learning capabilities. The accomplishments of deep learning or, more generally, machine learning are outstanding, rapidly reaching great fame among the general public.

AlphaGo succeeded in 2016 in beating the Go world champion using a combination of tree-search and reinforcement learning. After G. Kasparov lost against a trained machine specialized in chess, the game of Go was regarded as the last popular game to resist machines. The Deep Mind company developed the program to learn the game's rules from scratch. The program learned to play Go, Shogi, and chess without specialized heuristics [Schrittwieser *et al.*, 2020, 2021]. After learning, AlphaZero competed and won against the world champions in these games. Following this achievement, the next step was the development of MuZero. The program is probably an essential step toward bringing AI deeper into our lives. It combines a tree-based search with a learned model that predicts the quantities most directly relevant to the game: the reward, the action-selection policy, and the value function. In other words, the program can learn the game's rules with the perspective of applying such an approach to real-world planning tasks with complex and unknown dynamics, a mind-blowing perspective for unsupervised learning. The system learns entirely from demonstrations without interactions with the environment in new versions. Some long-standing problems, such as predicting protein folding and its structures, were recently solved through machine learning. Predicting the folding of a protein from its genetic sequence is a painstaking effort that requires months of work and has limited the number of protein structures. In natural language processing and related applications, systems using the transformer structure have replaced previous state-of-the-art recurrent networks for various reasons, including their capabilities to process the data parallelly. Massive deep learning systems have been developed and deployed in many applications. The architecture at the core of the BERT and GPT-3 machine learning technique from google and OpenAI with billions of parameters learned essentially from all the texts on the internet. BERT uses instances of self-supervised learning [Devlin *et al.*, 2018].

GPT-3 was recently extended in the OpenAI codex to create a computer game by receiving information in natural language. The system masks words in a phrase and learns to suggest words to fill the gap. A second system does the same on sentences, predicting the following sentence in a text. Self-learning will most likely boost the power of machine learning in the future. Applications include translations, question-answering, conversational agents (chatbots or virtual assistants), or patent classification [Lee and Hsiang, 2020]. Deep learning can also write an essay on a subject based on a few inputs (subject, task, main statements). Sentiment analysis, the capability of understanding the emotions conveyed in a text or a video, is another application of these systems, opening new methods to understand people's opinions or real feelings about products on an increasingly large scale, a worrying development at the societal level.

The first industrial deep learning applications appeared with embedded solutions for the HVAC and building market. One of the main challenges is deploying a solution developed on a large cluster into an edge processor with much less computing power. The three main approaches are network pruning, distillation, and splitting the problem between the learning and exploitation phases. Pruning consists of keeping only the most significant weights in the network (sometimes with a parallel reduction of its accuracy). Distillation designs an approach that trains a smaller neural network to have a similar answer to the large network. In the third approach, field data are transferred from a device to the cloud and processed with deep learning that learns system parameters fed back to the device.

A wavelet processing layer is often very efficient in analyzing a machine's acoustic signal, such as a bearing or an actuator [Kumar *et al.*, 2020], sometimes using a GAN [Liang *et al.*, 2020]. The analysis of EEG is also an application in which a multiresolution pre-processing of the signal makes much sense [Xu *et al.*, 2018]. We discuss in the following sections some of the main architectures and their connections to multi-resolution and wavelets. Finally, the use of wavelets in deep learning has been extended to second-generation wavelets using the lifting scheme described in the Annex of this book [Rodriguez *et al.*, 2020].

7.2. Convolutional Neural Networks (CNN) and multiresolution

The development of deep convolutional networks [LeCun and Bengio, 1995; LeCun *et al.*, 1998] has triggered a revolution in image processing and learning, profoundly impacting data processing. Convolutional networks use a cascade of simple linear filters (convolution filters) iteratively applied to neighboring pixels. Given the matrix

$$M = \begin{pmatrix} 1 & 2 & 1 \\ 1 & 1 & 3 \\ 1 & 4 & 3 \end{pmatrix} \text{ and the convolution filter } F = \begin{pmatrix} 1 & -1 \\ -1 & 1 \end{pmatrix}.$$

The matrix M' after convolution is

$$M' = \begin{pmatrix} -1 & 3 \\ 3 & -3 \end{pmatrix}$$

The resulting output is pulled (i.e., averaged with low-pass filters and subsequently sub-sampled), then subsequently processed with a nonlinear operator. After several filter stages, the resulting signals are downsampled enough to be processed with a classical classifier on the whole set of data. Learning often uses back-propagation. Deep convolutional networks successfully classify images and sounds, such as identifying objects or people in an image or a video. The success of the convolutional network architecture has baffled the specialists even more, though their success was tough to figure out mathematically. The work by Stephane Mallet has shed some light on why convolutional networks are so efficient in learning. His paper shows that several of the main features of deep convolution networks can be related to multiresolution analysis and wavelet theory. Mallat explains some of the properties of convolution networks using a wavelet filter as a convolution filter. He shows the necessity of combining a convolution, a nonlinear, and a low-pass filter stage (so-called pooling). Averaging the filtered data with a low-pass filter makes the filter robust against small deformations of the image. LeCun has repeatedly pointed out that deep convolutional networks do not work without a nonlinear filter at each stage. In other words, the low-pass filter 'washed out' the data, which results in some apparent loss of information. A nonlinear filter introduces frequencies that correspond to frequency differences in the unfiltered signal (for instance, a rectifier $\rho(x) = \max{(x + b, 0)}$). In other words, nonlinear filtering permits the recovery of some frequencies that the low-pass filter would filter out without it. By cascading several modules comprising a wavelet filter, a low-pass filter, and a nonlinear filter, the signal is analyzed at lower frequencies at each stage till no energy remains in the signal. The many layers serve to analyze the signal at many different frequencies so that it becomes possible to capture the main features at different resolutions. In other words, the combination of modules results in a translation-invariant multiresolution analysis. Wavelet-based deep networks perform well even if there are out-performed by state-of-the-art deep convolutional networks. The main difference between wavelet analysis and convolutional networks is how the system learns. The cascade of modules using the wavelet transform is similar to a convolutional neural network, and the filters are defined by fixed wavelet functions instead of learning from the data. Wavelet analysis furnishes an explanation for the efficiency of convolutional deep neural networks, and such an explanation may guide data scientists in their search for even more performing networks.

Convolutional Neural Networks (CNN) have triggered the deep learning revolution with applications to image processing. However, they have found in the meantime applications in a vast number of fields such as finance [Sezer, Gudelek and Ozbayoglu, 2020], medicine [Acharya *et al.*, 2018], fault analysis [Waziralilah *et al.*, 2019], weather prediction [Chattopadhyay, Hassanzadeh and Pasha, 2020]. Figure 7.1 shows a possible CNN architecture. The network alternates processing with convolution operators, a nonlinear operator such as a ReLu, and pooling, often consisting of a low-pass filter. The convolution operator slides on the image making the convolution shift-invariant. The ReLu operator is an identity operator for values above a threshold (-bias) and zero; otherwise. After pooling, the signal is downsampled by a factor, similarly to a dyadic wavelet transform. Roughly, the more layers, the more the signal contains low-frequency components primarily. A classifier processes the last feature maps. The system learns the weights of the convolution filters and classifier and the bias of the ReLu using generally trained through back-propagation. Typically, millions of labeled images are supplied to the network during the learning phase. A CNN performs very well on image processing tasks such as face recognition or object recognition in images.

Astonishingly, a CNN performs so well considering the very high dimension of the search space (Large images with as many dimensions as pixels). A possible explanation is that the data form patches within the search space and have underlying relatively simple structures.

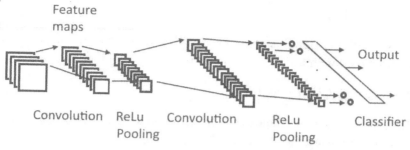

Feature maps

Convolution   ReLu   Convolution   ReLu   Classifier
          Pooling   Pooling

Fig. 7.1. Architecture of a Convolutional Neural Network (CNN).

Combinations of wavelets and convolution layers have shown promising results in image restoration [Liu *et al.*, 2000] or face super-resolution [Huang *et al.*, 2017]. Face super-resolution (SR) algorithms reconstruct high-resolution face images from low-resolution inputs. It is an important problem in face recognition tasks as the captured faces are of low resolution or lack facial details. Wavelet filters suit the task of processing a wave signal. Fujieda *et al.* [2018] proposed wavelet CNNs (WCNNs). They concatenate wavelet decomposition coefficients with the convolutional blocks' output. The authors suggest that the model is more interpretable than classical CNNs. Li *et al.* [2021] replace the first layer of the deep neural network with continuous wavelet convolution filters based on either the Mexican hat or Morlet wavelets. The best wavelet kernels are chosen from a dictionary. The authors apply the system to the problem of acoustically identifying defects in machines. A problem may be a missing tooth in a gear train or wear issues that may lead to a total failure and high costs. The CNN network processes the acoustic signals typical of defects. They convincingly show that the association between the different diagnosed defects and the kernels with the larger weights is consistent with the type of failure.

An essential aspect of Machine Learning using wavelet functions is that the wavelet's shape must be tuned for each specific task either adaptively, trial and error, or even per design. Tat Dat *et al.* [2020] have designed wavelets suited explicitly to analyze the complex development of an epidemic and apply them to the dynamics of Covid-19.

Mallat [2016] developed an understanding of CNN based on multiresolution analysis, filter theory, and invariants. Together with Bruna, he developed a new deep learning method based on their knowledge of some of the central features of CNN [Bruna and Mallat, 2013]. The network stacks several layers with a similar architecture based on the wavelet scattering transform (see part I). At the first level, a low-frequency scaling function filters the signal with:

S0 x[n] = x * φJ [n]   (7.1)

At the next level, the signal is convoluted with a wavelet function, and the result further convoluted with the scaling function

S1 x [n] = | x * ψ (λ1)| * φJ [n]   (7.2)

with the function ψ (λ1) belonging to a wavelet dictionary. The process is repeated after sub-sampling at the next level

S2 x [n] = || x * ψ (λ1)| * ψ (λ2)| * φ [n]   (7.3)

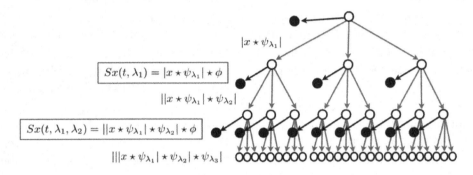

Fig. 7.2. The architecture of a wavelet scattering network (After Bruna and Mallat, [2013]).

A wavelet signal transform replaces the convolution filter. Instead of learning the convolution filters, the system chooses the most appropriate functions to describe the classification objective in a wavelet dictionary (Figure 7.2). The low-pass filter is the equivalent of pooling in CNN. Absolute values operators bring nonlinearity and replace the ReLu. The method has been applied to several problems in image processing with comparable results to some early CNN [Oyallon *et al.*, 2018].

Invariant scattering convolution networks have a structure similar to a CNN but with fixed filters. The network integrates a multi-resolution analysis using oriented wavelets and a pooling that makes the structure translation and rotation invariant and includes a nonlinear transformation. The system performs well on simple benchmarks such as handwriting recognition but still underperforms in more complex image classification compared to CNN. Zarka *et al* [2019] added a second chapter to the story. They add supplementary layers between the scattering and the classifier to generate a sparse code approximation of coefficients in a dictionary. The system learns both the dictionary and the classifier using gradient descent. Quite surprisingly, the network performs as well as AlexNet on image classification. Even if a state-of-the-art CNN performs much better, sparse coding improves the system considerably. Without going into the details of the network, let us introduce the new key element, the iterative soft/hard thresholding used for finding sparse representations.

Let us consider the inverse problem of determining x from the knowledge of the matrix A and the vector $Ax = y$. The Landweber [1951] algorithm recovers x of if A is singular and non-invertible. More precisely, the algorithm minimizes

$$min_{(x)} \|Ax - y\|^2 \tag{7.4}$$

Writing

$$f(x) = \|Ax - y\|^2 \tag{7.5}$$

the new value x_{k+1} can be upgraded with a gradient descent algorithm to

$$x_{k+1} = x_k - \omega \nabla f(x_k) \tag{7.6}$$

or equivalently

$$x_{k+1} = x_k - \omega A^*(Ax_k - y). \tag{7.7}$$

Daubechies, Defrise, and de Mol [2004] have extended the algorithm to search for a sparse representation of data on a matrix with $Ax = y + v$ with noise v. A regularization promotes a sparse solution with a low value of $\|x\|$. It penalizes a non-sparse solution using a parameter λ.

$$min_{(x)} \|Ax - y\|^2 + \lambda \|x\| \tag{7.8}$$

The soft/hard iterative thresholding (IST/IHT) introduced by Daubechies, Defrise, and de Mol [2004] is very efficient in getting a sparse representation. The descent algorithm becomes of the form,

$$x_{k+1} = T(x_k - \tau A^*(Ax_k - y)). \tag{7.9}$$

The algorithm is quite similar to the Landweber algorithm except for the thresholding. It converges toward x minimizing the penalty $\|Ax - y\|^2 + \lambda \|x\|$. The algorithm's convergence is slow, and a much faster version of the algorithm reduces lambda at each iteration [Jiao, Jin, and Lu, 2017]. Thresholded values are either zero (hard thresholding) or set to smaller values at each algorithm iteration. Let us conclude this introduction to soft/hard thresholding (Figure 7.3) by reminding the main equations for soft and hard thresholding.

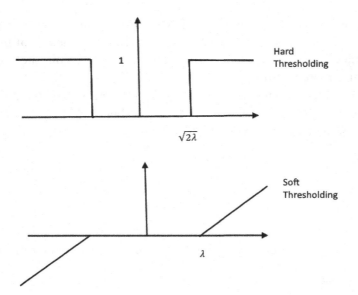

Fig. 7.3. Hard and soft thresholding function.

$$T_{hard(t)} = \chi_{\{|t| > \sqrt{2\lambda}\}}(t) \tag{7.10}$$

with χ the characteristic function.

For soft thresholding, one has

$$T_{soft(t)} = \max(|t| - \lambda, 0)\, sgn(t) \tag{7.11}$$

7.3. Generative Adversarial Networks (GAN)

A generative adversarial network (GAN) is a class of machine learning algorithms designed by Goodfellow *et al.* [2014]. Two neural networks, the generator, and the discriminator, compete in a game where one game agent gains another agent's losses. The discriminator D is trained to label the original images as accurate and the reconstruction by the generator G as fake. The generator G has the opposite goal: to generate images wrongly classified as real by the discriminator. Goodfellow *et al.* [2014] have shown that a GAN corresponds to a two-player zero-sum game.

$$\min_G \max_D V(DG)$$
$$= E_{x \sim p_{data}(x)}[\log(D(x)] + E_{z \sim p_z(z)}[\log(1 - D(G(z))] \tag{7.12}$$

D and G play a minimax game with a value function V. The first component is the log expectation that the discriminator has D as input with D equals one if the picture is real. The second term is related to the expectation that a picture is fake.

Goodfellow's original ideas have inspired innovative approaches and interpretations in terms of game theory. Gemp *et al.* [2020] used a network to learn Principal Component Analysis (PCA). The network corresponds to a multi-player game with k players that converge towards Nash equilibrium, the point at which no player has an incentive to change strategy. Each player is one of the top-k eigenvectors. The trick is to use a utility function so that its gradient maintains orthogonality between the vectors associated with each player.

Generative Adversarial Networks (GAN) are for supervised and unsupervised tasks. A GAN consists of pair of networks in competition with each other (Figure 7.4). The generator learns representations of the input data and generates fake data (images or sound) very similar to actual data furnished to the system. The discriminator receives both fake and authentic data and learns to distinguish them. The GAN trains the discriminator to maximize its classification accuracy and generate data, maximally confusing the discriminator. Recently, a GAN 'taught itself' to play games without ever getting the game's rules Kim *et al.* [2020].

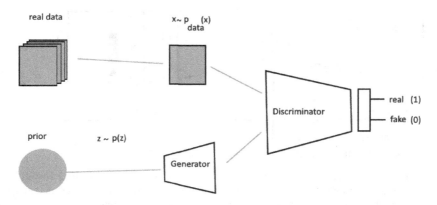

Fig. 7.4. Schematic principle of a generative antagonistic network (GAN). A generator transforms a vector drawn from a random distribution into an image or sound. The discriminator is supplied with both fake and real data and fake data from the generator and learns to distinguish them.

Practically, the generator tries to maximize a function V(G,D) while the discriminator tries to maximize it, both networks updating their weights depending on their success. The generator is optimal if the generated data distribution is similar to the real one. In that case, the generator has learned the real data distribution and fools the discriminator in 50% of the cases. If the learning data are quite specialized, for instance containing only faces, the network may converge to (Nash) equilibrium. The faces generated by the best systems are so realistic that they often fool both the discriminator and humans. GAN, as initially developed, had some flows like having a large proportion of fakes with two eyes of different colors. Such problems are solvable. The possibility of creating deep fakes is a concern for most AI researchers, especially in terms of mass manipulation and privacy. Some GAN applications may lead to increased privacy, such as anonymizing data. Beaulieu-Jones *et al.* [2019] have created a generator supplying realistic but fake patient data from systolic blood pressure trials. Once all security measures have proven to be sufficient, processing the data with GAN may permit sharing data without significant privacy concerns and create new examples. Classical (vanilla) GAN learns by supplying the network with pairs of images. Odena *et al.* [2017] proposed architecture to reduce the number of necessary labeled pictures. The system is capable of learning from different views.

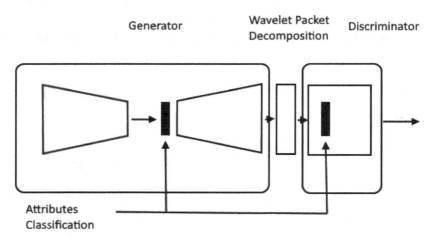

Fig. 7.5. Adding an attribute in a GAN system improves the classification quality. The attribute is provided as an input to both the generator and the discriminator, increasing the image generation's quality or image-to-image transformation. In the case of aging, the attribute may be gender or age.

The practical significance of GAN extended with CycleGAN [Zhu *et al.*, 2017]. Learning with CycleGAN can be done using unrelated pairs of images, and CycleGAN applies to image-to-image translation. The transformation of a horse into a zebra was one of the first examples.

In a CycleGAN, a first generator, G, learns the mapping from an image X into its transform Y. A second generator, F, learns the inverse transform. A consistency loss term tells if the inverse image transformation (Y→X) is consistent with the original images. The inversed image should contain recognizable horses! A surprising feature is that changing the animal's robe is not the only different feature. The quality of the grass changes from lush green to dark green as the system registered that horses roam in greener pastures compared to zebra. Let us give a few examples of some well-known applications. Landscape paintings of a famous artist are supplied to the system, say landscape from Van Gogh. After learning the system can transform pictures of a landscape into a painting in the style of van Gogh [Liu *et al.*, 2018]. One speaks of style transfer, an application explored by Gatys *et al.* [2016]. This research direction furnishes very spectacular results not only in image but also in speech processing.

A wavelet stage is sometimes introduced to better capture textures. The perceived quality of an image is much dependent on the high-frequency subbands, while the low-frequency subband has a significant effect on the objective quality of the image [Deng *et al.*, 2019]. This observation is often one of the reasons to integrate a wavelet stage in a system. Liu *et al.* [2019] have developed a system with attribute-aware face aging using a wavelet-based generative adversarial network. A wavelet packet module captures age-related textures at multiple scales (Figure 7.5 for the neural network's architecture).

Wavelet-based generative adversarial networks have resulted in excellent results in denoising. As seen in chapter 4, wavelet denoising can be a good approach to improving data quality. The system is trained with images containing two versions of an image, a noisy one and a wavelet-denoised one, and the system learns to transform the image from the noisy to the denoised style.

A CycleGAN efficiently denoises satellite images without supervision [Zhu *et al.*, 2017]. Wavelets and wavelet packages improve the performance of GAN for image reconstruction in MRI images [Chen, Firmin, and Yang, 2021] or to analyze cerebral vessels [Patel *et al.*, 2020]. In that last application, a multiresolution approach improves the accuracy of the segmentation of small blood vessels.

7.3.1. *Other related architectures related to generative networks*

7.3.1.1. *Autoencoders*

Autoencoder consists of an encoder that compresses the information and a decoder that reconstructs the original data with the lowest possible error. The encoded vector or matrix in the latent space is the input to the decoder. As shown in Figure 7.6, a variational auto-encoder associates a distribution with each code value, and the decoder creates a new image from a random vector.

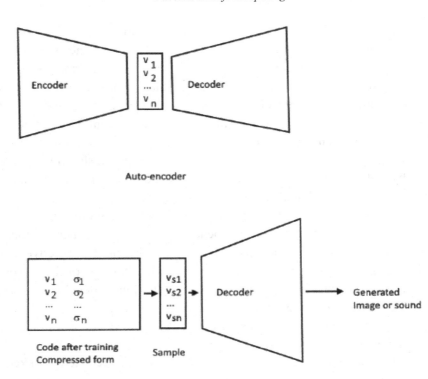

Fig. 7.6. Top: auto-encoder structure; bottom, the generator samples the data within a distribution.

7.3.1.2. *Transformer*

The generation of speech from a text is another application of generative networks. WaveNet was a breakthrough in Text-to-Speech systems, and it generates speech that well mimics a human voice [Oord *et al.*, 2016]. Yamamoto *et al.* [2020] report further progress using generative adversarial networks with a multiresolution spectrogram. The WaveNet combines multiresolution short-time Fourier transform (STFT) to effectively capture the realistic time-frequency distribution of natural speech to a Text-to-Speech acoustic model.

The processing of natural languages, either speak or text, has experienced a boost with the development of transformer networks with an encoder-decoder structure. In an already famous article, 'Attention is all you need, Vaswani *et al.* [2017] proposed the transformer network in which Attention is the main element.

Attention is a transformation that computes the similarity between a query and all keys (i.e., input in the text sequences). In the original paper, the Attention calculates the dot products of the query Q with all keys K and values V, dividing each by $\sqrt{d_k}$ with d_k the key dimension and applying a softmax function.

In matrix form, one has

$$Attention\ (Q, K, V) = softmax\left(Q\frac{K^T}{\sqrt{d_k}}\right)V \tag{7.13}$$

with the softmax function defined as

$$softmax(x_i) = exp(x_i) / \sum_{k=1}^{n} exp\ (x_k) \tag{7.14}$$

7.3.1.3. *Siamese networks*

Deep learning networks like GAN or U-nets need a lot of labeled data to learn. Labeling data are work-intensive to generate, and there is a strong need for networks that can learn from little data. Siamese networks are good candidates for learning with little data.

Figure 7.7 shows their structure. Two identical networks share their design, parameters, and weights. The constraint that both encoders have the same weights (W1=W2) is a constraint that forces the network to extract features characterizing

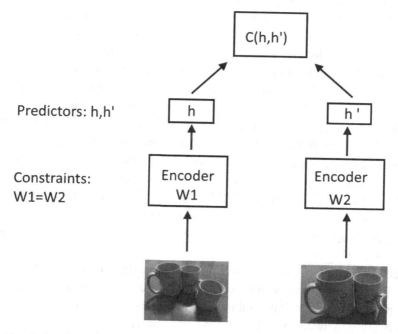

Fig. 7.7. Sketch showing a Siamese neural network. The two encoders are identical and use the same weights W=W1=W2.

the versions of images with the same label. Labeled versions of an image are generated by deforming them or adding sub-images [Leal-Taixé, Canton-Ferrer, and Schindler, 2016]. Presenting data at different resolutions is another possibility. Wang *et al.* [2017] use Siamese sub-networks [Bromley *et al.*, 1993] working parallel to accommodate the large variability in metastatic lesion sizes in spinal cancer. Three identical convolutional networks receive each an MRI image at a different resolution. The system aggregates the results at different resolutions. Learning with a limited number of data is still challenging as the system tends to collapse. In other words, the network is not capable of distinguishing different inputs.

Chen and He [2021] report that Siamese networks can learn meaningful representations without a very large number of images. The authors hypothesize that the chosen structure changes the learning by implementing an Expectation-Maximization (EM) algorithm.

7.4. U-nets and multiresolution

U-net has established itself quite rapidly among deep learning methods in medical applications. For image segmentation, U-net is becoming the state-of-the-art method, for instance, to diagnose a tumor. Figure 7.8 shows the architecture proposed by Ronneberger *et al.* [2015] based on the architecture of fully connected networks [Long, Shelhamer, and Darrell, 2015]. A cascade of convolution layers and ReLu filter the image in the encoding and the contracting path. In the original design, the number of filters doubles at each instance of downsampling. The signal is then upsampled starting from the lowest layer and concatenated with high-resolution features from the contracting path, helping localize the image features. The network got its name from its U-shape form, as seen in Figure 7.8. One part of the U is the contracting part, also defined as the encoder, while the second half is the expanding path or the decoder. The network is computationally very efficient and performs very well. In 2016 the U-net won several competitions and challenges on image segmentation by large margins. The network learns very efficiently with already a low number of images. These images are deformed to augment the training data.

U-nets' combinations of contracting and expanding paths remind us of the decomposition and reconstruction of wavelet architecture. Not completely, surprisingly, wavelet processing layers have led to very successful applications.

U-nets are enhanced in multiple ways by multiresolution analysis. Jahangard *et al.* [2020] insert multiresolution versions of the image at each level of the encoding part to improve segmentation. The low-resolution images are concatenated

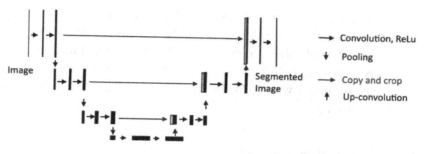

Fig. 7.8. U-net architecture. Each black box corresponds to a multi-channel feature map, and white boxes represent concatenated data. The arrows denote the different operations.

with convoluted downsampled layers. Multiresolution filters use the wavelet filters associated with the scaling functions. Compared to the state-of-the-art U-net, the network is faster in medical image segmentation.

Some architectures use wavelet decomposition layers between convolution layers in the encoding part of the U-net and wavelet reconstruction stages in the decoding part [Liu *et al.*, 2018]. The particularity is that both the low-frequency scaling and the wavelet coefficients are passed to the convolution layers resulting in an increase in the field of view compared to pure downsampling. The method is effective for image denoising, single image super-resolution, JPEG image artifacts removal, and object classification.

Another interesting architecture combines a wavelet decomposition path with a U-net. In Fu *et al.* [2021], the generator of a GAN uses two U-net in parallel, a conventional one and a second one using wavelet decomposition and reconstruction filters (Figure 7.9).

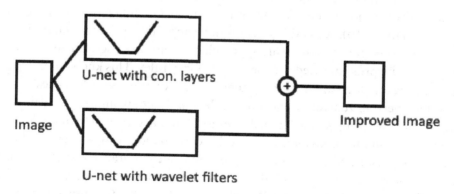

Fig. 7.9. The generator part of a GAN has two U-nets in parallel, the first one using a classical approach and the second wavelet filters.

Wang *et al.* [2020] report a U-net using multiresolution convolutional layers in the decoder. It serves as a general inverse problem solver for image(s)-to image(s) transformation with applications to enhance diffusely reflected images or denoise electron microscopy images. Here again, learning is faster and better than a classical U-net. Adding a wavelet or multiresolution image in a U-net improves the network's learning.

7.5. Fuzzy logic in deep learning

7.5.1. *Improving the interpretability of deep learning with neuro-fuzzy*

The interpretability of CNN or other types of neural networks is of crucial importance in many applications. The interpretability of CNN is a research topic by itself with interesting results but many open issues. Interpretability is essential to understand what the system has learned and detect bias during learning to prevent future generalization [Zeiler and Fergus, 2014].

A CNN was, for instance, trained to detect lipstick. During testing, replacing a person's mouth with another person's mouth without lipstick did not change the results. The detection of lipstick is probably correlated to other features, possibly earrings or eyelashes [Zhang and Zhu, 2018].

Several studies have tried to improve the interpretability of a deep neural network, typically a CNN, using fuzzy logic. The network architecture typically includes two paths, one using a neuro-fuzzy network and the second path consisting of a classical deep network. The system is decomposed into a first nonlinear description of the data with a limited number of fuzzy rules to simplify the interpretation of the system and a second path that works as a kind of black box to 'finish' the job of characterizing the data and complete the learning (first blocks of Figure 7.10). A hybrid system is quite appealing as a fuzzy classification already furnishes good results. This approach can learn from scratch and initialize the system with prior knowledge expressed as fuzzy rules. This knowledge permits designing the topology of the fuzzy system (number of rules, high-level description of the membership functions, and fuzzy rules) and initializing the system. After learning, one can compare the learned rules to the initial ones and try to understand the new rules and the convolution network's contribution, which is tricky. Fuzzy systems are very performant in many problems, such as traffic control or fuzzy classification of EEG signals. While the results are not completely convincing in terms of interpretability [Xi and Panoutsos, 2018, 2020], the direction is quite promising. We suggest completing the architecture, including multi-resolution in the neuro-fuzzy path using a fuzzy wavelet network (see Part 4).

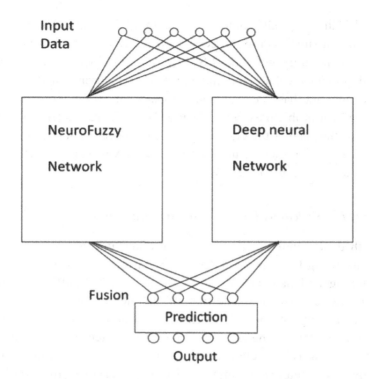

Fig. 7.10. The hybrid architecture combines a neuro-fuzzy framework with a deep neuronal network.

Figure 7.10 represents the neuro-fuzzy deep network architecture. The fusion layer is a densely connected:

$$x_i = w_d \ y_d + w_f \ y_f \qquad (7.15)$$

y_d is the output from the deep representation part, and y_f is the output from the fuzzy representation with weights w_d and w_f.

In some other applications, fuzzy processing is integrated at the prediction level to aggregate outputs from state-of-the-art pre-trained models. Fuzziness is introduced only in the fully connected prediction layer, replacing the softmax layer with a fuzzy layer to improve the interpretability of the system and the accuracy performance for image classification tasks [Price, Price, and Anderson, 2019]. Sentiment analysis is a growing field in data mining. There is a strong interest in automatic services to understand how peoples communicate on social media and react to new products and the emotions conveyed by their messages on the internet. The neuro-fuzzy layer improves the sentiment analysis quality and helps interpret the results [Es-Sabery *et al.*, 2021].

Bedi and Khurana [2020] choose a different architecture. The input data are first fuzzified and subsequently processed by a deep neural network, a so-called long-short-term memory network (LSTM). An LSTM cell receives the input's current and previous values and hidden states [Hochreiter and Schmidhuber, 1997]. The network has the excellent property of being more robust to the vanishing gradient problem as the number of layers increases (In CNN, the more layers one has, the smaller the gradient or learning becomes unstable). The output of the LSTM network is then defuzzified in the last layer. The network was applied to the IMDB dataset of movie reviews.

7.5.2. *Fuzzy layers deal with noisy data and uncertainty*

Dealing with data containing significant noise and uncertainty is another main motivation for using fuzzy logic in designing a deep network. Chen *et al.* [2018] take the Beijing taxi databank to predict and optimize traffic flow using the network in Figure 7.10. The addition of the neuro-fuzzy path significantly improves the quality of the traffic flow prediction with substantially better performance than state-of-the-art approaches. The system reduces the impact of data uncertainty that is characteristic of applications in flow control. Figure 7.11 shows another architecture combining neuro-fuzzy and CNN [Essa *et al.*, 2020].

7.5.3. *Deep fuzzy clustering*

Figure 7.12 shows the architecture of an auto-encoder using fuzzy clustering. The output of the encoder is fed to both the decoder and a clustering algorithm. The loss function (also called error function or cost function) is the sum of the loss on the reconstructed signal and the loss function for clustering. The reconstruction function quantifies how different the input and output signals of the encoders are, while the clustering loss function is related to the quality of the clustering results. Feng *et al.* [2020] use a fuzzy c-mean clustering algorithm, a common approach, but there are many alternatives and variants to that algorithm [Ruspini, Bezdek, and Keller, 2019]. The fuzzy c-mean clustering does not perform well at high dimensions.

Let us discuss a clustering approach to visualize and cluster high-dimensional data in a two or three-dimensional map. At a high dimension, the similarity between two points is given under the hypothesis of a Gaussian distribution and transforms a distance into a conditional probability. After two-dimensional

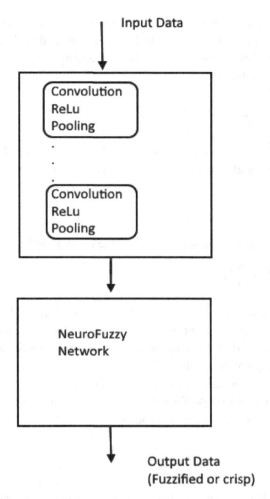

Fig. 7.11. A fuzzy deep network consists of the main blocks of a convolutional neural network in which a neuro-fuzzy network replaces the fully connected prediction block.

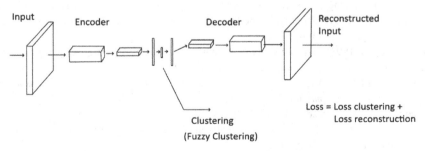

Fig. 7.12. Deep-clustering using an auto-encoder structure and a classifier.

projections, the distances are smaller between points, and van der Maaten and Hinton [2008] propose to use a heavy tail distribution to describe the probabilities. With the t-Student distribution, one has the probability of the point y_i in the cluster with centroid z_j given by

$$q_{ij} = \frac{(1+\|y_i-z_j\|^2)^{-1}}{\sum_{k \neq l}(1+\|y_k-z_l\|^2)^{-1}} \tag{7.16}$$

Guo *et al.*, 2017; Xi and Panoutsos, 2018 compute the center p_{ij} of the clusters (see original papers for the underlying assumptions):

$$p_{ij} = \frac{q_{ij}^2/\sum_i q_{ij}}{\sum_j(q_{ij}^2/\sum_i q_{ij})} \tag{7.17}$$

The Küllback-Leibler divergence quantifies the clustering loss:

$$Loss = \sum_i \sum_j p_{ij} \log\left(\frac{p_{ij}}{q_{ij}}\right) \tag{7.18}$$

They use this approach for unsupervised deep learning. Adding a loss function characterizing the quality of the reconstruction of the decoder forces the auto-encoder to preserve the data structure and information. It results in better clustering compared to a design with a single loss function. The fuzzy clustering of high-dimension data is knowingly a problematic task. Using the above architecture permits the development of performant fuzzy clustering on high-dimension data projected on two- or three-dimension spaces.

References

Acharya, U.R. *et al.* (2018). Deep convolutional neural network for the automated detection and diagnosis of seizure using EEG signals, *Computers in Biology and Medicine*, 100, pp. 270–278.

Beaulieu-Jones, B.K. *et al.* (2019). Privacy-preserving generative deep neural networks support clinical data sharing, *Circulation: Cardiovascular Quality and Outcomes*, 12(7), p. e005122.

Bedi, P. and Khurana, P. (2020). Sentiment Analysis Using Fuzzy-Deep Learning, *Proc. of ICETIT 2019* (Springer), pp. 246–257.

Bromley, J. *et al.* (1993). Signature verification using a "siamese" time delay neural network, *Advances in neural information processing systems*, 6.

Bruna, J. and Mallat, S. (2013). Invariant scattering convolution networks, *IEEE transactions on pattern analysis and machine intelligence*, 35(8), pp. 1872–1886.

Chattopadhyay, A., Hassanzadeh, P. and Pasha, S. (2020). Predicting clustered weather patterns: A test case for applications of convolutional neural networks to spatio-temporal climate data, *Scientific reports*, 10(1), pp. 1–13.

Chen, W. *et al.* (2018). A novel fuzzy deep-learning approach to traffic flow prediction with uncertain spatial–temporal data features, *Future generation computer systems,* 89, pp. 78–88.

Chen, X. and He, K. (2021). Exploring simple siamese representation learning, *Proc. of the IEEE/CVF Conference on Computer Vision and Pattern Recognition*, pp. 15750–15758.

Chen, Y., Firmin, D. and Yang, G. (2021). Wavelet improved GAN for MRI reconstruction, in *Medical Imaging 2021: Physics of Medical Imaging* (International Society for Optics and Photonics), p. 1159513.

Daubechies, I., Defrise, M. and De Mol, C. (2004). An iterative thresholding algorithm for linear inverse problems with a sparsity constraint, *Communications on Pure and Applied Mathematics: A Journal Issued by the Courant Institute of Mathematical Sciences*, 57(11), pp. 1413–1457.

Deng, X. *et al.* (2019). Wavelet domain style transfer for an effective perception-distortion tradeoff in single image super-resolution, *Proc. of the IEEE/CVF International Conference on Computer Vision*, pp. 3076–3085.

Devlin, J. *et al.* (2018). Bert: Pre-training of deep bidirectional transformers for language understanding, *arXiv preprint* arXiv:1810.04805 [Preprint].

Essa, E. *et al.* (2020). Neuro-fuzzy patch-wise R-CNN for multiple sclerosis segmentation, *Medical & Biological Engineering & Computing*, 58(9), pp. 2161–2175.

Es-Sabery, F. *et al.* (2021). Sentence-level classification using parallel fuzzy deep learning classifier, *IEEE Access*, 9, pp. 17943–17985.

Feng, Q. *et al.* (2020). Deep fuzzy clustering—a representation learning approach, *IEEE Transactions on Fuzzy Systems*, 28(7), pp. 1420–1433.

Fu, M. *et al.* (2021). DW-GAN: A Discrete Wavelet Transform GAN for NonHomogeneous Dehazing, *Proc. of the IEEE/CVF Conference on Computer Vision and Pattern Recognition*, pp. 203–212.

Fujieda, S., Takayama, K. and Hachisuka, T. (2018). Wavelet convolutional neural networks, *arXiv preprint* arXiv:1805.08620 [Preprint].

Gatys, L.A., Ecker, A.S. and Bethge, M. (2016). Image style transfer using convolutional neural networks, *Proc. of the IEEE conference on computer vision and pattern recognition*, pp. 2414–2423.

Gemp, I. *et al.* (2020). Eigengame: PCA as a Nash equilibrium, *arXiv preprint* arXiv:2010.00554 [Preprint].

Goodfellow, I. *et al.* (2014). Generative adversarial nets, *Advances in neural information processing systems*, 27.

Guo, X. *et al.* (2017). Deep clustering with convolutional autoencoders, *Proc. International conference on neural information processing* (Springer), pp. 373–382.

Hochreiter, S. and Schmidhuber, J. (1997) Long short-term memory, *Neural computation*, 9(8), pp. 1735–1780.

Huang, H. *et al.* (2017). Wavelet-srnet: A wavelet-based cnn for multi-scale face super resolution, *Proc. IEEE International Conference on Computer Vision*, pp. 1689–1697.

Jahangard, S., Zangooei, M.H. and Shahedi, M. (2020). U-Net based architecture for an improved multiresolution segmentation in medical images, *arXiv preprint* arXiv:2007.08238 [Preprint].

Jiao, Y., Jin, B. and Lu, X. (2017). Iterative soft/hard thresholding with homotopy continuation for sparse recovery, *IEEE Signal Processing Letters*, 24(6), pp. 784–788.

Kim, S.W. *et al.* (2020). Learning to simulate dynamic environments with gamegan, *Proc. IEEE/CVF Conference on Computer Vision and Pattern Recognition*, pp. 1231–1240.

Kumar, A. *et al.* (2020). Bearing defect size assessment using wavelet transform based Deep Convolutional Neural Network (DCNN), *Alexandria Engineering Journal*, 59(2), pp. 999–1012.

Landweber, L. (1951). An iteration formula for Fredholm integral equations of the first kind, *American journal of mathematics*, 73(3), pp. 615–624.

Leal-Taixé, L., Canton-Ferrer, C. and Schindler, K. (2016). Learning by tracking: Siamese CNN for robust target association, *Proc. IEEE Conference on Computer Vision and Pattern Recognition Workshops*, pp. 33–40.

LeCun, Y. *et al.* (1998). Gradient-based learning applied to document recognition, *Proc. IEEE*, 86(11), pp. 2278–2324.

LeCun, Y. and Bengio, Y. (1995). Convolutional networks for images, speech, and time series, *The handbook of brain theory and neural networks*, 3361(10), p. 1995.

Lee, J.-S. and Hsiang, J. (2020). Patent classification by fine-tuning BERT language model, *World Patent Information*, 61, p. 101965.

Li, T. *et al.* (2021). WaveletKernelNet: An interpretable deep neural network for industrial intelligent diagnosis, *IEEE Transactions on Systems, Man, and Cybernetics: Systems* [Preprint].

Liang, P. *et al.* (2020). Intelligent fault diagnosis of rotating machinery via wavelet transform, generative adversarial nets and convolutional neural network, *Measurement*, 159, p. 107768.

Liu, J. *et al.* (2000). Wavelet theory and its application to pattern recognition. World scientific.

Liu, P. *et al.* (2018). Multi-level wavelet-CNN for image restoration, *Proc. IEEE conference on computer vision and pattern recognition workshops*, pp. 773–782.

Liu, Y., Li, Q. and Sun, Z. (2019). Attribute-aware face aging with wavelet-based generative adversarial networks, *Proc. of the IEEE/CVF Conference on Computer Vision and Pattern Recognition*, pp. 11877–11886.

Long, J., Shelhamer, E. and Darrell, T. (2015). Fully convolutional networks for semantic segmentation, *Proc. of the IEEE conference on computer vision and pattern recognition*, pp. 3431–3440.

Mallat, S. (2016). Understanding deep convolutional networks, *Philosophical Transactions of the Royal Society A: Mathematical, Physical and Engineering Sciences*, 374(2065), p. 20150203.

Odena, A., Olah, C. and Shlens, J. (2017). Conditional image synthesis with auxiliary classifier gans, *Proc. International conference on machine learning* (PMLR), pp. 2642–2651.

Oord, A. van den *et al.* (2016). Wavenet: A generative model for raw audio, *arXiv preprint* arXiv:1609.03499 [Preprint].

Oyallon, E. *et al.* (2018). Scattering networks for hybrid representation learning, *IEEE transactions on pattern analysis and machine intelligence*, 41(9), pp. 2208–2221.

Patel, T.R. *et al.* (2020). Multi-resolution CNN for brain vessel segmentation from cerebrovascular images of intracranial aneurysm: a comparison of U-Net and DeepMedic, in *Medical Imaging 2020: Computer-Aided Diagnosis* (International Society for Optics and Photonics), p. 113142W.

Price, Stanton R, Price, Steven R and Anderson, D.T. (2019). Introducing fuzzy layers for deep learning, *Proc. 2019 IEEE International Conference on Fuzzy Systems (FUZZ-IEEE)*, (IEEE), pp. 1–6.

Rodriguez, M.X.B. *et al.* (2020). Deep adaptive wavelet network, *Proc. of the IEEE/CVF Winter Conference on Applications of Computer Vision*, pp. 3111–3119.

Ronneberger, O., Fischer, P. and Brox, T. (2015). U-net: Convolutional networks for biomedical image segmentation, *Proc. International Conference on Medical image computing and computer-assisted intervention* (Springer), pp. 234–241.

Ruspini, E.H., Bezdek, J.C. and Keller, J.M. (2019). Fuzzy clustering: A historical perspective, *IEEE Computational Intelligence Magazine*, 14(1), pp. 45–55.

Schrittwieser, J. *et al.* (2020). Mastering atari, go, chess and shogi by planning with a learned model, *Nature*, 588(7839), pp. 604–609.

Schrittwieser, J. *et al.* (2021). Online and offline reinforcement learning by planning with a learned model, *Advances in Neural Information Processing Systems*, 34.

Sezer, O.B., Gudelek, M.U. and Ozbayoglu, A.M. (2020). Financial time series forecasting with deep learning: A systematic literature review: 2005–2019, *Applied soft computing*, 90, p. 106181.

Tat Dat, T. *et al.* (2020). Epidemic dynamics via wavelet theory and machine learning with applications to Covid-19, *Biology*, 9(12), p. 477.

Van der Maaten, L. and Hinton, G. (2008). Visualizing data using t-SNE., *Journal of machine learning research*, 9(11).

Vaswani, A. *et al.* (2017). Attention is all you need, *Advances in neural information processing systems*, 30.

Wang, F. *et al.* (2020). Multi-resolution convolutional neural networks for inverse problems, *Scientific reports*, 10(1), pp. 1–11.

Wang, J. *et al.* (2017). A multi-resolution approach for spinal metastasis detection using deep Siamese neural networks, *Computers in biology and medicine*, 84, pp. 137–146.

Waziralilah, N.F. *et al.* (2019). A review on convolutional neural network in bearing fault diagnosis, in *MATEC Web of Conferences* (EDP Sciences), p. 06002.

Xi, Z. and Panoutsos, G. (2018). Interpretable machine learning: convolutional neural networks with RBF fuzzy logic classification rules, *Proc. 2018 International conference on intelligent systems (IS)* (IEEE), pp. 448–454.

Xi, Z. and Panoutsos, G. (2020). *Interpretable convolutional neural networks using a rule-based framework for classification, in Intelligent Systems: Theory, Research and Innovation in Applications* (Springer), pp. 1–24.

Yamamoto, R., Song, E. and Kim, J.-M. (2020). Parallel WaveGAN: A fast waveform generation model based on generative adversarial networks with multi-resolution spectrogram, *Proc. ICASSP 2020-2020 IEEE International Conference on Acoustics, Speech and Signal Processing (ICASSP)* (IEEE), pp. 6199–6203.

Zarka, J. *et al.* (2019). Deep network classification by scattering and homotopy dictionary learning, *arXiv preprint* arXiv:1910.03561 [Preprint].

Zeiler, M.D. and Fergus, R. (2014). *Visualizing and understanding convolutional networks, Proc. European conference on computer vision* (Springer), pp. 818–833.

Zhang, Q. and Zhu, S.-C. (2018). Visual interpretability for deep learning: a survey, *Frontiers of Information Technology & Electronic Engineering*, 19(1), pp. 27–39.

Zhu, J.-Y. *et al.* (2017). Unpaired image-to-image translation using cycle-consistent adversarial networks, *Proc. of the IEEE international conference on computer vision*, pp. 2223–2232.

Developing Intelligent Sensors with Fuzzy Logic and Multiresolution Analysis

Part 8

Chapter 8

Developing Intelligent Sensors with Fuzzy Logic and Multiresolution Analysis

8.1. Application of multiresolution and fuzzy logic to fire detection

Smoke detectors have suffered from the so-called *false alarms* problem [Thuillard, 1994]. A spectacular improvement resulted from more reliable components, better alarm organization, and signal processing. Smoke detectors implement sophisticated algorithms, and Fuzzy logic has had a central role in fire detection. The acceptance of fuzzy logic in fire detectors is quite large. Initially, fuzzy logic was used chiefly in classifiers, while with time, fuzzy logic described the alarm surface in multi-sensors detectors.

8.1.1. *Linear beam detector*

Commercial products have significantly benefited from fuzzy logic. The first example is a linear beam detector, and Figure 8.1 sketches its basic operating principle. A LED or a LASER emits a light pulse that travels a distance between typically 5 m to 150 m. The light is back-reflected to the detector by a high-quality retro-reflector. The detector goes into alarm if smoke attenuates the reflected signal.

Fuzzy algorithms can distinguish the signature of non-fire (signal intermission due to a moving object: a bird or a truck, signal attenuation caused by mixing of cold and hot air) and fire events. Significant signal features are extracted during the development phase. Fuzzy rules (Figure 8.2) combine prior knowledge with rules automatically generated. The fuzzy rules provide a differentiated diagnosis of potential problems to the operator and alarm criteria.

Data are collected in extensive field testing and fire testing. Data are classified using a constructive multiresolution approach. The algorithms were developed with a neuro-fuzzy method, using a multiresolution Kohonen type of network for

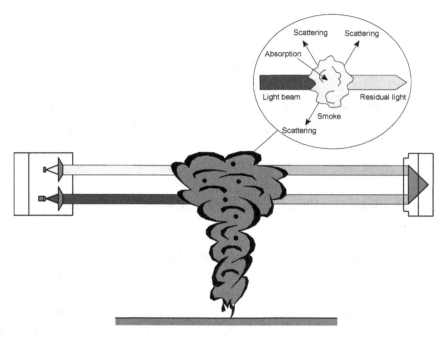

Fig. 8.1. A linear beam detector is a smoke detector, and light attenuation indicates the smoke level (alarm criterion).

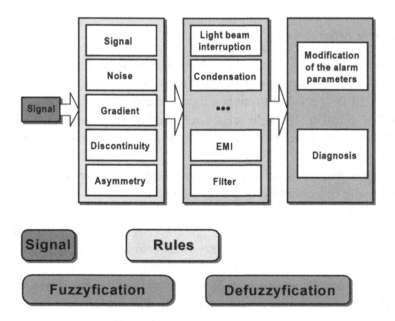

Fig. 8.2. The signal of the linear beam detector is analyzed online by a fuzzy system.

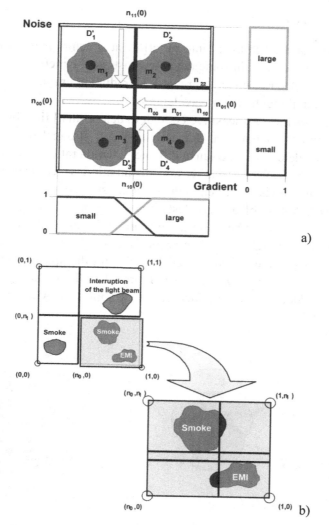

Fig. 8.3. a) A Kohonen-based neuro-fuzzy system optimizes a rule-based fuzzy system during product development. b) The system is refined by iteratively adding higher resolution membership functions.

signal classification. After initialization, it optimizes two membership functions per variable using a Kohonen network to determine the best partition and a simulating annealing method to optimize the shapes of the membership functions (Figure 8.3). The procedure is repeated by splitting the membership functions into two new ones to refine the fuzzy rules. Finally, field tests validate the rules.

8.1.2. *Flame detector*

Wavelet theory can be combined into an efficient spectral analysis method. We want to discuss an example in some detail to illustrate the method's power. Flame detectors use pyroelectric sensors to record the radiation emitted by flames in the infrared domain in three different wavelengths.

Flame detectors must be sensitive enough to detect small fires but must not be fooled by deceptive phenomena. Sun radiation and strong lamps are the main dangers for flame detectors. The sun and flame radiation ratio is much lower in the infrared than in the visible. For that reason, the radiation is measured in the infrared domain and not in the visible. Even in the infrared, sun radiation is typically much larger than the radiation of the smallest fires one wants to detect. Two features characterize a hydrocarbon fire. First, the flame pulsates, and second, the flame emits strongly around $4.3\mu m$, the emission line of CO_2 (Figure 8.4). The ratio between the signal at the different wavelengths and the spectral analysis of the flame fluctuations characterizes an actual fire [Thuillard, 2002]. The spectral analysis is embedded into the product, and it combines fuzzy logic with wavelet analysis (Figure 8.5).

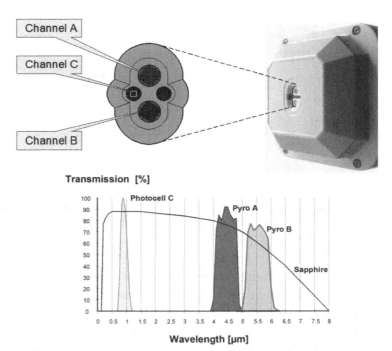

Fig. 8.4. A flame detector records the radiation of a flame at several wavelengths with pyro sensors. A fuzzy system analyzes the fluctuations of the radiations in the spectral domain and the frequency domain.

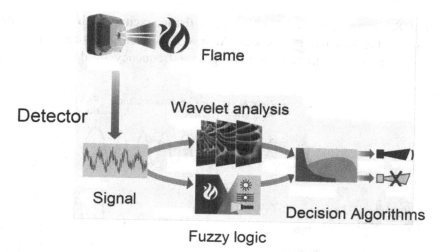

Fig. 8.5. Spectral analysis, feature extraction, and classification combine fuzzy logic and wavelet analysis.

Under laboratory conditions, a hydrocarbon fire pulsates at a very regular frequency between 0.5 Hz to 13 Hz. The larger the fire, the smaller the pulsation frequency. A simple law describes the pulsation frequency. The pulsation frequency is inversely proportional to the square root of the fire's diameter. Amazingly, the pulsation frequency is practically independent of the fuel in the first approximation. A hydrodynamics instability causes the flame to oscillate. This instability is due to the density difference between hot air and the surrounding airflow, resulting in an unstable gravity wave. We have suggested that the regular flame pulsation results from a resonant effect that sets when the wavelength of the gravity wave is in a simple ratio to the fire's diameter.

In the field, wind or air droughts perturb the regular flame pulsation, for instance, if a window is open. We found that flame pulsation still has some typical features even under those circumstances. To understand the reason, we did carry out many controlled experiments with oscillating membranes. We showed that external perturbations are parametrically coupled to the flames with such experiments.

A self-excited van der Pol oscillator can quite well model flame pulsation with parametric coupling [Thuillard, 2002]:

$$X'' + \omega_0{}^2 \cdot X + a \cdot (X^2 - K) \cdot X' = F(\omega, t) \cdot X \tag{8.1}$$

with $F(\omega, t)$ describing the perturbation, a and K constants, ω_0 the natural pulsation and X the average flame radiation.

Figure 8.6 compares the pulsation of a flame excited with an oscillating membrane to the van der Pol model. At low excitation, the flame frequency synchronizes to the membrane oscillating at a frequency of the order of the

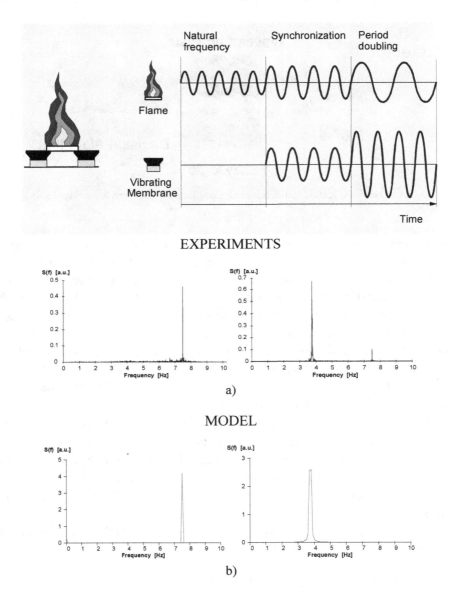

Fig. 8.6. Fundamental research on the physics and dynamics of flames led to a new flame pulsation model. a) In an experiment, a flame was excited with an oscillating membrane, and depending on the oscillation amplitude, the flame synchronizes on the excitation frequency or a multiple of it; b) The experiment can be modeled qualitatively with a forced van der Pol model.

natural flame pulsation frequency. As one increases the excitation amplitude, a bifurcation to the subharmonic occurs. The flame begins to pulsate at exactly half the excitation frequency. The comparison of many experiments with very different excitations did furnish a qualitative understanding of real-world situations. The outcome of this research was a catalog of the possible flame fingerprints.

The exploitation of these fundamental research results required an efficient spectral analysis method to recognize the different fingerprints. Short-time Fourier transforms in combination with a classifier were considered. The necessary power was too high for the microcontroller at our disposal (The main limitation is the electric power required for computation, not the computing power of the microcontroller. Low electric power is allowed in fire detection to permit battery operation in emergencies, where the regular power supply may be down!).

Wavelets furnish an alternative to the Fourier transform. The approach with a filter cascade does not require much computing power. For orthogonal wavelets, the energy conservation relation holds. It follows that the low-pass and the high-pass filters corresponding to the two decomposition filters for the first level of decomposition fulfill the power complementarity condition, as illustrated in Figure 8.7.

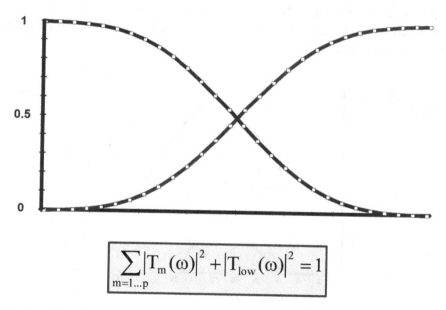

$$\sum_{m=1...p} \left|T_m(\omega)\right|^2 + \left|T_{low}(\omega)\right|^2 = 1$$

Fig. 8.7. The filtered signals after a one-level wavelet decomposition fulfill the power complementarity condition, and it allows a fuzzy interpretation of the transmission function as low and high-frequency membership functions.

$$\sum_{m=1...p}|T_m(\omega)|^2 + |T_{low}(\omega)|^2 = 1 \qquad (8.2)$$

After low-pass filtering and decimation, the signal is filtered with the same two filters in wavelet decomposition, splitting the low-frequency filter band into two new subbands.

At any decomposition level, the corresponding filters fulfill the power complementary condition. Figure 8.8 provides a fuzzy interpretation of the filter transmission functions as *low-frequency* or *high-frequency subbands*. The degree of membership μ_{T_m} are estimated from the wavelet coefficients by the expression [Thuillard, 1998, 2002]:

$$\mu(T_m) = \sum_n(d_{m,n})^2 / (\sum_{m=1}^{p}\sum_n(d_{m,n})^2 + \sum_n(c_{low,n})^2) \qquad (8.3)$$

The multiresolution approach furnishes an easy way to use fuzzy logic for spectral analysis. After classification, a set of fuzzy rules of the form describe the different cases in the form:

If (frequency in spectral band 1) is A AND ... then ... $\qquad (8.4)$

This approach makes fuzzy rules in the frequency domain simple and computationally efficient. The fuzzy system includes rules describing other essential criteria in flame detection, such as the degree of correlation between the signals in the different spectral bands.

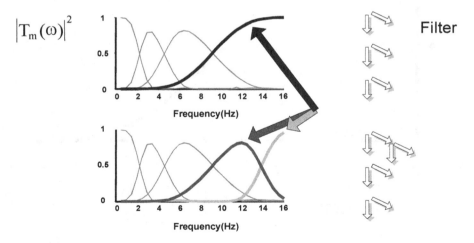

Fig. 8.8. A series of filters fulfilling the power complementarity condition is obtained by cascading filters. The transmission functions can be interpreted linguistically as membership functions.

The spectral analysis can be flexible by extending the method to wavelet packets. The complementary power condition is preserved, though it does introduce two new variables. Figure 8.8 gives an example. Several research projects continue that line of research [Kushnir and Kopchak, 2021], expanding the number of bands or finding out the best emplacement for the detectors [Zhen *et al.*, 2019]. Much research is on fire detection using deep learning [Shen *et al.*, 2018; Saeed *et al.*, 2020; Ryu and Kwak, 2021]. Zhong *et al.* [2018] use a convolutional network for flame detection of video surveillance.

Today, intelligence applies to human performance and is also connected to many products. Most technical products include computational intelligence, and this section will explain how to use soft computing techniques during product development.

From the industrial point of view, the success of fuzzy logic has much to do with the fact that it permits the translation of knowledge into linguistically expressed mathematical expressions. Translating this knowledge into a fuzzy system is not as simple as initially claimed at the beginning of the *fuzzy wave*. Development engineers have learned that the fine-tuning of a fuzzy system can be quite time-consuming if the number of implemented rules describing the system is extensive. Therefore, the most significant development in the field has been the appearance of new methods to train fuzzy systems automatically. There are three main soft computing methods to train fuzzy systems: neural networks, genetic algorithms, and multiresolution-based techniques. Fuzzy logic is well suited to fusing information from data and human experts. It is generally easier for a human operator to express his knowledge with linguistical rules than under a purely mathematical form. Fusing the two sources of information and testing the compatibility between the fuzzy rules formulated by a human expert and a databank are two of the main issues in learning.

8.2. Transparency

The primary motivation behind fuzzy rules is keeping the human factor within the loop. Better methods than fuzzy logic exist for self-learning systems without any human supervision. Fuzzy learning is justified when a human expert is part of the modeling or the validation process. Fuzzy learning provides methods to fuse human expert knowledge with experimental knowledge and measurements. It is generally easier for a human operator to express his expertise with linguistic rules than in a purely mathematical form. Fuzzy logic is well suited to fusing information from human experts and databanks. Depending on the operator's confidence in human expertise, the rules generated by the human expert can be integrated as hard or soft constraints. During automatic learning, one eliminates data in contradiction with hard constrained rules. Soft-constrained rules are included in different forms. For instance, data points can be generated from the rules formulated by the expert and added to the experimental data (Figure 8.9), possibly using type-2 fuzzy rules. Another possibility is to look for a compromise solution between the rules obtained from experimental data and the rules formulated by human experts.

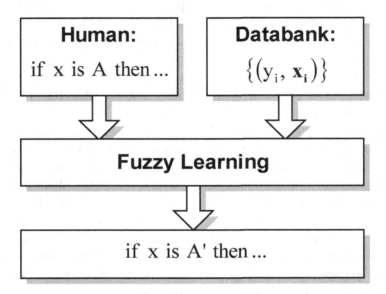

Fig. 8.9. The linguistic formulation of fuzzy logic simplifies the fusion of human expert rules with information extracted from a databank. The transparency of the resulting rules is of crucial importance, and transparency has been a primary motivation behind learning methods combining multiresolution analysis with fuzzy logic.

Some of the most successful fuzzy learning methods are formally equivalent to a classical modeling technique. Spline modeling is used to develop fuzzy systems within the Takagi-Sugeno formalism. The central contribution of the fuzzy approach lies in a series of methods that ensure either an intuitive interpretation of the rules by human experts or at least an easy inclusion of expert knowledge to the experimental knowledge under the form of a databank. As mentioned above, fuzzy logic cannot be separated from its linguistic context, and a good compromise between accuracy, transparency, and complexity must be found. Let us discuss that aspect of fuzzy modeling within the context of function approximation.

The first limitation of fuzzy modeling is that the dictionary of local functions for modeling is restricted to functions having a linguistic interpretation, and functions with negative values do not have a simple linguistic interpretation. Therefore, a fuzzy approximation is sub-optimal for accuracy and complexity.

For a given accuracy, the lowest complexity description of a fuzzy system is achieved by optimizing the shape and position of the membership functions. For good interpretability, the constraint that the membership functions form a partition of unity is often necessary. This condition is rarely fulfilled by the lowest complexity solution; therefore, adding that constraint increases the complexity of the solution.

Multiresolution-based fuzzy methods furnish a new approach to the problem of transparency and linguistic interpretability. Linguistic interpretability is included per design using pre-defined membership functions forming a multiresolution. Membership functions are chosen from a dictionary and describe terms that do not change during learning. A fuzzy system developed with that method consists of rules with clear linguistic interpretations of membership functions. Linguistic interpretability and transparency are two slightly different concepts. Linguistic interpretability refers to the quality of rules to have a natural linguistic interpretation, such as *if the temperature is low, then the heater is on.* Transparency describes the quality of a system to be understood by the human operator. A preliminary condition to transparency is the natural linguistic interpretability of rules. A second condition is that the number of rules and the number of different levels in a hierarchical fuzzy system is still manageable by human experts. In other words, the results should not be too complex and linguistically transparent to give enough insight into the results.

We have seen that complexity and accuracy are often contradictory. In many systems, transparency is lost if high accuracy is required. A possible solution consists of using two fuzzy modeling results, one at a low accuracy that preserves transparency for human validation and a second very accurate model for computational validation. The high-resolution approximation is obtained from the low-resolution description by adding rules representing small corrections.

Transparency is significantly increased by removing unnecessary terms through the fusion of rules or by using constructive methods. Fusing rules in wavelet-based methods is simple as the membership functions form a multi-resolution. A low-resolution approximation can be computed using the fast wavelet decomposition's approximation coefficients at high resolution. The energy contained in the wavelet coefficients characterizes the error introduced by lowering the resolution. The resolution is chosen locally based on the maximal tolerated local error conditions.

8.3. Man, sensors, and computer intelligence

The multiresolution learning methods presented in the last two parts are implemented in various products. Implementations were in the domain of sensors and, more precisely, in fire detection. Sensorics is especially interesting, representing a typical case of distributed intelligence. Learning starts from a databank containing knowledge on fires and deceiving phenomena collected through field testing and laboratory (Figure 8.10).

An alarm surface separating the alarm from the non-alarm conditions is extracted from data for fire and non-fire situations. The alarm surface is translated into fuzzy rules.

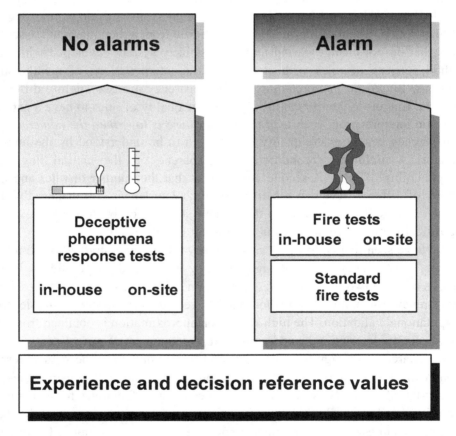

Fig. 8.10. Intelligent fire detectors are developed by extracting information from large databanks containing fire and non-fire situation measurements.

The different rules are checked against human experts using a computer-assisted development tool—the program checks for the consistency between experimental data and expert know-how. The program proposes also compromise solutions in case of incompatibility.

One of the most exciting stages in the development process is fusing the knowledge extracted from data with existing expert knowledge. The compatibility between the different experts is checked before knowledge fusion (Figure 8.11). Comparing specialist knowledge is not too difficult, and it relies on a geometrical interpretation of knowledge. A series of fuzzy linguistic rules can always be expressed as surfaces (in n-dimensions surfaces for n input variables). In this geometrical approach, information processing from different sources compares surfaces and studies how they complete each other and overlap. Therefore, the compatibility between fuzzy rules generated by human operators and data can be assessed by comparing the corresponding hypersurfaces.

Suppose that we have two experts who express their knowledge linguistically on a specific process using fuzzy rules. The first possibility is that the two experts know two different parts of the process. In this case, their knowledge completes

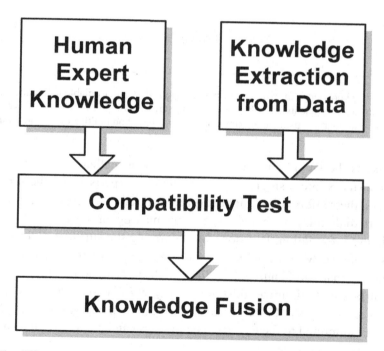

Fig. 8.11. The different rules are checked for compatibility before knowledge from various experts is fused.

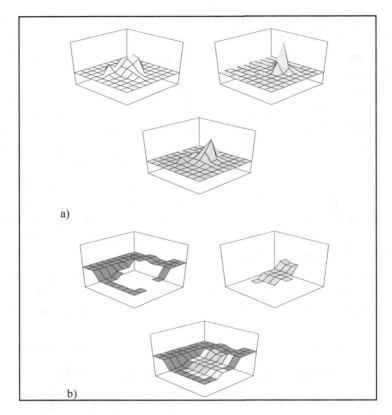

Fig. 8.12. a) The knowledge of two experts can be analyzed by a deformable template method using the fuzzy-wavelet coefficients describing the control surface as input. b) The partial knowledge of two experts is summarized using approximation methods based on multiresolution analysis.

each other, as shown in Figure 8.12b. It corresponds mathematically to fusing two different surfaces into a single surface. If the two experts know the same part of the process, their information might partially contradict. In this case, the computer might start dialoguing with the experts by making proposals to reconcile the contradicting information. It is done by deforming the surfaces corresponding to expert knowledge with a minimum of pre-defined operations, such as surfaces becoming comparable [Thuillard, 1998]. Each deformation results in a penalty, and the surface that minimizes the total penalty $\pi(T)$ is proposed as a compromise solution (Figure 8.12a). The deformed surface can then be translated into linguistic expressions submitted to the experts. The process can be iterated till an agreement between the experts is reached.

Our approach is, in some aspects, similar to wavelet-based deformable templates techniques. Expert knowledge is expressed as a surface with as few spline coefficients as reasonable. The expert knowledge' surfaces are deformed using three operations on spline functions:

Translation by n an integer
Dilation by 2^m, m integer
Change the value of a spline coefficient

A penalty corresponds to each deformation. Given two deformed surfaces T1 and T2, the score Sc is defined by:

$$Sc = \boldsymbol{max}(\textstyle\sum_x(T_1(x) - T_2(x))^2, K) \cdot \pi(T) \tag{8.5}$$

with $\pi(T)$ the total penalty function and K a constant. The best compromise between the penalty function associated with surfaces' transformations of two original surfaces, S_1 and S_2, and their dissimilarities characterized by $max(\sum_x(T_1(x) - T_2(x))^2, K)$ is obtained by minimizing the score function Sc with, for instance, evolutionary-based techniques or Monte-Carlo methods. The result is interpreted as follows:

1) If $max(\sum_x (T_1(x) - T_2(x))^2, K) =K$ then the synthesis between the two experts can be expressed by the average value:
$T_a(x) = (T_1(x) + T_2(x))/2.$

2) If $max(\sum_x (T_1(x) - T_2(x))^2 K) >K$, then one considers that the two experts contradict each other. They are several possibilities:

One expert is wrong
Expert's knowledge is not described with sufficient precision.

8.3.1. *Local model failure*

The deformable surface approach permits reconciling different experts' knowledge and detecting problematic regions.

Learning is dynamic, and field testing is a central part of the development process. As the experts' knowledge expands, one acquires new information that completes missing data at other locations. Field testing is central to rule' validations.

A considerable advantage of such a working process is that it takes advantage of the available computing power while always keeping the human in the loop. The human experts are not run over by the computer (Figure 8.13). Cross-checking the computer results is possible since the information is under a linguistic form at the end. Such control of the computer results by human experts is necessary, as one should never forget

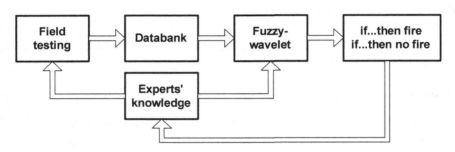

Fig. 8.13. Field testing is an essential part of development, and field testing collects new information on the sensors and validates the fuzzy rules describing the alarm surface.

that the results furnished by the computer can only be as good as the data supplied to it.

In conclusion, the computer-assisted development of *intelligent* products with fuzzy rules is standard today, and it is particularly true in today's multi-disciplinary working environment.

8.4. Constructive modeling

Constructive methods often reduce the complexity of models. Adaptive Spline Modeling of Observational Data (ASMOD) has been successfully implemented in many modeling problems, such as ship docking or helicopter guidance [Harris, Hong, and Wilson, 1999]. Kavli [1993] proposed the ASMOD scheme (Adaptive Spline Modeling of Observation Data) to tackle the *curse of dimensionality*. With ASMOD, the model structure is constructed iteratively through successive model refinements. The resulting model is a linear sum of several low-dimensional sub-models. Let us describe ASMOD within the setting of neuro-fuzzy modeling. The model is refined in several ways. A performance indicator balances the increased complexity associated with the refinement and the reduction of the model. The Bayesian and Akaike's s information criteria compare the performance of the different refinements and choose the most appropriate one.

ASMOD applies very well to fuzzy-wavelet modeling. The model refinement starts with a straightforward model, typically a one-dimensional sub-model. Each refinement step corresponds to choosing among three possibilities. Two refinement procedures are part of the ASMOD scheme: adding new one-dimensional sub-models and forming tensor products sub-models. The third refinement procedure consists of splitting a membership function into membership functions at one higher level of resolution.

8.5. From a sensor to a smart sensor network with multicriteria decisions

The previous sections focused on the analysis of sensor signals for fire detection. Fire protection includes decision-making tools, such as the analytic network process [Saaty and Vargas, 2013], to decide on a scenario based on available information. Fusing the information provided by smoke or flame detectors and video signals raises the detection capacities to new levels [He *et al.*, 2021]. Video detection of forest fires through cameras or satellite imaging is increasingly implemented [Abedi Gheshlaghi, Feizizadeh, and Blaschke, 2020]. Toledo-Castro *et al.* [2018] propose a network of sensors connected through a wireless network. Their system analyzes the information at different locations using a fuzzy system assessing the risk based on meteorological parameters and vegetation.

References

Abedi Gheshlaghi, H., Feizizadeh, B. and Blaschke, T. (2020). GIS-based forest fire risk mapping using the analytical network process and fuzzy logic, *Journal of Environmental Planning and Management*, 63(3), pp. 481–499.

Harris, C., Hong, X. and Wilson, P. (1999). An intelligent guidance and control system for ship obstacle avoidance, *Proceedings of the Institution of Mechanical Engineers, Part I: Journal of Systems and Control Engineering*, 213(4), pp. 311–320.

He, Z. *et al.* (2021). Scenario-based comprehensive assessment for community resilience adapted to fire following an earthquake, implementing the analytic network process and preference ranking organization method for enriched evaluation II techniques, *Buildings*, 11(11), p. 523.

Kavli, T. (1993). ASMOD-an algorithm for adaptive spline modelling of observation data, *International Journal of Control*, 58(4), pp. 947–967.

Kushnir, A. and Kopchak, B. (2021). Development of Multiband Flame Detector with Fuzzy Correction Block, *Proc. 2021 IEEE XVIIth International Conference on the Perspective Technologies and Methods in MEMS Design (MEMSTECH)*, IEEE, pp. 58–63.

Ryu, J. and Kwak, D. (2021). Flame Detection Using Appearance-Based Pre-Processing and Convolutional Neural Network, *Applied Sciences*, 11(11), p. 5138.

Saaty, T.L. and Vargas, L.G. (2013). The analytic network process, *Decision making with the analytic network process*. Springer, pp. 1–40.

Saeed, F. *et al.* (2020). Convolutional neural network based early fire detection, *Multimedia Tools and Applications*, 79(13), pp. 9083–9099.

Shen, D. *et al.* (2018). Flame detection using deep learning, *Proc. 2018 4th International conference on control, automation and robotics (ICCAR)*, (IEEE), pp. 416–420.

Thuillard, M. (1994). New methods for reducing the number of false alarms in fire detection systems, *Fire Technology*, 30(2), pp. 250–268.

Thuillard, M. (1998). Fuzzy-wavelets: theory and applications, *Proc. Sixth European Congress on Intelligent Techniques and Soft Computing (EUFIT'98)*, pp. 2–1149.

Thuillard, M. (2002). A new flame detector using the latest research on flames and fuzzy-wavelet algorithms, *Fire Safety Journal*, 37(4), pp. 371–380.

Toledo-Castro, J. *et al.* (2018). Fuzzy-based forest fire prevention and detection by wireless sensor networks, in. *The 13th International Conference on Soft Computing Models in Industrial and Environmental Applications*, Springer, pp. 478–488.

Zhen, T. *et al.* (2019). A mathematical programming approach for the optimal placement of flame detectors in petrochemical facilities, *Process Safety and Environmental Protection*, 132, pp. 47–58.

Zhong, Z. *et al.* (2018). A convolutional neural network-based flame detection method in video sequence, *Signal, Image and Video Processing*, 12(8), pp. 1619–1627.

Multiresolution and Wavelets in Graphs, Trees, and Networks

Part 9

Chapter 9

Multiresolution and Wavelets in Graphs, Trees, and Networks

9.1. Wavelet decomposition on a graph

This chapter focuses on wavelet and multiresolution analysis applications on graphs and trees. The interest in graph theory is very high due to its importance in connection to the internet and social media, and deep learning on graphs is a rapidly developing field. Several recent papers review deep learning on trees and graphs [Su *et al.*, 2022; Zhang *et al.*, 2020; Zhou *et al.*, 2020; Wu *et al.*, 2020]. Some of the main applications are text and image classification, the modeling of chemical biochemical structures, physics modeling, and robotics. Combinatorial optimization, search, and classification on graphs are also major topics. The study of deep learning in graphs is challenging, but it opens new research directions to tackle the curse of dimensionality using invariance and symmetries [Bronstein *et al.*, 2021]. Deep neural networks in the spectral domain have been developed using the Laplacian of a graph and transforming it into the Fourier or wavelet domain. The next sections in this chapter succinctly explain these new approaches.

A large section of this chapter covers phylogenetic trees and networks from a multiresolution perspective starting from the treelet approach to classification. After introducing phylogenetic trees and phylogenetic networks (outerplanar networks), we will present new applications of wavelet analysis in classification. The last sections show how to apply these methods to classifying galaxies or world mythologies.

9.1.1. *Fourier and wavelet transforms on graphs*

A graph consists of a set of vertices $(1 \leq i \leq n)$ connected by some edges $\{1 \leq i, j \leq j\}$. The adjacency matrix A furnishes a matrix representation of the graph:

$$A_{i,j} = \begin{cases} 1 & \text{if the vortices i, j are connected by an edge} \\ 0 & \text{otherwise} \end{cases} \tag{9.1}$$

L = D-A with D the matrix with the degree of each vertex in its diagonal

$$D_{i,j} = \begin{cases} \Sigma_{1 \le i \le n} A_{i,j} & i = j \\ 0 & otherwise \end{cases} \tag{9.2}$$

The Laplacian has a central importance in the spectral analysis of a graph. Consider the graph in Figure 9.1, in which each node has a value f(m,n). The Laplacian of the element (m,n) can be seen here as an approximation of the negative of $-\nabla^2(f)$ what permits us to relate the Laplacian intuitively to the Fourier transform.

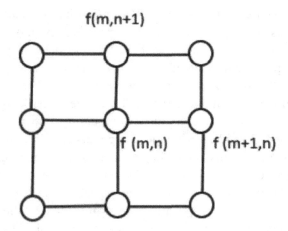

Laplacian: 4 f(m,n)- f(m+1,n)- f(m-1,n)- f(m,n+1)- f(m,n-1) $\sim -$

Fig. 9.1. The Fourier transform of a graph is related to the graph Laplacian, which is itself related to the second derivative.

The Laplacian can be related to the Fourier transform if one recalls that e^{iwx} is the eigenfunction of the one-dimensional Laplacian function $\frac{d^2}{dx^2}$. The inverse Fourier transform corresponds to the projection of f on the eigenfunctions of the Laplacian operator:

$$f(x) = \frac{1}{2\pi} \int \hat{f}(\omega) e^{i\omega x} d\omega \tag{9.3}$$

The graph Laplacian matrix contains all the necessary information to perfectly reconstruct a graph or approximate the undirected graph using the largest eigenvalues. The eigenvectors of the Laplacian are orthogonal, and the eigenvalues are real and non-negative: $0 \leq \lambda_0 < \lambda_1 \leq \lambda_1 \leq \cdots$. The multiplicity of the zero eigenvalues corresponds to the number of connected components in the graph. Given the eigenvectors v_l of a graph Laplacian with N nodes, the lth component $\hat{f}(l)$ of the graph Fourier, transform of a signal f is

$$\hat{f}(l) = <v_l^*, f> = \sum_{n=1}^{N} v_l^*(n) \ f(n) .$$

$$(9.4)$$

The eigenvectors are orthogonal, and the decomposition is invertible.

$$f(n) = \sum_{l=0}^{N-1} \hat{f}(l) \ v_l(n) .$$

$$(9.5)$$

Hammond *et al.* [2011] have developed the graph wavelet transform. They define it by transforming each of the graph Fourier coefficients with a function g using an operator T with $T_g(v_i) = g(\lambda_i) \ v_i$. The wavelets are not fixed but constructed on the eigenvectors of the Laplacian. In other words, the wavelet function depends on the details of the adjacency matrix:

$$\psi_{s,n}(m) = \sum_{l=0}^{N-1} g(s \ \lambda_i) \ v_i^*(n) \ v_l(m).$$

$$(9.6)$$

One refers the reader to Hammond *et al.* [2011] to construct the wavelet kernel g.

The above graph decomposition permits extending deep learning methods to graphs [Yu *et al.*, 2018].

9.1.2. *Graph wavelet neural networks*

Graphs are ubiquitous in connection to the internet as they describe relationships between users in social networks or may be used to connect sites or scientific articles. Developing performant neural networks on a graph is not a simple task. Bruna *et al.* [2013] use neural networks with learnable filters in the frequency domain. The original networks were computationally inefficient, and methods based on the Chebyshev polynomials have made computation much more tractable [Hammond *et al.*, 2011; Defferrard *et al.*, 2016; Kipf and Welling, 2017]. Xu *et al.* [2019] have presented a multiresolution neural network based on learnable heat kernels $\exp(-\lambda s)$ with λ an eigenvalue of the Laplacian [Coifman and Maggioni, 2006]. The network is very performant on semi-supervised node classification tasks such as the Citeseer and Pubmed graphs. The network is called a Graph Wavelet Neural Network (GWNN). We expect the field to develop and mature in the coming years, boosted by the significant commercial interest in analyzing networks. The main challenge consists of extracting useful information from the results as the interpre-tation of the wavelet decomposition in the context of graphs is everything but straightforward.

9.1.3. *Spectral ordering*

A second important application of the Fourier decomposition is the ordering problems. A graph is often well approximated using the Fourier components with its lowest eigenvalues. The multiplicity of the smallest non-zero eigenvalue (i.e., the number of eigenvectors associated with the eigenvalue) furnishes the number of independent components [Fiedler, 1975]. Fiedler showed that the smallest non-zero eigenvalue of the Laplacian contains much information. Let us consider a symmetric matrix A' and a matrix A obtained by permutation of the index of the column fulfilling the condition

$$A_{i,j} \leq A_{i,k} \qquad j < k < i$$

$$A_{i,j} \geq A_{i,k} \qquad i < j < k \qquad\qquad (9.7)$$

Section 9.3 explains the importance of Eq. 9.7 in the context of classification. Fiedler proved that the eigenvector corresponding to the smallest non-zero eigenvalue furnishes a method to find a permutation of the indices satisfying (9.7). The algorithm is simple for an eigenvalue with a multiplicity of one:

1. Order the values of the eigenvector in ascending order;
2. Reorder the indices of A according to the above order.

9.2. Treelet

A tree representation of data naturally induces a multiresolution analysis (MRA). In its simplest version [Donoho, 1997], the decomposition is on a fixed tree with a Haar-like wavelet basis. The procedure is illustrated in Figure 9.2 using a rooted tree.

The treelet decomposition [Lee and Nadler, 2008] constructs both a tree and a multiresolution representation directly from unstructured data. The correlation coefficient determines which variables to merge in the tree. The similarity score is given by

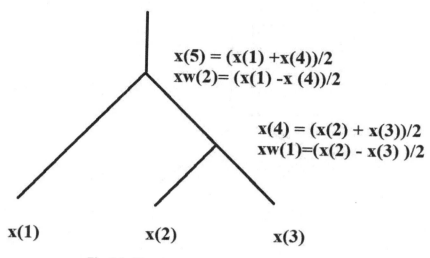

Fig. 9.2. Haar wavelet decomposition on a fixed tree.

$$M_{i,j} = C_{i,j} / \sqrt{C_{ii} C_{jj}}$$

with $C_{i,j}$ the covariance defined as

$$C_{i,j} = E(v_i - Ev_i)(v_j - Ev_j)^T$$

The treelet construction uses a greedy algorithm, searching for the two characters with the largest correlation at each step.

$$i_m, j_m = \arg\max{}_{i,j} (M_{i,j})$$

The two characters are then processed with a local PCA. The first and second components are used respectively as scaling and detail functions, and only the scaling function is further processed. The method is very useful for clustering correlated data but not appropriate for constructing a phylogenetic tree from data. Other methods are better suited; this is the topic of the next sections.

9.3. Phylogenetic trees and networks

First, let us discuss data classification defined by a distance matrix compatible with a phylogenetic tree. As illustrated in Figure 9.3, the distance from a reference node n to the last common node between nodes i and j is

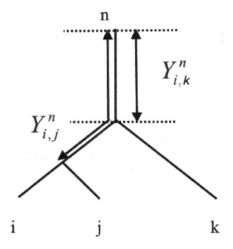

$$Y_{i,j}^n = \tfrac{1}{2}\left(d(x_i, x_n) + d(x_j, x_n) - d(x_i, x_j)\right)$$

Fig. 9.3. The distance matrix Y defined in (9.8) fulfills the ordering conditions (9.7).

$$Y_{i,j}^n = 1/2\,((d(x_i, x_n) + d(x_j, x_n) - d(x_i, x_j)) \tag{9.8}$$

with $d(x_i, x_j)$ the distance between the end nodes i and j of the tree.

For simplification, let us write $d(x_i, x_j)$ as d(i,j). The distance matrix $Y_{i,j}^n$ describes the distance on a tree from a reference node n to the last common node between nodes i and j. A phylogenetic network or a tree, defined by a distance matrix, with a circular ordering of the taxa fulfills Eq. (9.9), the so-called Kalmanson inequalities (compare these equations to Eq. 9.3)

$$Y_{i,j}^n \geq Y_{i,k}^n \qquad\qquad i < j < k < n$$

$$Y_{k,j}^n \geq Y_{k,i}^n \qquad\qquad i < j < k < n \tag{9.9a}$$

or equivalently

$$d(i,j) + d(k,n) \geq d(j,k) + d(i,n)$$

$$d(i,k) + d(j,n) \geq d(i,j) + d(k,n) \tag{9.9b}$$

A perfect order is an order of X, the set of end nodes so that the distance matrix fulfills the Kalmanson inequalities [Kalmanson, 1975]. Bandelt and Dress [1992) showed that a set of characters characterized by a distance matrix d satisfying (9.9) is perfectly represented (i.e., without loss of information) by an outerplanar network (see next section and Figure 9.7 for an example), a phylogenetic tree generalization. While a phylogenetic network fulfills the Kalmanson inequalities, a phylogenetic tree fulfills the Kalmanson inequalities and the four-point condition. The last condition states that any four end nodes (i,j,k,n) satisfy the inequality:

$$d(i,j) + d(k,n) \leq max\{d(i,k) + d(j,n), d(j,k) + d(i,n)\} \qquad (9.10)$$

Fiedler's approach works well on a distance matrix Y fulfilling (9.9). Better methods exist for ordering matrices that only approximately meet conditions (9.9).

9.3.1. *Effect of lateral transfers on phylogenetic trees and networks*

Phylogenetic trees are widely used outside of biology to describe the evolution of some cultural traits. Transmission of cultural elements may occur within a population or through cultural interaction between different peoples. Lateral (or horizontal) transfer describes the transmission of characters between individuals without a direct vertical inheritance from parents to their offspring. A lateral transfer from taxon A to taxon B corresponds to replacing some proportion α of taxon B with a segment of A. A phylogenetic tree is a too crude representation of the relationships between taxa (i.e., end nodes) in many applications with lateral transfers. While lateral transfers destroy a perfect phylogenetic tree structure, a phylogenetic network is quite robust against it.

Many classification problems deal with binary characters defining, for instance, a mythological motif absence or presence among some traditions. Let us consider binary characters and a planar representation of a phylogenetic tree. For binary characters (0/1, -1/1, black/white), Eq. (9.9) is equivalent to the circular consecutive-one property. Figure 9.4 shows an example of a matrix that fulfills, after ordering, the circular consecutive-one property. After ordering the taxa, all 'one' states are consecutive in a circular order. The first character is consecutive to the last one in a circular order.

An arrow from an origin node represents a lateral transfer to a target node on a phylogenetic tree. A lateral transfer corresponds to the replacement of some states on the target node by the corresponding character states of the origin node of the transfer. For binary characters, one readily understands (see Figure 9.5 for an illustration) that lateral transfers between consecutive nodes in a planar representation of a tree do not disrupt the consecutive-one property.

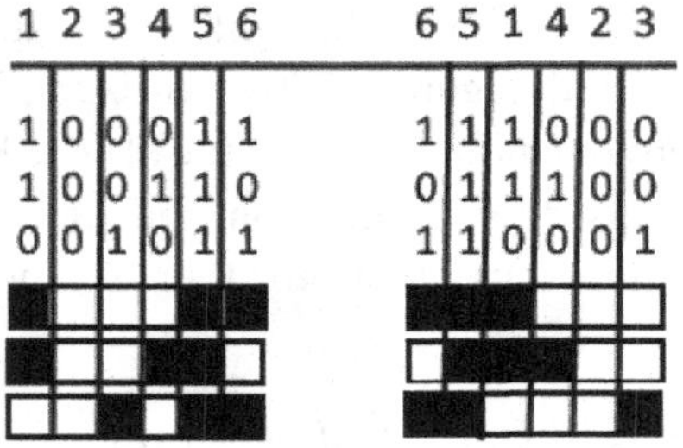

	1	2	3	4	5	6		6	5	1	4	2	3
	1	0	0	0	1	1		1	1	1	0	0	0
	1	0	0	1	1	0		0	1	1	1	0	0
	0	0	1	0	1	1		1	1	0	0	0	1

Fig. 9.4. After ordering, the matrix is so that each character is so that all 'one' states (one=black) are consecutive in a circular order (i.e., the first character is consecutive to the last one in a circular order).

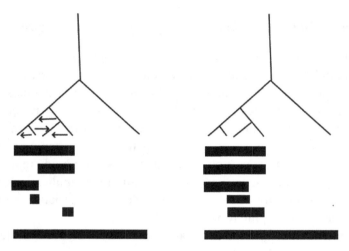

Fig. 9.5. Example of lateral transfers preserving the circular order of the tree. Left: without transfer; right: with lateral transfer.

More generally, the circular order of a phylogenetic tree is robust against lateral transfer. Indeed, suppose all lateral transfers are between adjacent nodes in a circular order of the end nodes compatible with a tree. In that case, an outerplanar network can perfectly represent the resulting distance matrix [Thuillard, 2009].

Figure 9.6 shows the robustness of the circular order of a tree using the degrees of liberty on the planar representation of a tree. All lateral transfers are after the reordering of the taxa between consecutive nodes. An outerplanar network perfectly describes the tree with the lateral transfer. Figure 9.7 shows an example with, in general, no order satisfying the Kalmanson inequalities. There is no order in which all lateral transfers are between adjacent trees on the tree, and no outerplanar describes perfectly the tree with lateral transfers.

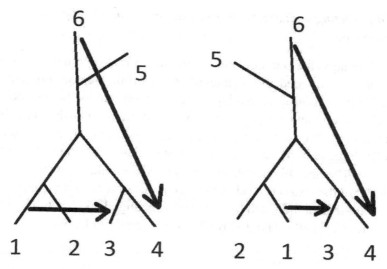

Fig. 9.6. By reordering the end nodes, there is a circular order so that all lateral transfers represented by an arrow are between adjacent end nodes of the tree. The distance matrix associated with the perturbed tree fulfills the Kalmanson inequalities, and an outerplanar network can exactly represent the distance matrix.

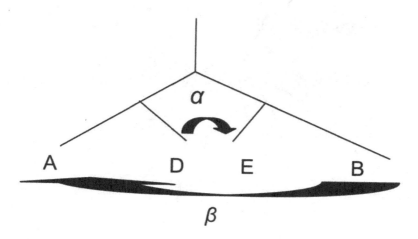

Fig. 9.7. Perfect order cannot be guaranteed if there is no order with all lateral transfers between adjacent taxa on the tree.

In conclusion, lateral transfers fundamentally disrupt the topology of a phylogenetic tree. As long as there is a planar representation of the tree with lateral transfers between adjacent taxa, then the circular order of the taxa is preserved. In other words, the circular order is a relevant classification criterium.

9.3.2. *Constructing a phylogenetic tree and outerplanar network from data*

Neighbor-Joining is the standard method to build a tree from data described by a distance matrix. Provided the character' states fulfill the four-point condition, Neighbor-Joining constructs a phylogenetic tree representing the distance matrix.

Figure 9.8 shows an outerplanar network resulting from analyzing a family of myths classified as 'Cosmic hunt.' A hunter pursues an animal, and he escapes into the sky, often transforming into a star or a constellation. Each end node corresponds to a tradition. The grey blobs indicate clusters with similar character states and a circular order of the taxa (i.e., traditions). A circular order is, for instance, obtained by starting at the taxa indicated by a '1' and scanning clockwise (arrow) the taxa. See Thuillard, Le Quellec and d'Huy [2018] for details and Annex C.

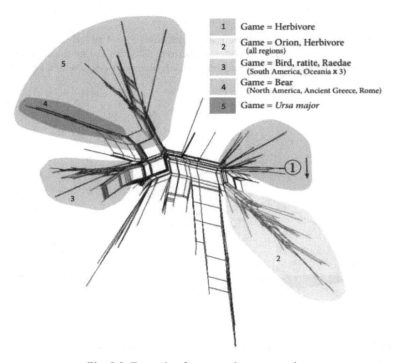

Fig. 9.8. Example of an outerplanar network.

Each end node corresponds to a tradition. The outerplanar network is constructed with NeighborNet as defined below.

Let us now describe these essential algorithms.

Neighbor-Net and Neighbor-Joining

Init:

$\mu(i) = 1 \; \forall i$ and C(i)={i}. Each cluster contains a unique taxon
Step 1:
Compute for each pair of taxa (i,j) the value $Q(i,j)$:

$$Q(i,j) = \sum_{C_m} ((n-2)D_m(C(i), C(j))) - \sum_{i \neq k} D_m(C(i), C(k)) - $$

$$\sum_{j \neq k} D_m(C(j), C(k))$$

With n the number of taxa (or clusters), and

$$D_m(\,C(i), C(j)\,) = \sum_{\substack{i \in C(i) \\ j \in C(j)}} \mu(i)\,\mu(j)\,\delta(i,j)$$

with
$$\delta(i,j) = \begin{matrix} 0 & s(i) = s(j) \\ 1 & otherwise \end{matrix}$$

The clusters (i,j) minimizing Q are merged into a new cluster C(new). The new weights are actualized so that $\sum_{i \in C(new)} \mu_i = 1$ multiplying all weights in C(i) by α and the second by (1-α). The value α can be adaptively chosen so that α is proportional to the cluster cardinality. The iteration of the first step results in a phylogenetic tree. A second step is necessary to order the taxa in the construction of an outerplanar network,

Step 2: Ordering (Neighbor-Net only)
Search the order among the four possible ordering of the taxa in C(i) and C(j), the one minimizing the contradiction defined for a binary character as

$$Contradiction = \sum_{\substack{i < j < k \\ i,j,k \, \epsilon C \, (i) \cup C(j) \\ l \notin C(i) \cup C(j)}} \max(Y_{i,k}^l - Y_{i,j}^l, 0)$$

For a perfect phylogenetic network, the approach is equivalent to minimizing

$$Q_2(i^*, j^*) = (n - 4 + |C(i)| + |C(j)|)\, d(i^*, j^*) - $$

$$\left(\sum_{k \neq i} d(i^*, C(k)) + \sum_{j \neq i} d(j^*, C(k)) \right) - $$

$$\left(\sum_{k \neq i, k \in C(i) \cup C(j)} d(i,k) + \sum_{k \neq j, k \in C(i) \cup C(j)} d(j,k) \right)$$

For a proof of the perfect reconstruction of an outerplanar network with NeighborNet, see Bryant and Moulton [2004] and Levy and Pachter [2011]. Several algorithm versions construct the best outerplanar network if data only approximatively correspond to a perfect outerplanar network. Our experience shows that the minimum contradiction principle leads to excellent results.

Depending on the problem and computing power, different forms of contradiction may be implemented. Below we introduce the contradiction within a multiresolution framework.

9.4. Multiresolution approach to phylogeny

9.4.1. *Finding the best phylogenetic network*

The treelet method belongs very clearly to multiresolution analysis. The treelet approach has the disadvantage of not being a phylogenetic approach, which limits its scope. We show below how multiresolution analysis may contribute to phylogeny analysis and classification. A set of binary characters fitting an outerplanar network is so that there is an order of the taxa for which each character fulfills the consecutive-one condition. After ordering, each character has values that fit a unique Haar function. The critical step in the analysis is identifying the best Haar function fitting the ordered values of a character. Let us consider the wavelet function

$$\Psi_{i,j}(\mathrm{k}) = \begin{cases} \frac{1}{2(j-i)} & if\ j \geq k \geq i, i \neq j \\ \frac{-1}{2(n-(j-i))} & otherwise \end{cases}. \tag{9.11a}$$

In the following, we will use two equivalent types of binary codings: the function S corresponds to the binary characters' states (1,0) of the ordered taxa, while one defines the function G on the states (1,-1) by the transformation $1 \to 1; 0 \to -1$. The best Haar function fitting the data maximizes the scalar product $< G, \Psi_{i,j} >$ with values in $[-1,1]$ (We exclude the trivial case with all one or zero values). One obtains the local deviation to a perfect outerplanar network by analyzing the residual R with

$$R = 1 - < G, \Psi_{k,l} > \tag{9.11b}$$

and $(k,l) = argmax(< G, \Psi_{i,j} >)$

R is a value defined on a given character. The residue allows selecting the characters describing best the outerplanar network. After removing the characters with a random distribution, one generally obtain a better description of the data in term of an outerplanar network. A strong indication that data do not fit a tree or an outerplanar network is when only a few characters fulfill the consecutive-one condition.

The residue can also be defined for each point 1 (or taxon) by computing $r1 = 1 - S(l)$ and $r2 = S(l)$ defined respectively on the positive resp. negative values of $\Psi_{k,l}$. Figure 9.9 illustrates the procedure. Further, the residue can be decomposed on Haar wavelets, and the signal energy characterizes locally for each character the deviation to a perfect phylogeny.

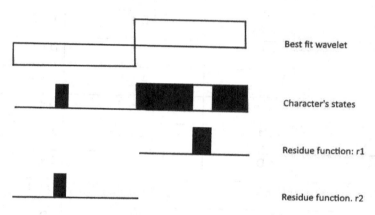

Fig. 9.9. The multiresolution search algorithm determines the largest deviations iteratively to a perfect phylogenetic network. In a perfect network, the residue has all zero values.

9.4.2. *Clustering noisy data with NeighborNet*

The following section explores the clustering property of NeighborNet, and it suggests an enhancement of the algorithm using an unexploited degree of liberty on the computation of the distance matrix. As shown below, varying this parameter is useful for analyzing noisy data to search for the parameter's value preserving best the consecutive-one property.

For binary characters, one generally defines the distance between two states as equal to zero if both states are identical and one otherwise. A different distance matrix leads to interesting algorithms for noisy data. Here the distance between the state $(0,0)$ is set to D.

$$d(i,j) = 0 \qquad S_i = 1;\ S_j = 1$$
$$d(i,j) = 1 \qquad S_i = 1;\ S_j = 0;\ \text{or } S_i = 0;\ S_j = 1 \qquad (9.12)$$
$$d(i,j) = D \qquad S_i = 0;\ S_j = 0$$

Table 9.1 shows that the distance matrix fulfills the Kalmanson inequalities (9.9) for $0 \leq D \leq 2$.

Table 9.1: The Kalmanson inequalities are fulfilled on any quartet of 4 taxa fulfilling the consecutive-one property if the parameter D is within [0,2].

Four characters: i,j,k,n	d(i,k) + d(j,n)	>=	d(i,j) + d(k,n)	d(j,k) + d(i,n)
1100	1 + 1		0 + D	1 + 1
0011	1 + 1		D + 0	1 + 1
1001	1 + 1		1 + 1	D + 0
0110	1 + 1		1 + 1	0 + D
1000	1 + D		1 + D	D + 1
0100	D + 1		1 + D	1 + D
0010	1 + D		D + 1	1 + D
0001	D + 1		D + 1	D + 1
0000	2D		2D	2D
1111	2		2	2

For D larger than 2, the distance matrice Y does not fulfill the Kalmanson inequalities, and the algorithm does not properly reconstruct a perfect outerplanar network from a distance matrix. For D=0, the minimum Q value (see section 9.3.2) corresponds to the two instances in Figure 9.10 with two taxa with identical states and all the other ones with opposite states. A character state pair (0,1) has zero contribution to Q.

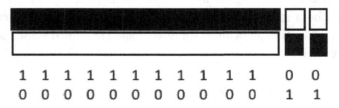

$$\begin{array}{ccccccccccc|cc}
1 & 1 & 1 & 1 & 1 & 1 & 1 & 1 & 1 & 1 & 1 & 0 & 0 \\
0 & 0 & 0 & 0 & 0 & 0 & 0 & 0 & 0 & 0 & 0 & 1 & 1
\end{array}$$

Fig. 9.10. The two characters with binary characters (1/0 or black/white) maximize the contribution to Q (D=0).

Table 9.2 shows that the differential contribution of two identical pairs $((0,0)$ and $(1,1)$ with $D<2$) equals $-(2-D)(N(1)-N(0))$. It follows that D does not influence the relative contribution of taxa with identical states as $(2-D)$ is simply a multiplicator of $(N(0)-N(1))$.

Table 9.2: Contribution to one character's $Q(i,j)$ depends on the state's pair.

	(0,0)	(1,1)	(0,1) or (1,0)
d(0,0)=0	-2 N(1)	-2 N(0)	0
d(0,0)=0.5	-(N(0)/2 + 3/2 N(1))	-2 N(0)	-0.5 N(0)
d(0,0)=1	-n	-2 N(0)	-N(0)
d(0,0)=2	-2 N(0)	-2 N(0)	-2 N(0)
D	-D N(0) - (2-D) N(1)	-2 N(0)	-D N(0)

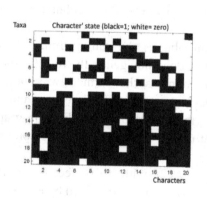

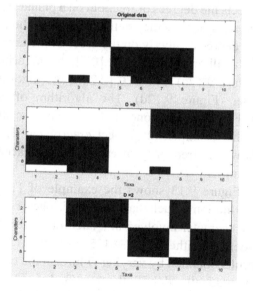

Fig. 9.11. The robustness of the classification increases with D if the data form two clusters of randomly distributed data (left). Conversely, the robustness to disruption by a character not fulfilling the consecutive-one property decreases with D (right).

The D factor determines the contribution of (1,0) states. For D=0, a (0,1) state has no contribution to the Q factor. For D=2, the contribution of each state (0.1), (1,0), (0,1), and (0,0) are equal, and the algorithm does not make any sense. As one increases D, the ordering becomes more robust against noise but more prone to disruptions of a perfect order by a single non-ordered character (Figure 9.11).

Using the multiresolution approach, one may determine the best parameter (section 9.4.1), minimizing the contradiction with the multi-resolution approach in section 9.4. An advantage of the approach is that it directly includes the search for lateral transfers.

9.4.3. *Automatic identification of simple instances of lateral transfer*

Let us show that simple instances of lateral transfers can be automatically discovered by varying the parameter D. Figure 9.12a corresponds to a simple tree defined on binary characters. The associated graph shows the taxa that are adjacent in a circular order. In all instances, the taxa pairs (1,2), (3,4), (5,6), and (7,8) are always adjacent. The taxa (1,3), (1,4), (2,3), and (2,4) have an equiprobability (25%) of being adjacent, while a pair (1,8) has a probability of 12.5%. The result reflects the degrees of freedom on a planar representation of a tree. In Figure 9.12b, one adds two characters that transform the tree into a perfect outerplanar without any degree of liberty on the order of the taxa.

In all trials with $D \in [0,2[$, the algorithm obtains the same circular order (Figure 9.12c). For $D \in [2,2.5]$, the algorithm does not generally find the best order (Figure 9.12d). The algorithm often connects the further-away nodes. In Figure 9.12e, one adds a character that relates the characters 3 and 6. In that example, no perfect outerplanar describes the data perfectly. The graph shows the frequency of each pair of adjacent nodes. Figure 9.13 focuses on that example.

Figure 9.13 shows the example of Figure 9.12e with no perfect order; the distribution is such that the order is one of the perfect orders obtained by removing one character involved in a lateral transfer in the tree. In those two cases, the best orders are either (1, 2, 3, 4, 5, 6, 7, 8) or (1, 2, 4, 3, 6, 5, 7, 8). In other words, the results obtained by varying D furnish the two best orders. Further, the analysis can automatically identify the taxa (3, 4, 5, 6) involved in lateral transfers resulting in a non-zero contradiction. The algorithm is a typical soft computing approach. It furnishes, in simple cases, the lateral transfers but does not identify them always all as the problem is notoriously NP-hard [Thuillard and Moulton, 2011].

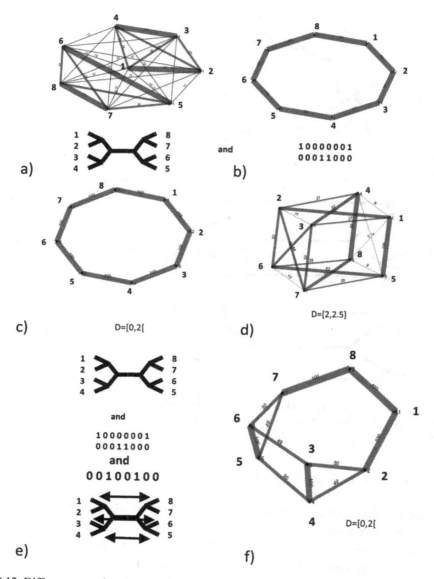

Fig. 9.12. Different examples show the consecutive taxa proportion as a weighted adjacency graph. a) Phylogenetic tree (D=0); b) with the addition of two characters (D=0); c) like b) with D=[0,2[; d) like b) but D=[2,2.5]; e) with the addition of a character introducing a contradiction in the best order; f) Circular orders with D=[0,2[.

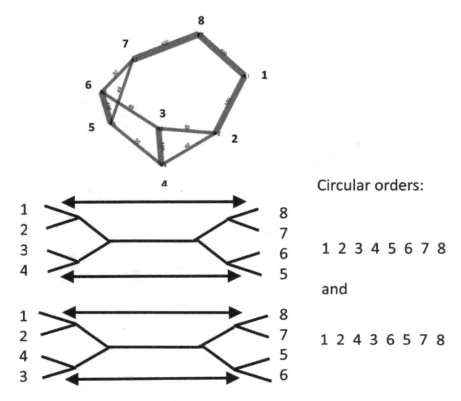

Fig. 9.13. Figure 9.12e (top) graph becomes a perfect outerplanar network if one removes one of the characters. The adjacency map on the circular order furnishes the two circular orders compatible with the two perfect outerplanar networks.

9.5. Applications to phylogeography

Phylogeography refers to the historical processes responsible for the geographic distribution of a genealogical lineage and is applied to genetic systems, cultural traits, or languages. Very schematically, there are two main models, one assuming population migration and the one assuming a diffusion process with their associated mathematical models based on random walks generated phylogenetic trees and the diffusion equations.

Bayesian phylogenetics is widely used to determine the evolution of large language families. Bouckaert *et al.* [2018] use the 'break-away' model to study the origin and expansion of Pama–Nyungan languages across Australia. This model is the basis of many approaches to the evolution of cultural traits and describes their evolution in a migratory scheme based on recently collected data. Let us consider a collection of cultural traits moving with the population. At some time, part of the population breaks away and settles at another location. A phylogenetic tree models the process very well (Figure 9.14a,b). The end nodes describe the actual states. In the case of a single migration origin and no back-migration, each geographic location is associated with one or some consecutive end nodes. Theoretically, it is possible to reconstruct the origin of a trait from the present cultural traits. Simulations show that reconstructing the origin place and states is quite tricky [Neureuther, 2021], even in the case of a single origin of cultural traits. In the case of multiple migrations, finding the different origins of cultural traits is impossible without ancient time-stamped data. An outerplanar network is a better model for motifs with multiple origins, as illustrated in Figure 9.14c,d.

The knowledge of historical data improves the quality of the simulations. Russel *et al.* [2014] modeled the spread of farming in the Bantu-speaking regions based on a linguistic approach completed in several instances with archeological information. The results align with ancient DNA studies showing the importance of migrations.

Figure 9.15 illustrates the disruption of the matching between the geographic ordering on a map and the phylogenetic tree in the break-away model if migration paths cross.

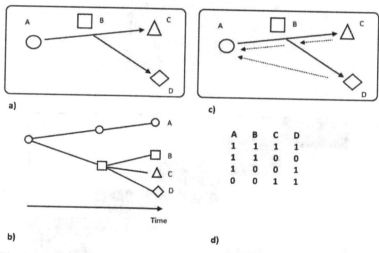

a)

c)

b)

A	B	C	D
1	1	1	1
1	1	0	0
1	0	0	1
0	0	1	1

d)

Fig. 9.14. The 'break-away' model describes the propagation of cultural traits; a) Geographic map associating a node to each tradition in space; b) The model represents both the evolution in time (same symbols) as well in space (end nodes); c) In case of multiple origins of traits, it is generally impossible to reconstruct the original state or its origin; d) With multiple origins of a trait, an outerplanar representation is often a better model as the data often fulfill the circular consecutive-one condition.

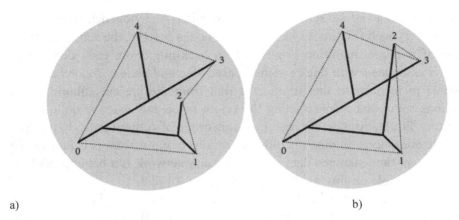

a)   b)

Fig. 9.15. a) Migration paths are not crossing, and the phylogenetic tree or network describing the different myth's versions has the same circular order as the migration tree. The line connecting adjacent taxa in a circular order forms a single loop; b) The migratory paths intersect at some point. If one assumes no interaction at the intersection, then the evolution of the myth is described by a tree, but geographic circularity is not preserved (i.e., the circular path along the geographic locations has crossing lines).

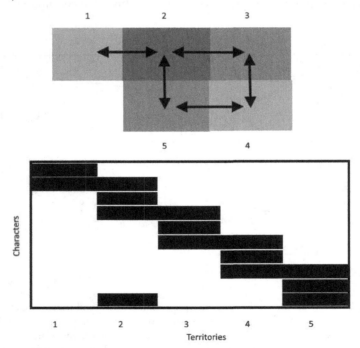

Fig. 9.16. Top: a sketch of a geographic map with five territories. Bottom: Geographic distribution of the characters. The example is discussed in the text.

Outerplanar networks model cultural traits propagation through diffusion and population migrations. In that sense, the model is independent of the details of the cultural traits. The phylogenetic tree preserves geographic neighbor relationships if the tree reported on a geographic map is so that no two branches intersect. As the search for the origin is out of scope, the model does not require any clock model and removes a significant difficulty in modeling the evolution of cultural traits. Figure 9.16 shows an example where the data do not perfectly fit an outerplanar network but for which one may reconstruct the propagation of cultural traits between geographic regions (Figure 9.16a). The diffusion paths in Figure 9.16 are obtained from the ordering minimizing the contradiction. The circular order of the end nodes (1, 2, 3, 4, 5) matches the order drawn on a sketched geographic map.

9.5.1. *Application on the classification of myths' motifs*

Julien d' Huy [2013] had the idea to apply phylogenetic networks to the study of mythology, particularly the Polyphemus myth type, in which a person gets into a homestead of a master of animals' or a monstrous shepherd. The hero escapes by sticking to the hair of an animal. The Greek version is the most famous one, but other versions are found all over Eurasia and North America. The phylogenetic network permitted identifying non-tree-like descent processes and helped discuss relationships between the different versions.

Other works followed [Le Quell ec, 2015; d' Huy and Berezkin, 2017; Thuillard, Le Quellec, d' Huy, 2018] in the footsteps of Yuri Berezkin's systematic analysis of myth's motifs in world mythology [Berezkin 2005; Berezkin, 2017 and references thereein]. This section shows how the methods presented in previous sections apply to different applications.

Berezkin's [2015] database is the most comprehensive collection of myths' motifs, and it includes motifs from all populated continents. The corpus contains over 2264 motifs from over 934 different peoples from all over the world. The presence or absence of a motif among traditions is binary coded and was analyzed using the methods in the previous section. After ordering with the algorithms, the contradiction analysis showed that a subset of characters was well ordered and fulfilled to a good level the consecutive-one condition (Figure 9.17). Deviations to the consecutive-one condition are very informative. For instance, the Sub-Saharan cluster (4) contains motifs specific to Africa and some shared with Eurasia, East, and West Africa.

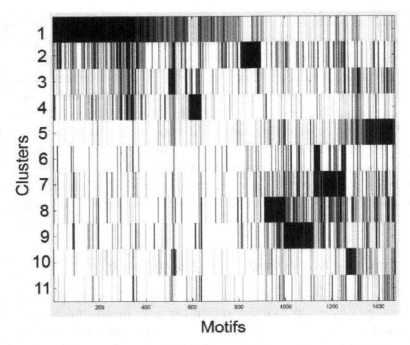

Fig. 9.17. Graphic representation of the average value on each of the 11 clusters (White: zero; Black: value larger than 0.15).

The characters and taxa were ordered with the algorithms defined in the previous section; the different characters formed eleven clusters:

1. Eurasia, North- and East Africa
2. Circumpolar Eurasia
3. Southeast Asia (part of Oceania)
4. Sub-Saharan Africa
5. South America (together with Papua, New Guinea)
6. Circumpolar America
7. Bering Strait
8. Northwest N. America
9. Central and East N. America
10. Pacific Coast (South- and North America), Mesoamerica
11. Oceania.

NeighborNet ordered both taxa and characters in separate runs. The ordering of the characters was quite efficient, even though the characters do not fit perfectly an outerplanar network topology. The reader may consult the original article to visualize the different clusters on a map [Thuillard, Le Quellec, d' Huy, 2018].

About half the characters are compatible with the classification. Quite surprisingly, the classification of the remaining motifs results in a second subset of motifs well described by a second outerplanar network, different from the first one. The analysis of the two networks shows that 'Creation myths,' origin motifs, and well-known motifs such as the cultural hero or the rainbow snake are a core concern in the first corpus of motifs.

In contrast, celestial bodies (moon and the sun) are a central focus in the second corpus, together with animals and trickster stories. The second corpus contains most motifs with an extended geographical distribution, and it includes many motifs present in most regions.

Subsequent analysis showed that the two clusters contain motifs with a different geographic distribution. While many motifs are found in many continents, their distribution is biased toward two large areas, as shown in Figure 9.18.

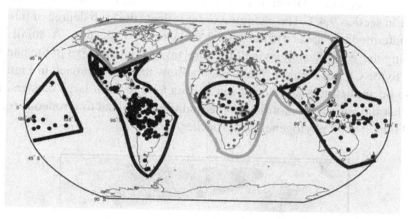

Fig. 9.18. Two corpora include the most widespread world myths' motifs. The traditions with gray dots have an over-proportion of motifs associated with the first corpus, with many motifs linked to women, men, animals, or death. The black dots represent traditions with an over-proportion of motifs associated with the second corpus containing many motifs related to the sun and the moon.

The above study demonstrates the power of the contradiction approach to identify deviations to an outerplanar structure at the single taxon or character level or as a whole. Low contradiction values define characters that define clusters in well-defined regions. Validation is key to the proper interpretation of the results, and the contradiction approach is well suited to it. Another learning is that Neighbor-Net is an excellent tool for clustering. Many characters cluster in some large regions (Figure 9.17). Within such a region, the distribution of characters is primarily random and does not fit an outerplanar network. Neighbor-Net identifies the clusters, and the outerplanar network structure describes how the different regions connect. Neighbor-Net is significantly better than the treelet method for taxa ordering. The treelet algorithm does not always find a circular order associated with a matrix satisfying the consecutive-one property. Therefore, the algorithm is not well-suited to data fitting an outerplanar network. For character ordering, treelet furnished comparable results.

Let us now show an example using the methods in section 9.4. Berezkin's database contains many motifs associated with ancient traditions, and the characters present in at least one old tradition are selected. Most ancient traditions (Sumer, Akkad, Babylon, Phoenicia, ancient Italy, and Egypt) with few motifs in the databank show a very high level of contradiction after classification and are here not further discussed. The ancient traditions (ancient Greece, China, and early Scandinavian literature) with the most motifs (resp. 177, 117, 74 motifs) are embedded in the three regions in Figure 9.19. The white spots represent areas that are difficult to classify. The main clusters are stable, but their order depends on the D factor in section 9.4.1. The changing order reflects the high degree of interaction in the intermediate areas (white areas) and between clusters. A small cluster containing the 'early Scandinavian literature' taxon contains taxa in the band from Iceland to the Chinese region. These results show that the approach in Figure 9.12 can also be applied to a large databank as data tend to form large clusters. It also shows that the paucity of motifs in some traditions can lead to erroneous results, a general issue for all phylogenetic approaches.

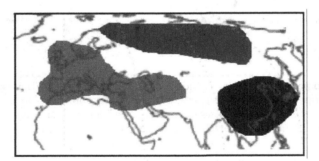

Fig. 9.19. Classification of ancient motifs. Three clusters form around taxa containing early Chinese literature (black) and ancient Greece (light gray), and North Eurasian taxa. The white regions include traditions that are often difficult to classify with their position in a circular order depending significantly on the coefficient D.

9.6. Continuous characters: Classification of galaxies

For continuous characters, another condition replaces the consecutive-one requirement.

Condition for an outerplanar network with continuous character' states:
A curve relating consecutive values of the circular order is so that a horizontal line crosses the curve at most twice [Thuillard and Fraix-Burnet, 2009]. If each character/variable fulfills this condition, an outerplanar network perfectly describes the data (Figure 9.20).

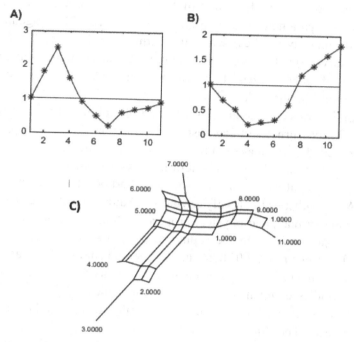

Fig. 9.20. The two characters in A and B fulfill the Kalmanson inequalities (9.9) as any horizontal line crosses the curve at most twice. An outerplanar network can perfectly represent the two characters.

Galaxies are incredibly complex systems, and classification based on morphology alone is insufficient. Hubble [1926] proposed a morphological classification scheme of galaxies. Hubble classified the galaxies into three principal families, the elliptical, the spirals, and the barred spirals. Fraix-Burnet [2004] pioneered a classification approach integrating morphological features with different physical and chemical parameters using phylogenetic methods. The approach is known as Astrocladistics. In biology, cladistics group organisms into clades based on their similarities in an evolution scheme. After classifying the galaxies' characters, the different objects correspond to the end nodes of a tree and show the proximity relation between families of galaxies. A good validation strategy consists of comparing the results obtained by different approaches. In a study, six parameters were selected (central velocity dispersion, the disc-to-bulge ratio, the effective surface brightness, the metallicity, and the line indices NaD and OIII). The study used different approaches to classify the data. The various techniques resulted in an excellent agreement with the cladistics approach. The minimum contradiction approach described in the last section is one of these techniques. After having tested the method on a small sample of 100 galaxies, the approach was applied to the above six parameter-space [Fraix-Burnet *et al.*, 2012] together with the cladistic and other approaches (see Fraix-Burnet, Thuillard, and Chattopadhyay [2015] for a survey on classification methods). The paper suggests an explanatory classification of galaxies based on various physical properties instead of a descriptive, morphological classification.

Other applications include the classification of globular clusters [Fraix-Burnet *et al.*, 2009; Fraix-Burnet and Davoust, 2015], Gamma-Ray bursts [Cardone and Fraix-Burnet, 2013], and quasars [Fraix-Burnet *et al.*, 2017].

In recent years, other fields did benefit from Astrocladistics. Jofré *et al.* [2017] describe the chemical evolution of solar neighborhood stars. Holt *et al.* [2018, 2021] use Astrocladistics to classify Jovian and Saturnian satellites based on their physical, compositional, and physical properties. A more recent study focuses on the Jovian Trojan swarms. In the Jupiter orbit, two swarms of solar objects are close to the Lagrange point, 60° head and 60° behind Jupiter. The Lagrange points are the positions in space where objects tend to stay as the gravitational attraction of two large bodies compensates. By convention, these objects are named after one hero of Greek mythology. In 2021, the catalog of Jovian Trojans contained over 9800 objects. The Lucy space probe, successfully launched in 2021, is on a 12 years journey to seven Jovian trojan asteroids. The cladistic study integrates different properties of the asteroids and provides a more refined classification. The results suggest a hierarchical structure of the objects, with the larger clusters of objects having a possible common origin. With the next-generation wide-field surveys and the Lucy mission, the knowledge of the Jovian Trojans will massively expand, and the astrocladistics approach may help classify the future findings.

9.7. Outlook

The analysis of graphs is very important to information theory, and many research resources are dedicated to finding better learning and classification methods. The difficulty of learning in the context of a graph is that its topology also has to be learned. Deep learning on images with convolution networks is already difficult, but imagine learning on images with randomly selected pixels! Let us focus on tree topologies to explain some of the problems. A classification or learning problem on a tree consists of intertwined stages: determining the neighborhood between nodes (i.e., an order in trees and networks), finding and verifying the underlying topology. We have discussed the power of spectral analysis for ordering and have succinctly discussed multiresolution approaches for deep learning. For complex topologies, the difficulty with the spectral approach is that the underlying wavelets are not very intuitive, and the results are often not simple to interpret.

Ideally, after learning, one may want to visualize a tree at different resolutions. The simplest approach consists of pruning the tree to contain only a few low-resolution branches, while high resolutions furnish a more detailed view. The problem is not as simple as it may look. Roughly speaking, the question is how to prune the tree. Treelet is a possible answer to that problem. The algorithm constructs both a tree and a multiresolution representation directly from unstructured data. The correlation coefficient determines which variables to merge in the tree. The algorithm is not optimal on all trees and networks.

Sections 9.3-9.4 indicate another research direction. Some data do fit approximately to a tree topology. Ordering the different branches in a circular order leads naturally to a multiresolution approach (see sections 9.3 and 9.4). The contradiction in the circular order is a simple loss function on the order of the taxa. The loss function is useful for classifying data, selecting data fitting best a tree or a network topology, and deciding how to prune a tree in a classification task.

Interestingly, there is a connection between the spectral approach and ordering the taxa on a tree and network through Fiedler's analysis described in 9.1.3. For a perfect outerplanar network, ordering using the spectral approach and NeighborNet approach furnish identical results. Numerical simulations show that the spectral approach is less robust against noise than NeighborNet. At least for the ordering problem, the non-spectral approach is better than the spectral one. The difficulty with non-spectral approaches is the localization of the neighbors to a node. NeighborNet elegantly solves that issue in phylogenetic trees and networks. Once that issue is solved, multiresolution analysis becomes simple. Defining a node's neighborhood can become very challenging for more complex topologies, and more research work is needed.

References

Bandelt, H.J., Dress, A.W. (1992). Split decomposition: a new and useful approach to phylogenetic analysis of distance data, *Mol. Phylogenet Evol.*1:242-52.

Berezkin, Y.E. (2005). Cosmic Hunt: Variants of Siberian-North American Myth, *Folklore: Electronic Journal of Folklore*, (31), pp. 79-100.

Berezkin, Y.E. (2012). Folklore parallels between Siberia and South Asia and the mythology of the Eurasian steppes, *Archaeology, Ethnology and Anthropology of Eurasia*, 40(4), pp. 144-155.

Berezkin, Y.E. (2015). Folklore and mythology catalogue: its lay-out and potential for research, *The Retrospective Methods Network*, (S10), pp. 58-70.

Berezkin, Y.E. (2017). *Peopling of the New World from data on distributions of folklore motifs*, in Maths meets myths: quantitative approaches to ancient narratives (Springer) pp. 71-89.

Bouckaert, R.R., Bowern, C. and Atkinson, Q.D. (2018). The origin and expansion of Pama–Nyungan languages across Australia, *Nature ecology & evolution*, 2(4), pp. 741-749.

Bronstein, M.M., Bruna, J., Cohen, T. and Veličković, P. (2021). Geometric deep learning: Grids, groups, graphs, geodesics, and gauges, *arXiv preprint arXiv:2104.13478*.

Bruna, J., Zaremba, W., Szlam, A. and LeCun, Y. (2013). Spectral networks and locally connected networks on graphs, *arXiv preprint* arXiv:1312.6203.

Bryant, D. and Moulton, V. (2004). Neighbor-net: an agglomerative method for the construction of phylogenetic networks, *Molecular biology and evolution*, 21(2), pp. 255-265.

Cardone, V.F. and Fraix-Burnet, D. (2013). Hints for families of gamma-ray bursts improving the Hubble diagram, *Monthly Notices of the Royal Astronomical Society*, 434(3), pp. 1930-1938.

Coifman, R.R. and Maggioni, M. (2006). Diffusion wavelets, *Applied and computational harmonic analysis*, 21(1), pp. 53-94.

Defferrard, M., Bresson, X., & Vandergheynst, P. (2016). Convolutional neural networks on graphs with fast localized spectral filtering, *Advances in neural information processing systems*, 29, 3844-3852.

Donoho, D.L. (1997). CART and best-ortho-basis: a connection, *The Annals of Statistics*, 25(5), pp. 1870-1911.

Fiedler, M. (1974). Eigenvalues of nonnegative symmetric matrices, *Linear Algebra and its Applications*, 9, pp. 119-142.

Fraix-Burnet, D. (2004). First phylogenetic analyses of galaxy evolution, in *Penetrating Bars through Masks of Cosmic Dust* (Springer, Dordrecht). pp. 301-305

Fraix-Burnet, D., Chattopadhyay, T., Chattopadhyay, A.K., Davoust, E., and Thuillard, M. (2012). A six-parameter space to describe galaxy diversification, *Astronomy & Astrophysics*, 545, p. A80.

Fraix-Burnet, D. and Davoust, E. (2015). Stellar populations in ω Centauri: a multivariate analysis, *Monthly Notices of the Royal Astronomical Society*, 450(4), pp. 3431-3441.

Fraix-Burnet, D., d'Onofrio, M. and Marziani, P. (2017). Phylogenetic analyses of quasars and galaxies, *Frontiers in Astronomy and Space Sciences*, 4, p. 20.

Fraix-Burnet, D., Thuillard, M. and Chattopadhyay, A.K. (2015). Multivariate approaches to classification in extragalactic astronomy, *Frontiers in Astronomy and Space Sciences*, 2, p. 3.

Hammond, D.K., Vandergheynst, P. and Gribonval, R. (2011). Wavelets on graphs via spectral graph theory, *Applied and Computational Harmonic Analysis*, 30(2), pp. 129-150.

Holt, T.R., Brown, A.J., Nesvorný, D., Horner, J. and Carter, B. (2018). Cladistical analysis of the Jovian and Saturnian satellite systems, *The Astrophysical Journal*, 859(2), p. 97.

Holt, T.R., Horner, J., Nesvorný, D., King, R., Popescu, M., Carter, B.D. and Tylor, C.C. (2021). Astrocladistics of the Jovian Trojan Swarms, *Monthly Notices of the Royal Astronomical Society*, 504(2), pp. 1571-1608.

Hubble E.P. (1926). Extra-galactic nebulae, Contributions from the Mount Wilson Observatory/ Carnegie Institution of Washington.

d'Huy, J. (2013). Polyphemus (Aa. Th. 1137): A phylogenetic reconstruction of a prehistoric tale, *Nouvelle Mythologie Comparée/New Comparative Mythology*, 1(1), http-nouvellemythologiecompare e.

d'Huy, J. and Berezkin, Y. (2017). How did the first humans perceive the starry night? On the Pleiades, *The Retrospective Methods Network Newsletter*, (12-13), pp. 100-122.

Jila, N. (2006). Myths and traditional beliefs about the wolf and the crow in Central Asia: examples from the Turkic Wu-Sun and the Mongols, *Asian Folklore Studies*, pp. 161-177.

Jofré, P., Das, P., Bertranpetit, J. and Foley, R. (2017). Cosmic phylogeny: reconstructing the chemical history of the solar neighbourhood with an evolutionary tree, *Monthly Notices of the Royal Astronomical Society*, 467(1), pp. 1140-1153.

Kipf, T.N. and Welling, M. (2016). Semi-supervised classification with graph convolutional networks, *arXiv preprint* arXiv:1609.02907.

Le Quellec, J.L. (2015). Peut-on retrouver les mythes préhistoriques? L'exemple des récits anthropogoniques, *Comptes rendus des séances de l'Académie des Inscriptions et Belles-Lettres*, 159(1), pp. 235-266. (in French)

Lee, A.B., Nadler, B., and Wasserman, L. (2008). Treelets: an adaptive multi-scale basis for sparse unordered data, *Annals of Applied Statistics*, 2(2):437-471.

Levy, D. and Pachter, L. (2011). The neighbor-net algorithm, *Advances in Applied Mathematics*, 47(2), pp. 240-258.

Neureiter, N., Ranacher, P., van Gijn, R., Bickel, B. and Weibel, R. (2021). Can Bayesian phylogeography reconstruct migrations and expansions in linguistic evolution?. *Royal Society open science*, 8(1), p. 201079.

Russell, T., Silva, F., & Steele, J. (2014). Modelling the spread of farming in the Bantu-speaking regions of Africa: an archaeology-based phylogeography, *PLoS One*, 9(1), e87854.

Su, X., Xue, S., Liu, F., Wu, J., Yang, J., Zhou, C., Hu, W., Paris, C., Nepal, S., Jin, D. and Sheng, Q.Z. (2022). A comprehensive survey on community detection with deep learning, *IEEE Transactions on Neural Networks and Learning Systems*.

Thuillard, M. (2009). Why phylogenetic trees are often quite robust against lateral transfers, in *Evolutionary Biology* (Springer, Berlin, Heidelberg), pp. 269-283.

Kalmanson K. (1975). Edgeconvex circuits and the traveling salesman problem, *Can. J. Math.* 27:1000-10.

Thuillard, M. and Fraix-Burnet, D. (2009). Phylogenetic applications of the minimum contradiction approach on continuous characters, *Evolutionary Bioinformatics*, 5, pp.EBO-S2505.

Thuillard, M. and Moulton, V. (2011). Identifying and reconstructing lateral transfers from distance matrices by combining the minimum contradiction method and neighbor-net, *Journal of bioinformatics and computational biology*, 9(04), 453-470.

Thuillard, M., Le Quellec, J.L., d' Huy, J. and Berezkin, Y. (2018). A large-scale study of world myths, *Trames: A Journal of the Humanities and Social Sciences*, 22(4), pp. A1-A44.

Wu, Z., Pan, S., Chen, F., Long, G., Zhang, C. and Philip, S.Y. (2020). A comprehensive survey on graph neural networks, *IEEE transactions on neural networks and learning systems*, 32(1), pp. 4-24.

Xu, B., Shen, H., Cao, Q., Qiu, Y., & Cheng, X. (2019). Graph Wavelet Neural Network, *In International Conference on Learning Representations (ICLR 2019)*.

Yu, B., Yin, H. and Zhu, Z. (2018). Spatio-temporal graph convolutional networks: a deep learning framework for traffic forecasting, *Proceedings of the 27th International Joint Conference on Artificial Intelligence*. pp. 3634-3640.

Zhang, Z., Cui, P. and Zhu, W. (2020). Deep Learning on Graphs: A Survey, *IEEE Transactions on Knowledge & Data Engineering*, (01), pp.1-24.

Zhou, J., Cui, G., Hu, S., Zhang, Z., Yang, C., Liu, Z., Wang, L., Li, C. and Sun, M. (2020). Graph neural networks: A review of methods and applications, *AI Open*, 1, pp. 57-81.

Genetic Algorithms and Multiresolution

Part 10

Chapter 10

Genetic Algorithms and Multiresolution

The primary purpose of this part is to explain the connections between genetic algorithms and multiresolution analysis. Genetic algorithms relate centrally to multiresolution analysis in problems using binary coding of integers. Bethke [1981] made a significant first step in that direction by introducing Walsh partition functions in the field of genetic algorithms. Essential insights into the working of genetic algorithms, particularly the building block hypothesis, have been unraveled using Walsh functions. Haar wavelets better capture the building block hypothesis than Walsh's partition. In this chapter, a simple wavelet-based genetic algorithm is constructed and discussed within the framework of Haar wavelets. The algorithm uses a single operator that shares some features of the crossover and mutation operators. The wavelet-based genetic algorithm is methodologically interesting and simple enough to furnish some analytical results while preserving some essential features of genetic algorithms.

10.1. The standard genetic algorithm

The standard genetic algorithm is undoubtedly a good prototype algorithm for genetic algorithms [Goldberg, 1991] though not the algorithm of choice in applications. The standard genetic algorithm uses strings described by a binary alphabet B={0,1} to encode possible solutions to an optimization or search problem. The different strings form what is called a population. At each generation, the algorithm selects new strings according to their fitness. Some of them are modified with the crossover and mutation operators and included in the next generation.

The standard genetic algorithm is often explained based on the fundamental theorem of genetic algorithms. This theorem furnishes a bound to the probability of a schema H defined on the alphabet S={0,1,*}. The alphabet S corresponds to the alphabet B together with the symbol *, which represents *any symbol in B*. For example, consider the schema H=(1,0,*,0). It contains the two strings (1,0,0,0) and (1,0,1,0).

Wavelets in Soft Computing

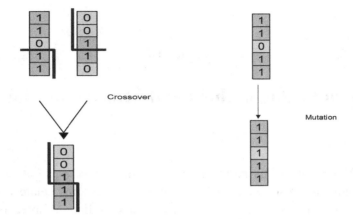

Fig. 10.1. The standard genetic algorithm uses the crossover and the mutation operator.

The standard genetic algorithm uses two operators: crossover and mutation. The crossover operator splits two strings at a given point and exchanges one segment with the other string (Figure 10.1). Crossover tends to preserve compact and short substrings.

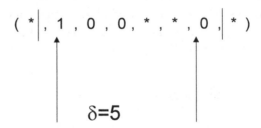

Fig. 10.2. A schema consists of a string of symbols belonging to the alphabet S={0,1,*}. The useful length of the string δ is the distance (or the number of positions) between the first and the last symbol in the schema belonging to the alphabet B={0,1}. The number of symbols in the schema belonging to the alphabet B is called the order O of the schema.

The smaller the useful length, the smaller the chance that a crossover will disrupt a schema (The useful length δ is the distance, or the number of positions, between the first and the last symbol in the schema belonging to the alphabet B). In the above example (Figure 10.2), the crossover will only disrupt the schema if the splitting point is at one of the two positions given by the line. A crossing point at any other location may result in a disruption of the schema.

The mutation operator modifies one bit (also called allele by analogy to biology) in the string. A schema is disrupted by a mutation only if the symbol is different from *. The number of symbols in the schema belonging to the alphabet B is called the order O of the schema. Mutations tend to preserve low-order schemata.

In the standard version of the genetic algorithm, the survival probability of a string s is chosen proportional to f(s)/f with f(s) the fitness of the string s and f the average fitness over all strings. The fundamental theorem of genetic algorithms states that the expectation of the number of instances of a given schema H, m(H, t), can be written under the form of the following inequality [Holland, 1992]:

$$E(m(H, t + 1))$$
$$\geq m(H, t) \cdot f(H)/f \cdot [1 - p_c \cdot \delta(H)/(l - 1) - p_m \cdot O(H)] \quad (10.1)$$

with p_c the crossover probability, p_m the mutation probability, f(H) the average fitness of the schema, and f the average fitness over all strings.

Short schemata with an above-average fitness and a short useful length will increase in number very rapidly, while high order schemata with below-average fitness values rapidly disappear. Genetic algorithms find excellent solutions to many optimization problems by assembling parts of good solutions. This hypothesis is often called the building block hypothesis. Short, low-order schemata with above-average fitness combine to form better solutions. Despite the many successes of genetic algorithms, many challenges stay. One of them is finding out which problems fulfill the building block hypothesis. Partition functions furnish the first approach to this question [Bethke, 1980, 1980; Horn and Goldberg, 1995]. Using the Walsh partition functions, Goldberg [1989] did construct functions that do not fulfill the building block hypothesis. These so-called deceptive functions offer insight into the working of genetic algorithms.

10.2. Walsh functions and genetic algorithms

10.2.1. *Walsh functions*

Walsh functions take only a value of 1 or -1 on the support of length L. Figure 10.3 shows the Walsh functions with L=8.

In matrix form, the Walsh transform W of a vector x is given by

$$W = M \cdot x \quad (10.2)$$

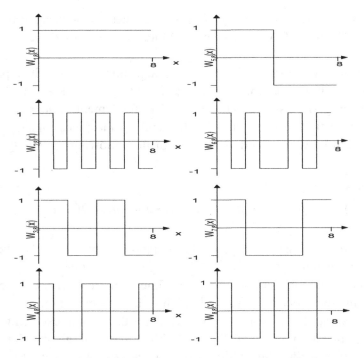

Fig. 10.3. Walsh functions on the support of length L=8.

The following expression defines the matrix M:

$$M_{i,j} = -1^{bc(i,j)} \tag{10.3}$$

with bc(i,j) the number of 1 set in the string defined by the expression bit AND (i,j).

Walsh partition functions form an orthonormal basis. A vector can therefore be decomposed on the Walsh functions and reconstructed losslessly. The decomposition is given by

$$\omega_i = (M \cdot x)_i \tag{10.4}$$

The Walsh coefficient ω_i corresponds to its projection on the ith Walsh partition function. From the Walsh coefficients, one reconstructs the original vector:

$$x = 1/(i_{max} + 1)\sum_i \omega_i M_i \tag{10.5}$$

Example:
The Walsh basis functions for i,j ={0,1,2,3} is:

$$M = \begin{pmatrix} 1 & 1 & 1 & 1 \\ 1 & -1 & 1 & -1 \\ 1 & 1 & -1 & -1 \\ 1 & -1 & \boxed{-1} & 1 \end{pmatrix}$$

Let us verify this with (i = 2, j = 3, circle). The expression bit AND (2,3) is

bit AND[(1,0),(1,1)] = (1,0)

The number of 1 in the bit AND expression is bc(i,j) = 1 and M(2,3) = -1. Consider as an example the decomposition of the vector x = (1,0,1,0). The Walsh coefficients ω_j (j = 0...,3) corresponding to the projection on the different Walsh functions are given by $\omega_i = (M \cdot x)_i$. One obtains $\omega_0 = 2$; $\omega_1 = 2$; $\omega_2 = 0$; $\omega_3 = 0$ and it is easily verified that ¼ (2 M_1 + 2 M_2) = x with M_i the ith column of M corresponding to the ith Walsh partition function.

10.2.2. *An alternative description of the Walsh functions using the formalism of wavelet packets*

Walsh functions are related to Haar wavelets and can be deduced from the multiresolution Haar decomposition independently from (10.3). The following section introduces the Walsh functions using the formalism of wavelet packets. Recall that a tree composed of low-pass and high-pass filter cascades represents the dyadic wavelet decomposition. Figure 10.4 shows an example giving the tree representation of a three levels wavelet decomposition.

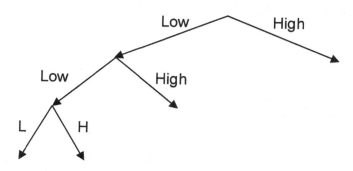

Fig. 10.4. Tree representation of a wavelet decomposition.

The wavelet decomposition can be generalized to wavelet packets, represented in Figure 10.4 by a subtree of the complete decomposition tree. The complete decomposition tree corresponds to all possible dyadic decompositions of a signal with two filters fulfilling the power complementarity condition. Figure 10.5 shows the complete tree for a 3-levels decomposition.

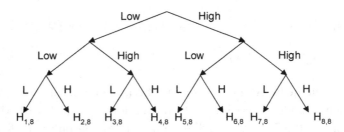

Fig. 10.5. Full decomposition tree.

One observes a correspondence between the Walsh wavelet packets and the complete decomposition tree for the Haar function. At the Jth level of decomposition, each function on which the signal is projected, corresponds to one basis Walsh function of support $L=2^J$.

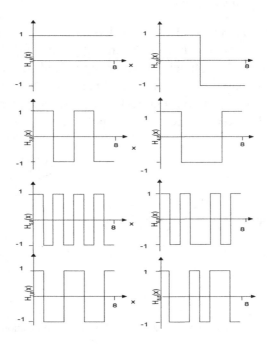

Fig. 10.6. Functions corresponding to the end nodes of the complete decomposition tree in Figure 10.5 with L=8.

Assume a signal of length L and a full decomposition tree using a Haar wavelet as the mother wavelet. The L functions of support L corresponding to the end nodes of the full tree are the Walsh functions. Figure 10.6 shows it for J=3, and the result holds for Walsh functions of any order. One can verify that the functions in Figure 10.6 are the same as in Figure 10.3. It follows that signal decomposition on Walsh functions is lossless and invertible. The original signal can be perfectly reconstructed starting from the coefficients at the last decomposition levels.

10.2.3. *On deceptive functions in genetic algorithms*

Binary coding transforms a number into a string. The integer i is coded as an L bits string in base 2: <a_1,...,a_L> with

$$i = \sum_{k=1}^{L} a_k \cdot 2^{L-k} \tag{10.6}$$

Assume that a fitness function $f(a_1, \ldots, a_L)$ can be associated to all strings $(a_1, \ldots, a_L)$. The average fitness value on all strings f (*,...,*) is given by the expression:

$$f(*, \ldots, *) = 1/2^L \cdot \sum_{all\ strings} f(a_1, \ldots, a_L) \tag{10.7}$$

or in terms of the first Walsh function:

$$f(*, \ldots, *) = 1/2^L \cdot \sum_{allstrings} f(a_1, \ldots, a_L) \cdot H_{1,L} \tag{10.8}$$

Similarly, the average fitness function of strings of the form (0,*,...,*) is

$$f(0, *\ldots, *) = 1/2^{L-1} \cdot \sum_{all\ strings} f(a_1, \ldots, a_L) \cdot (H_{1,L} - H_{2,L}) \tag{10.9}$$

A genetic algorithm may be deceived by a function with low order schemata of high average fitness containing no optimal solution. Goldberg [1989, 1991] designed intrinsically difficult problems for genetic algorithms using the Walsh functions. The building block hypothesis does not hold for such examples, and genetic algorithms are generally worse than a random search.

The Walsh functions are a conceptually powerful tool for understanding genetic algorithms. Many subtrees of the full decomposition tree in Figure 10.5 are suited for discussing the building block hypothesis. In particular, the Haar wavelet basis, as defined by the subtree in Figure 10.4, is more adapted to the discussion of some genetic algorithms. The following section presents such an algorithm.

10.3. Wavelet-based genetic algorithms

This section discusses a very simple genetic algorithm that captures many of the ideas behind evolutionary computing in the context of multiresolution. The algorithm uses an operator that combines some of the crossover's main features and the mutation operator. This genetic algorithm is conceptually interesting as mathematical expressions for the expectation of schemata of the type $<a_1,...,a_i,*,...,*>$ can be exactly computed in terms of a Haar wavelet decomposition. The proposed algorithm is simple enough to be explained with multiresolution analysis. Despite its simplicity, the algorithm still captures the essence of the standard genetic algorithm.

As in the previous sections, one uses binary coding. Let us consider a function f of one variable. The function $f(x_i)$ is a function of the integer 'i' and can be interpreted as a_i's fitness with $a_i = <a_1,...,a_4>$ and $i = \sum_{k=1}^{4} a_k \cdot 2^{4-k}$.

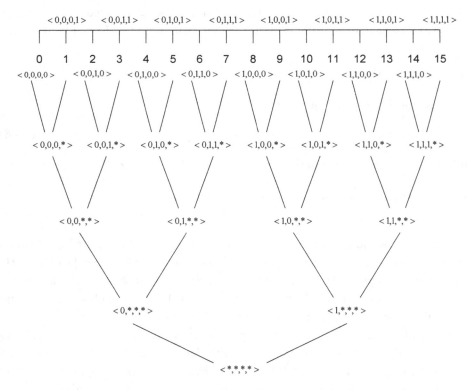

Fig. 10.7. The multiresolution structure of schemata $H=<a_1,..,a_j,*,...*>$ is illustrated for L=4. Integers in the range $[0,2^L-1]$ are expressed in base 2.

Figure 10.7 shows the multiresolution character of the schema formulation. The fitness of an L bits schema $<a_1,...,a_k,*,*,*>$ corresponds to the average value of the fitness function on 2^{L-k} adjacent values. The average fitness can be computed using a 2^{L-k} dilated Haar function.

The wavelet-based genetic algorithm works as sketched in Figure 10.8. A string of fitness f_i is replicated on average $\gamma \cdot f_i$ times. Each string in the new generation is modified with probability P_m by an operator O_m, $(m = \{0,1,...,L\})$. The operator O_m randomly replaces the last m bits in the strings. If m=0, all bits are randomly replaced, while the string is kept unchanged for m=L (L is the number of bits in the string). The probability of splitting the string at position m is described by the values P_m, satisfying

$$\sum_{m=0}^{L} P_m = 1.$$

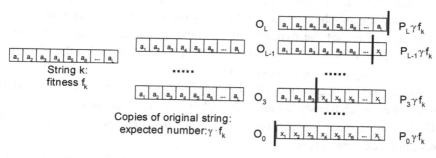

Fig. 10.8. A simple wavelet-based genetic algorithm is designed by replacing the crossover and the mutation operators in the standard genetic algorithm with a single operator. The operator O_m replaces the last m bits randomly.

10.3.1. *The wavelet-based genetic algorithm in the Haar wavelet formalism*

Understanding when and why genetic algorithms work well is a complicated question. On the one hand, numerous successful applications of genetic algorithms tend to prove the efficiency of genetic algorithms in many situations. On the other hand, theoretical considerations have led to a number of no free lunch theorems that clearly show that the blind application of genetic algorithms on a randomly chosen problem has a chance of less than 50% to be better than a random search, Much research has been done to understand emergent behaviors in genetic algorithms to escape that apparent paradox. Several researchers have followed this line, and here one should mention the work by Vose [1999]. He dedicated a book to a mathematical discussion of the so-called simple genetic algorithm. This model is very similar to the standard genetic algorithm from Holland. The main difference is that only one gene is kept after crossover. This minor simplification makes the system solvable.

The expectation of the number of strings at generation (p+1) can be computed from the expectation at step p by applying an operator G. The iterative application of the operator G defines the trajectory of the expected population. Different behaviors may be expected, depending on the number and the type of fixed points of the transform. If the matrix is irreducible and the coefficients of the matrix G are everywhere positive, then there exists a unique eigenvector with positive coefficients. In the limit of an infinitely large population, the population follows the trajectory defined by G and converges towards a fixed population. If the vector G has several eigenvectors, it can be shown that in the limit of an infinite population, the system will spend most of the time in the vicinity of the fixed points. Despite its many successes, the study of the simple genetic algorithm did not contribute much to reducing the gap between applications and theory. The main reason is that the dynamic of the simple genetic algorithm is often so complex that it is difficult to draw general conclusions. As soon as the system has several positive eigenvectors, the relevance of the results to understanding small population dynamics is questionable. This problem leads us to consider a simpler algorithm, the wavelet-based genetic algorithm described in the previous section. The discussion of the wavelet-based algorithm furnishes results that may guide choosing the free parameters.

A lesson of past years is that it is necessary to precisely define the coding method of the solutions and the genetic operators. The genetic algorithm's efficiency generally depends very centrally on the choice of the coding method [Reeves, 2014]. We explain the wavelet-based genetic algorithm using binary coding of integers in the following. Let us point out here that most results in the subsequent sections are not specific to Haar wavelets. Many of the results apply to a large class of wavelet-based algorithms with a multiresolution search space structure. The multiresolution subdivision of the search space defines proximity relationships between the strings: Two close strings belong to the domain of definition of a well-localized, high-resolution Haar function. In contrast, distant strings belong only to the common domain of low-resolution Haar functions. A non-trivial example is given in annex B, based on a nonlinear wavelet construction.

In the two following sections, we will relate the wavelet-based genetic algorithm to wavelet theory and filtering theory in the framework of the infinite population approach. Assuming an infinite population simplifies the analysis. Due to the algorithm's simplicity compared to the simple genetic algorithm, the behavior of infinite populations provides a general framework to qualitatively understand the more complex and practically only relevant case of finite population sampling.

The probabilities P_m determine the evolution of the population. The evolution equation of a schema of the form $H = a_1 a_2 \ldots a_k *, \ldots, **$ can be computed. Without limitations and simplifying the notations, we assume that $a_1 = a_2 = \ldots = a_k = 0$. The expected number of strings n_H with H at generation p+1 is

$$E(n_{a_1 a_2 a_3 \ldots a_k * \ldots **}) = \gamma \cdot [(\sum_{m=0}^{k-1} \sum_{i=1}^{N \cdot 2^{-m}} 2^{m-k} \cdot f_i \cdot n_i) \cdot P_m +$$
$$\sum_{m=k}^{L} (\sum_{i=1}^{N \cdot 2^{-m}} f_i \cdot n_i) \cdot P_m] \tag{10.10a}$$

For k=0, one obtains

$$E(n_{* \ldots ***}) = \gamma \cdot (\sum_{i=1}^{N} f_i \cdot n_i) \tag{10.10b}$$

n_i is the number of strings at generation p representing the solution with integer value i, f_i the corresponding fitness value, and $N = 2^L$. After some manipulations, one obtains the first main result, namely an expression relating the expectation of schemata to the detail coefficients $d_{k,j}$ of the Haar wavelet decomposition of $f(a_i) \cdot n(a_i)$ at the previous generation:

$$E(n_{a_1 a_2 \ldots a_k = 0 * \ldots **}) - E(n_{a_1 a_2 \ldots a_k = 1 * \ldots **}) = d_{k,j} \cdot \gamma \cdot \sum_{m=k}^{L} P_m \tag{10.11a}$$

$$E(n_{* \ldots **}) = \gamma \cdot (\sum_{i=1}^{N} f_i \cdot n_i) = \gamma \cdot c_{1,1} \tag{10.11b}$$

From (10.11a), one concludes that the expectation of

$$n_{a_1 a_2 a_3 \ldots a_k = 0 * \ldots **} - n_{a_1 a_2 a_3 \ldots a_k = 1 * \ldots **}$$

is proportional to the corresponding Haar detail coefficient $d_{k,j}$ of $fn(a_i) = f(a_i) \cdot n(a_i)$.

Figure 10.9 illustrates this result with one example. In this example, a uniform probability distribution gives the disruption point: $(P_0 = \ldots = P_{k+1} = 1/(k+1))$. At each generation, the algorithm obtains a population from a random sampling with a probability proportional to the distribution of the values. At generation p, a population with a random distribution $fn(a_i) = f(a_i) \cdot n(a_i)$ is taken. The population at step p+1 is obtained using the genetic algorithm with a uniform distribution of disruptions points. The distribution of the different schemata is estimated from the average of a large number of simulations. The empirical distribution was subsequently decomposed into its wavelet coefficients and compared to the wavelet coefficients of $fn(a_i) = f(a_i) \cdot n(a_i)$. Both wavelets coefficients are to a factor identical.

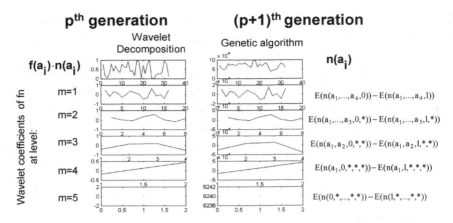

Fig. 10.9. The expectation of a schema $<a_1,...a_j,*,...*>$ at the $p+1^{th}$ generation is inferred from the wavelet coefficients of the function $fn(a_i) = f(a_i) \cdot n(a_i)$ at generation p.

10.3.2. *The connection between the wavelet-based genetic algorithm and filter theory*

We have just shown that a schema expectation at the $p+1^{th}$ generation depends on the wavelet coefficients of the function $fn(a_i) = f(a_i) \cdot n(a_i)$ at generation p, with a_i the string coding for the number i. The relation to filter theory is straightforward. The dyadic wavelet decomposition with Haar wavelets corresponds to a filter tree. Figure 10.10 represents this procedure graphically. The expectation value of a given string at the $p+1^{th}$ generation can be computed by first decomposing the function $fn(a_i) = f(a_i) \cdot n(a_i)$ with Haar wavelets. In a second step, the algorithm multiplies the wavelet coefficients by a level-dependent factor $W_k = \sum_{m=k}^{L} P_m$. The signal is reconstructed using the wavelet reconstruction algorithm in the last step. As the weighting factor increases at a lower resolution, $1 = W_0 \geq W_1 \geq ... \geq W_L$. The effect corresponds to filtering the fitness-weighted distribution fn with a low-pass filter and leads us to the second main result: on average, low-order schemata with high fitness are privileged by wavelet-based genetic algorithms. The low-frequency part of the population distribution f_n is weighted more than the high-frequency part in the population of a new generation. More precisely, the weighting factor W_i increases at lower resolution: $1 = W_0 \geq W_1 \geq ... \geq W_L$.

The building block hypothesis can now be formulated for this genetic algorithm model. Low-order schemata of high average fitness guide the search, and the wavelet-based genetic algorithm favors regions with high average fitness values. The algorithm is a reasonable method for functions with maximal fitness values corresponding to regions with high average fitness. The search algorithm may be deceived by functions for which an optimum belongs to a region with a low average fitness at low resolution (This topic is developed further below).

Let us illustrate Eq. (10.10) with a second example showing the significant influence of the disruption probabilities P_m on the search. The following disruption probabilities P_m were chosen: $P_0=P_1=P_3=P_4=0$; $P_2=1$. At generation p, the algorithm generates a population with a random distribution proportional to $fn(a_i) = f(a_i) \cdot n(a_i)$. The algorithm uses a fixed disruption point after the second bit. The average of many simulations (Figure 10.11) furnishes an estimation of the expectation of the different schemata. One observes, as expected, that, on average, the sampling rate is almost constant over each of the four domains.

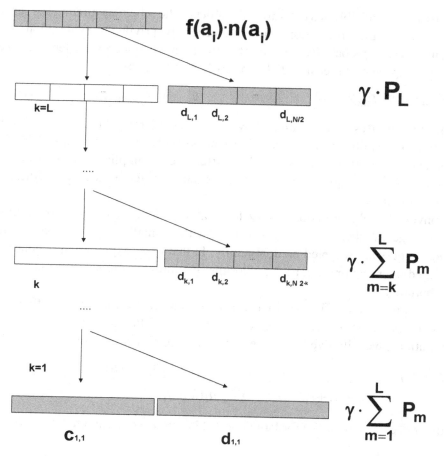

Fig. 10.10. The expectation value of a given string at the p+1th generation can be computed by first decomposing the function $fn(a_i) = f(a_i) \cdot n(a_i)$ with Haar wavelets, then multiplying the wavelet coefficients by a level-dependent factor (right) to reconstruct the signal finally from the weighted wavelet coefficients. This whole process corresponds to low-pass filtering of the original signal.

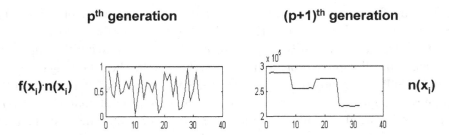

pth generation   **(p+1)th generation**

Fig. 10.11. Left: example showing the fitness-weighted number of strings $f(x_i)$ $n(x_i)$. The second level (P_2=1) generates four search regions. Right: schemata distribution at the $(p+1)^{th}$ generation at the pth generation. The operator randomly replaces the last 3 bits at each generation (P_2=1).

The disruption probabilities determine the order of the schemata guiding the search very centrally. Low-resolution sampling generally privileges exploration over exploitation. The probability P(not a) of a string *a* not being drawn after S samples in a search space of dimension 2^N has a low bound given by

$$P(not\ a) \leq S \cdot P_0/2^N \tag{10.12}$$

The probability P_0 sets, therefore, a lower limit to exploration. Large values of the disruption probability at low resolution tend to flatten the expected distribution curve, and Figure 10.11 shows this. The difference in sampling rates between the different regions is quite small despite the large differences in the fitness of individual strings.

Conversely, if one chooses very low values of the disruption probabilities P_m for large m, then high fitness strings with a small neighborhood of high average fitness are sampled predominantly. In that case, exploitation is generally privileged over exploration, as the algorithm explores mostly solutions in a small neighborhood.

Let us discuss the efficiency of a wavelet-based genetic algorithm starting from the evolution equation (10.11) expressed under the following form (To simplify the notations, we will give here the equation for the first string only):

$$n_1(k+1, f_1) = \gamma \cdot (P_L \cdot n_1(k) \cdot f_1 + P_{L-1} \cdot 1/2 \cdot \Sigma_{i=1}^2 n_j(k) \cdot$$
$$f_j + \ldots + P_0 \cdot 1/2^N \cdot \Sigma_{i=1}^{2^N} n_i(k) \cdot f_i) \tag{10.13}$$

As the trajectory converges for large k, (10.13) can be approximated by

$$0 \approx \alpha \cdot \frac{n_1(k+1, f_1)}{\bar{n}(k+1)} - \alpha \cdot \frac{n_1(k, f_1)}{\bar{n}(k)} =$$
$$\gamma \cdot ((P_L \cdot f_1 - \alpha/\gamma) \cdot n_1(k, f_1)/\bar{n}(k) + 1/\bar{n}(k) \cdot$$
$$(P_{L-1} \cdot 1/2 \cdot \Sigma_{i=1}^2 n_j(k) \cdot f_j + \ldots + P_0 \cdot 1/2^N \cdot \Sigma_{i=1}^{2^N} n_i(k) \cdot f_i)) \tag{10.14a}$$

with $\alpha = \lim_{k \to \infty} \bar{n}(k+1)/\bar{n}(k)$ and it follows

$$n_1(k, f_1)/\bar{n}(k) \cdot \approx 1/(\beta - P_L \cdot f) \cdot (P_{L-1} \cdot 1/2 \cdot$$

$$\sum_{i=1}^{2} n_j(k)/\bar{n}(k) \cdot f_j + \ldots + P_0 \cdot 1/2^N \cdot \sum_{i=1}^{2^N} n_i(k)/\bar{n}(k) \cdot f_i) \qquad (10.14b)$$

with $\beta = \alpha/\gamma$.

Equation (10.14) shows that at equilibrium, the distribution of the population follows locally a $\Delta_i/(\beta - P_L \cdot f)$ law, with Δ_i a constant depending on the disruption probabilities. The form of the function determines the search's efficiency. A constant value of Δ_i over the whole search space makes the distribution of a string independent of its neighbors. It is impossible to extract information from past samples, and the wavelet-based genetic algorithm is worse than a random search. Generally speaking, the wavelet-based genetic algorithm is only efficient if the objective string(s) is within a region of high average fitness. In that case, the algorithm focuses the search on those areas. In other words, an efficient search strategy is so that the objective string(s) must coincide with regions having a value of Δ_i well above average. A second condition for an efficient search of the objective string is that the values of the denominator $(\beta - P_L \cdot f)$ are small in comparison to Δ_i. Figure 10.12 illustrates this with a simple example. In that example, sampling is limited to the first and the last two resolution levels. Figure 10.12b represents the inverse of the sampling probability at equilibrium for the fitness distribution in Figure 10.12a. For each of the two regions in Figure 10.12a, the $\Delta_i/(\beta - P_L \cdot f)$ relationship predicted by (10.14) is observed.

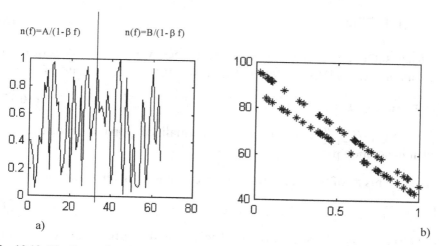

a)

b)

Fig. 10.12. The fitness function in a) is sampled with P0=0.3; P1=0.4; P7=0.3; P2=...=P6=0. b) The inverse of the distribution function at equilibrium is plotted as a function of the fitness value. The points are aligned on two lines; each line corresponds to one of the two segments in a).

In the example of Figure 10.12, the search will be quite inefficient, whatever the objective is, because Δ_i in both regions are quite similar and therefore the distribution function is essentially given by the denominator.

10.4. Population evolution and deceptive functions

The concept of deceptivity is central to genetic algorithms. The minimal objective of a genetic algorithm is to perform, on average better on a class of problems than a random search. If this minimal condition does not hold, we will say that the problem is deceptive for the considered algorithm. Let us estimate the different strings' expectations analytically to discuss deceptivity later. We have seen that the expectation $E^{(1)}(a_i)$ of a string a_i after a single generation is of the form

$$E^{(1)}(a_i) = G[f(a_i)] \tag{10.15}$$

with $G[f(a_i)] = \gamma \cdot (f_0 + \sum_{m,n} d_{m,n} \cdot (\sum_{j=m}^{L} P_j) \cdot \psi_{m,n}(i))$

with $\psi_{m,n}(i)$ the value of the corresponding Haar wavelet at the position of the string a_i. If the initial population is sampled from a uniform population, then $d_{m,n}$ corresponds to the wavelet coefficients of the filtered fitness-weighted distribution function $f(a_i) \cdot n(a_i)$. In the limit of a very large population, one may compute the outcome of the wavelet-based genetic algorithm. The expectation at generation p is given recursively by

$$E^{(p)}(a_i) = G[f \cdot E^{(p-1)}(a_i)] \tag{10.16}$$

Let us discuss the iteration process's convergence within the framework of heuristic random search [Vose 1999] and express (10.16) under a matrix form:

$$z[p + 1] = G_M(z[p]) \tag{10.17}$$

with $z[p] = n(x_i)/(\sum_{i=1}^{Pop} n(x_i)/Pop)$, the normalized population distribution expected at generation p.

Stable fixed points z_s of the transform G_M corresponds to eigenvectors of G_M:

$$G_M[z_s] = \lambda \cdot z_s \tag{10.18}$$

The matrix G_M has only positive coefficients and is irreducible (assuming $f_i \geq 0, \forall i; P_0 \neq 0$). The conditions for the Frobenius-Perron theorem are fulfilled [Gantmacher, 1959]. The theorem states that an irreducible matrix with only positive coefficients has a positive eigenvalue corresponding to a unique eigenvector with only positive values. As there is a unique eigenvector with only positive values, the iterative application of the transform G_M converges towards a single stable point, z_s. Figure 10.13 provides an example, showing a fitness function, the normalized eigenvector of the transform G_M, and the distribution obtained from the iterative application of (10.17). For comparison, Figure 10.13b shows the equilibrium stable fixed distribution function obtained by solving the eigenvector problem (10.18). Both populations are almost identical.

Let us introduce here a working definition of deceptiveness. A genetic algorithm is deceptive for a given objective if the search of strings fulfilling the objective is, on average, less efficient than a random search.

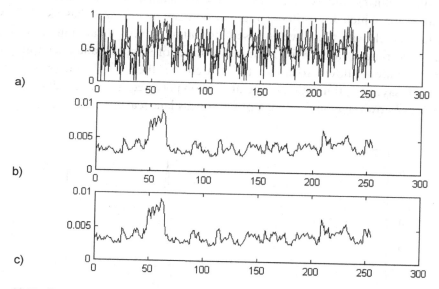

Fig. 10.13. Example showing the stable distribution of the population ($P_0 = \ldots = P_8 = 1/9$): a) Fitness of the different strings, the second line shows the expected distribution after one generation; b) Population after 100 iterations using (10.17); c) Stable population computed with (10.18).

Different objectives are possible. The objective may be a string or several strings with a fitness above a given threshold. A reasonable objective may also be to discover regions of high average fitness. This latter objective is relevant to many control problems in which stability of the solution is an issue.

In summary, deceptivity depends on an objective. Suppose that the algorithm is less efficient than a random search at each generation in the infinite-population limit. In that case, simulations show that the finite-population case is also deceptive already for a reasonably large number of samples (Proving or refuting this conjecture may be interesting, though we will not embark on this!).

The deceptiveness of a fitness function also depends on the chosen free parameters. The disruption probabilities $P_0,..., P_L$ are the main parameters relevant to the wavelet-based genetic algorithms, and their choice determines the algorithm's performance. A fitness function may be deceptive for a given objective at a specific resolution and non-deceptive at another resolution. Figure 10.14 illustrates this. The different curves show the equilibrium distribution for four sets of disruptions probabilities on the same fitness function.

At the lowest resolution, the highest peak is washed out through filtering. From this example, one understands that changing the resolution during learning may positively affect the efficiency of the search. In particular, changing the disruption probabilities during the search may be recommended in multi-modal fitness landscapes for which high-fitness regions correspond to large basins. A low-resolution search with the wavelet-based algorithm permits localizing regions of high average fitness values with a limited number of samples, and a sampling at higher resolution allows focusing the search on these high-fitness regions. Needless to say, an optimization of the disruption parameters P_m necessitates some preliminary knowledge on the shape of the fitness landscape.

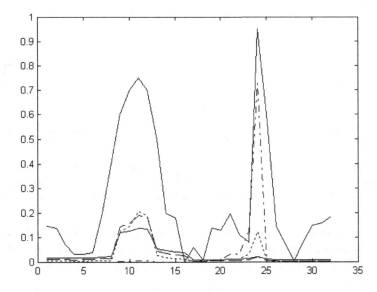

Fig. 10.14. The equilibrium distribution function of the distribution of strings is defined by the fitness function given by the solid upper line. The disruption probabilities are chosen proportional to $P_m \propto 1/(2 + (L - m))^\alpha$: a) $\alpha = 0$ (solid line); b) $\alpha = 1$ (long dash); c) $\alpha = 2$ (short dash); $\alpha = 3$ (dash-dot). The high-frequencies are less filtered as one goes from a) to d).

Before addressing the question of the relevance of the infinite-population description to the finite-population case, let us first summarize the above discussion.

We have presented a wavelet-based genetic algorithm that makes explicit some of the connections between Haar wavelets and genetic algorithms. The algorithm uses a single operator that tries to catch some of the main features of the crossover and mutation operators. The model's simplicity allows the derivation of analytical results, a rare case in genetic algorithms. In particular, the expected population is expressed in terms of the wavelet coefficients of the fitness function. As wavelet theory has an equivalent formulation within filter theory (subband coding), the results can also be formulated in terms of filtering.

The search performance depends critically on the disruption probabilities. The disruption probabilities determine the importance of exploitation and exploration to a considerable extent. Large probabilities for low-resolution sampling result in exploration being privileged on exploitation, while the reverse holds if sampling is performed in the neighborhood of the fittest strings. The algorithm's efficiency depends centrally on a good correlation between the objective strings and the regions of high average fitness. The algorithm is efficient if the search is guided towards the 'best' string by sampling regions with high average fitness. We have presented an example (Figure 10.15) in which a fitness function is deceiving for a particular setting of the disruption probabilities and a given objective string. A slight modification of the disruption probabilities for that specific case leads to a very efficient algorithm.

Let us now discuss the finite population case. In the infinite-population model, the distribution converges towards a stable equilibrium distribution. The dynamic of the wavelet-based genetic algorithm is much simpler than the simple genetic algorithm by Vose. The simple genetic algorithm's dynamics can be rich, and the infinite-population distribution's relevance to the standard genetic algorithm in *real-world applications* is unclear. The existence of an equilibrium distribution in the wavelet-based genetic algorithm represents a basis for discussing the finite population model. The infinite-population model's equilibrium distribution can help understand the algorithm in a finite population's only practically relevant case. A central but difficult question is to know to which extent the equilibrium distribution characterizes the population well enough. In the finite but large population case, the distribution moves in many generations from a random distribution given by the initial population to an average distribution described approximately by the equilibrium distribution. The larger the population, the better the average distribution is approximated by the equilibrium distribution. If the equilibrium distribution is qualitatively different from the transient infinite-population distributions, any discussion of the algorithm's performance in the finite population case is highly speculative. To what extent does the first generation distribution correlate to the equilibrium distribution? Simulations show that the correlation is not perfect, but a significant trend exists.

10.5. Multiresolution search

The wavelet-based genetic algorithm, presented in the last sections, captures much of the essence of the standard genetic algorithm while being analytically tractable. Besides being simple, the wavelet-based algorithm is also interesting as it is a prototype algorithm of a larger class of search algorithms presented below. This last section is conceptually important. It extends wavelet-based genetic algorithms to a broader class of search algorithms based on multiresolution techniques in both the continuous and the discrete domain. We propose to describe these techniques by the generic term of *multiresolution search*.

Let us extend the simple wavelet-based genetic algorithm presented in the last sections to a continuous search space parameter by expressing it under a more general form. At the pth generation, a finite subset of the search space $\{x_1,...,x_n\}$ has a fitness $f(x_i)$. The following procedure generates the candidate solutions for the next generation.

1) A solution of fitness f_i is replicated on average $\gamma \cdot f_i$ times.
2) An operator modifies each element of the subset created in (1) Θ_m (m = 0,...,L). The probability of using the mth operator m is P_m ($\sum_m P_m = 1$). The operator Θ_m transforms an element x_i into x with a probability density function $\theta_m(x_i \to x)$.

$$\theta_m(x_i \to x) \propto 1/2^{L-m} \cdot \sum_n H_{m,n}(x_i) \cdot f(x_i) \cdot H_{m,n}(x) \qquad (10.19)$$

with $H_{m,n}$ the scaling function associated with the Haar wavelet. It is not difficult to show that, for binary coding, the operator Θ_m is equivalent to the operator O_m, replacing the last m bits in the strings. The cumulative effect of the different operators Θ_m can be described by the operator Θ that transforms an element x_i into x with a probability density function $\theta(x_i \to x)$ given by:

$$\theta(x_i \to x) \propto \sum_m P_m \cdot 1/2^{L-m} \cdot \sum_n H_{m,n}(x_i) \cdot f(x_i) \cdot H_{m,n}(x) \qquad (10.20)$$

A multiresolution search on a (continuous or discrete) search space is so that at each generation, the algorithm tests a finite subset of the search space $\{x_1,...,x_n\}$.

In a new subset of elements, the algorithm replicates each x_i on average $\gamma \cdot f_i$ times, with f_i its fitness. The value γ may be a constant or modified from generation to generation. An operator subsequently transforms each element of the new subset Θ_m (m=0,...,L). The probability of using the mth operator m is P_m ($\sum_m P_m = 1$). The operator Θ_m transforms an element x_i into x with a probability density function of the form $\theta_m(x_i \to x) \propto \sum_n F_{n,m}(x_i) \cdot f(x_i) \cdot G_{n,m}(x)$ with $F_{n,m}(x) = F(2^m \cdot x - n)$; $G_{n,m}(x) = G(2^m \cdot x - n)$.

The resulting subset defines the search subspace at the next generation.

Figure 10.15 summarizes the algorithm (see Figure 10.17 for a practical example).

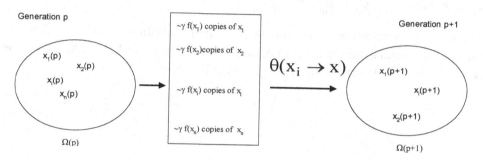

Fig. 10.15. General description of a multiresolution search.

The above formulation of the wavelet-based genetic algorithm in terms of a multiresolution search extends the algorithm to continuous search spaces. It includes multiresolution searches based on different wavelet constructions than the Haar wavelets. A wavelet-based multiresolution search uses an operator Θ that transforms an element x_i into x with a probability density function of the form:

$$\theta(x_i \to x) \propto \sum_m P_m \cdot 1/2^{L-m} \cdot \sum_n \tilde{\varphi}_{m,n}(x_i) \cdot f(x_i) \cdot \varphi_{m,n}(x) \qquad (10.21)$$

The functions $\tilde{\varphi}$ and φ are respectively the dual scaling functions and the dual scaling functions corresponding to the biorthogonal wavelets $\tilde{\psi}$ and ψ. The probabilities P_m must be appropriately chosen such as to ensure non-negative values of θ as $\tilde{\varphi}$ or φ have negative values for any scaling function except the Haar scaling function. A modified probability density function is used to obtain non-negative density functions, assuming for simplicity that $min(\varphi_{m,n}(x)) \geq 0$ one may use the function:

$$\theta_m(x_i \to x) \propto \frac{1}{2^{L-m}} \cdot \sum_n (\tilde{\varphi}_{m,n}(x_i) + \delta) \cdot f(x_i) \cdot \varphi_{m,n}(x), m > 0 \qquad (10.22a)$$

$$\theta_0(x_i \to x) = 0 \qquad (10.22b)$$

If $\delta \geq -min(\tilde{\varphi}_{m,n}(x))$ then the values of the density functions are always non-negative. In that formulation, the operator transforms an element x_i into x with a probability density function $\theta(x_i \rightarrow x)$ proportional to:

$$\theta(x_i \rightarrow x) \propto \sum_{m\neq 0} P'_m \cdot 1/2^{L-m} \cdot \sum_n (\tilde{\varphi}_{m,n}(x_i) + \delta) \cdot f(x_i) \cdot \varphi_{m,n}(x)$$

$$(10.23)$$

Equation (10.23) is almost equivalent to (10.21). The difference is that the constant δ contributes to the lowest resolution sampling (Figure 10.16). By equating (10.23) to (10.22), one has:

$$P_0 = \delta/(1+\delta); \quad P'_m = P_m/(\sum_{m\neq 0} P_m \cdot (1+\delta)) \tag{10.24}$$

The value of δ determines the amount of random sampling. A value of $\delta = 0.2$ means, for instance, that random sampling is chosen in about 16% of the case. For some orthogonal wavelets, the value of δ is quite small.

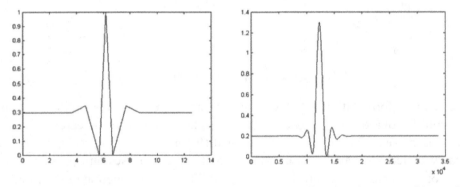

Fig. 10.16. After normalization, an offset is added to the scaling functions to avoid negative probabilities. The offset determines the proportion of randomly chosen elements at each generation. Left: biorthogonal 4.2 spline (Its main advantage: the lifting scheme furnishes boundary scaling functions, see Annex), Right: Coifman 8 (the offset corresponds to a small amount of random search of the order of 16%).

The main results of the previous sections can be translated to the continuous case (in the limit of an infinitely small quantization step!), and we will limit the discussion to stating two results in the infinite population limit:

The probability density function $N(x,p)$ of a candidate solution x at generation p can be estimated recursively. The probability density function converges with p towards an equilibrium distribution.

The probabilities P_m determine the respective importance of exploitation and exploration to a considerable extent. Large probabilities for low-resolution sampling result in exploration being privileged on exploitation, while the reverse holds if sampling focuses on the neighborhood of the fittest strings.

The algorithm's efficiency depends centrally on a good correlation between acceptable solutions and the regions of high average fitness. The algorithm is efficient if the search is guided towards high-fitness solutions by sampling regions with high average fitness.

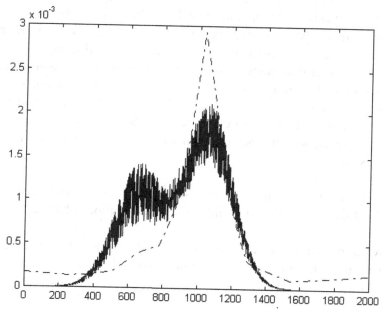

Fig. 10.17. Example showing a normalized fitness function (solid line) and the sampling probability distribution on the search space at equilibrium (dash) for $P_0=0.3$; $P_6=7/40$; $P_5=7/40$; $P_4=7/40$; $P_3=7/40$ (P_k corresponds to the projection on the 2^{L-k} dilated scaling function; P_0 to the contribution of random sampling (Search space $[0,2^L=2048]$).

10.6. Searching for a good solution: How to beat brute force

Humans and nature apply complex strategies to gather and organize useful information based on experience, knowledge, partial information, in-born capabilities, or even intuition. One other important strategy is trial-and-error. Adaptive search methods represent a tentative to apply in computation the trial-and-error approach. The basic idea behind an adaptive search is to extract information from the previously sampled points and to include that information, either implicitly or explicitly, in the search strategy. New adaptive search methods inspired by nature created much interest in the soft computing community. Examples are genetic algorithms, multiresolution search algorithms, ants' optimization, and simulated annealing. A large number of questions in optimization and search problems reduce to the following problem: consider a hypersurface in $\mathfrak{R}^n$ (or in Z^n). Assume that the surface can be described by an expression of the form $y = f(x)$, with $x \in \mathfrak{R}^{n-1}$ (or Z^{n-1}), in which f(x) is a measure of the fitness or goodness of a solution x, taking values between zero and one typically. Find values of x for which either f is maximal or at least within a small range of the maximal value. Without preliminary knowledge, the optimal search method avoids testing a possible solution twice. It is only possible to "beat brute force" if some a priori information on the fitness function is available. The mechanisms and assumptions behind adaptive search are far from perfectly-identified or understood. The most important general question is determining what information permits to elaborate an efficient adaptive search strategy? Knowing some relationships between good solutions permits the design of efficient search strategies. The relationships characterizing good solutions in the search space cover many different possibilities. Let us give here a few examples:

- Fitness is either a monotonously increasing or decreasing function of a variable
  A gradient-descent type of algorithm will lead to a good solution.

- A correlation exists between good solutions and regions of high average fitness
  A stochastic gradient descent combined possibly with a random search might do

- The problem is separable in two or more of its variables
  Evolutionary algorithms may be a good choice. Alternatively, some dimensionality reduction methods like PCA lower the problem's complexity depending on the data structure.

The above statements have in common: they are all expressions in which the knowledge of many sample points permits to exclude possibilities, limiting the range of parameters, or lead the search algorithm to regions in which good solutions are likely to be found. By doing so, the cumulative probability of sampling good solutions increases compared to a random approach. Therefore, a central question on the research agenda is to determine which information characterizes a particular type of search problem and how to use that information to reduce the computing power necessary to achieve one's goal. There is an answer to that question in only a few cases. Most adaptive search methods are based on one of the following assumptions:

- A proximity relation exists between good solutions.
- The problem can be decomposed into small sub-problems whose solutions can be combined to generate good candidate solutions to the general problem.
- An algorithmic relation allows predicting the location of good solutions.

Some of the most successful search and optimization approaches use stochastic elements. Examples are genetic algorithms, stochastic multiresolution search, gradient search, and simulated annealing. The performances of these algorithms depend significantly on the choice of some free parameters. To determine these parameters, one still relies on "good practices" obtained through numerical experiments on typical problems. A disturbing fact is that even if the fitness function is known, it is often impossible to determine if the chosen parameters were appropriate or even sometimes if the search is, on average better than a search with brute force. The computing of average performance values often requires prohibitive computing time!

For genetic algorithms, an approach based on the Walsh partition function [Bethke, 1981] provided insight into the aspects that determine the likelihood of successful GA performance. There is no free lunch, and one needs information to beat brute force! The reader finds several examples using multiresolution searches and a further discussion in Thuillard [2004a, 2004b]. The following section transfers the above learning to swarm intelligence.

10.7. Swarm intelligence

Swarm intelligence is the collective behavior of decentralized and self-organized swarms. Ants, birds, and bees show impressive examples. Ants mark their path with pheromones that guide other ants to a possible food source. If food is absent, the ants will search in different directions, and the scent of the pheromone dissipates. In artificial intelligence, algorithms inspired by ants have successfully optimized problems on a network or a graph [Dorigo *et al.*, 1999]. As an illustration, let us take the example of the traveling salesman person problem, which consists in finding a maximum fitness path (or the path of total minimum weight on a weighted graph) starting from a node and including each other node once before returning to the starting node. The pheromone level depends on the fitness of tested solutions on the edges. The pheromone is washed away with time so that the search does not get stuck in a sub-optimal region. The pheromone trace is like a leaky memory. Ants' optimization algorithms have good performances on the TSP problem, though best-in-class algorithms outperform them. They efficiently solve routing problems [Li *et al.*, 2019] and generally multi-objective problems.

The beauty and fascination of swarm intelligence translate the very successful behaviors of a group of animals into simple algorithms. One often speaks of collective intelligence, meaning that a group of animals' capabilities are superior to individuals. Bio-inspired swarm optimization techniques have been increasingly used [Bonyadi and Michalewicz, 2017; Li *et al.*, 2019]. Kennedy and Eberhart [1995] introduced **Particle Swarm Optimization (PSO)** and Karaboga [2005] the Adaptive Bee Colony (ABC). PSO and ABC have been successfully used in many optimization problems, for instance, for learning weights in a neural network predicting heating and cooling loads of residential buildings [Zhou *et al.*, 2020]. The field is active with applications in many different areas, from routing communication networks [Jacob and Darney 2021] to medicine [Rusdi *et al.*, 2018].

These search algorithms are looking for an optimal balance between exploratory behavior of new regions in the search space and exploitative behavior to get closer to a (possibly local) optimum. A particle moves at speed in swarm optimization, depending on the tested solution(s) 's fitness and general swarm behavior. Many complex optimization problems benefit from PSO and ABC techniques, including learning in many types of neural networks. Some algorithms simulate the growth of a bee population with applications dealing with optimizing warehouse or traffic control [Jung 2003; Arun and Kumar 2017; Hao *et al.*, 2018], to cite a few recent exciting applications. As summarized by Karaboga and Bartuk [2007], the bee algorithm tries to mimic the behavior of a colony of bees. The algorithm can be described from the bee perspective in its simplest version. One has three types of bees:

1) The <u>employed</u> bees search for food sources within their neighborhood.
2) The <u>scouts</u>. Once the food source in their area is tarnished, the employed bees transform into scouts and search randomly for new sources in the whole space or into onlookers.
3) The <u>onlooker</u> bees search their food probabilistically depending on the information provided by the employed bees,

One recognizes several features discussed in the context of multiresolution learning. The exploitation concentrates on attractive regions within the range of the best solutions, and exploratory behavior corresponds to a random search. In its main lines, the Markov-multiresolution search discussion also applies here. The algorithm is better than brute force if excellent solutions are found around regions in the search space having a few good solutions. The ABC algorithm adds an essential element. A procedure decides on transforming the employed bees (exploitation) into scouts or onlookers (probabilistic search) within the most promising region. The ABC corresponds to a multiresolution search with a memory in the multiresolution framework. The discussion on the multiresolution search helps capture the spirit of ABC.

In summary, much of the discussion on multiresolution search is relevant to understanding the effect of the different parameters in an ABC search and estimating the potential advantage of the ABC approach compared to brute force. The success of bio-inspired algorithms and their inspiration to an extensive community show that their simple formulation permits to focus on the ingredients that lead to an efficient search, namely having information on the fitness functions.

References

Arun, B., & Kumar, T.V. (2017). Materialized view selection using artificial bee colony optimization, *International Journal of Intelligent Information Technologies (IJIIT)*, 13(1), pp. 26-49.

Bethke, A.D. (1980). *Genetic algorithms as function optimizers* (Ph.D. University Michigan).

Bonyadi, M.R., & Michalewicz, Z. (2017). Particle swarm optimization for single objective continuous space problems: a review, *Evolutionary computation*, 25(1), pp. 1-54.

Dorigo, M., Di Caro, G., & Gambardella, L.M. (1999). Ant algorithms for discrete optimization, *Artificial life*, 5(2), pp. 137-172.

Gantmacher, F. (1959). *The theory of matrices*, Vol II, (Chelsea, New York).

Goldberg, D.E. (1989). Genetic algorithms and Walsh functions: Part I, a gentle introduction, *Complex systems* 3, pp. 129–152.

Goldberg, D.E. (1991). Genetic algorithms as a computational theory of conceptual design, in *Applications of Artificial Intelligence in Engineering VI*. (Springer), pp. 3-16.

Holland, J.H. (1992). Adaptation in natural and artificial systems: an introductory analysis with applications to biology, control, and artificial intelligence. (MIT Press).

Horn, J. and Goldberg, D.E. (1995). Genetic algorithm difficulty and the modality of fitness landscapes, in *Foundations of genetic algorithms* (Elsevier), pp. 243-269.

Jacob, I.J., & Darney, P.E. (2021). Artificial Bee Colony Optimization Algorithm for Enhancing Routing in Wireless Networks, *Journal of Artificial Intelligence*, 3(01), pp. 62-71.

Jung, S.H. (2003). Queen-bee evolution for genetic algorithms, *Electronics letters*, 39(6), 575-576.

Karaboga, D. (2005). An idea based on honey bee swarm for numerical optimization (Vol. 200, pp. 1-10), *Technical report-tr06*, Erciyes university, engineering faculty, computer engineering department.

Karaboga, D., & Basturk, B. (2007). A powerful and efficient algorithm for numerical function optimization: artificial bee colony (ABC) algorithm, *Journal of global optimization*, 39(3), pp. 459-471.

Kennedy, J., & Eberhart R. (1995). Particle swarm optimization, *Proc. ICNN'95-international conference on neural networks*. Vol. 4. (IEEE), pp. 1942-1948.

Li, Y., Soleimani, H., & Zohal, M. (2019). An improved ant colony optimization algorithm for the multi-depot green vehicle routing problem with multiple objectives, *Journal of cleaner production*, 227, pp. 1161-1172.

Reeves, C.R. (2014). *Fitness landscapes, in Search methodologies* (Springer), pp. 681-705.

Rusdi, N.A., Yahya, Z.R., Roslan, N., & Wan Muhamad, W.Z.A. (2018). Reconstruction of medical images using artificial bee colony algorithm, *Mathematical Problems in Engineering (online)*.

Thuillard, M. (2004a). Adaptive multiresolution and wavelet-based search methods, *International Journal of intelligent systems*, 19(4), pp. 303-313.

Thuillard, M. (2004b). Adaptive multiresolution search: How to beat brute force? *International Journal of approximate reasoning*, 35(3), pp. 223-238.

Vose, M.D. (1999). The simple genetic algorithm: foundations and theory (MIT Press).

Wolpert, D.H., & Macready, W.G. (1997). No free lunch theorems for optimization, *IEEE transactions on evolutionary computation*, 1(1), pp. 67-82.

Zhou, G., Moayedi, H., Bahiraei, M., & Lyu, Z. (2020). Employing artificial bee colony and particle swarm techniques for optimizing a neural network in prediction of heating and cooling loads of residential buildings, *Journal of Cleaner Production*, 254, 120082.

Annexes

Annex A: Lifting scheme

Introduction

The Fourier approach has been the main method to construct wavelets for quite some time. The situation has changed with the discovery of the lifting scheme [Sweldens, 1995]. In the lifting scheme, wavelets are derived in the spatial space. The lifting scheme has led to the development of wavelets defined on a sphere, wavelet constructions to process boundaries, and multiresolution schemes on irregular intervals. All these new constructions are regrouped under the concept of second-generation wavelets. All wavelet constructions obtained in the Fourier domain are derived in the spatial domain by using the lifting scheme [Daubechies and Sweldens, 1998]. For that reason, the lifting scheme is often considered a generalization of wavelet theory, and therefore the denomination of *second-generation wavelet* was introduced.

In this introduction to second-generation wavelets, the goal is to give the flavor of the method and present constructions used in this book. The lifting scheme is quite intuitive. Consider a function $y_n = f(x_n)$ with 2^n samples. The lifting scheme aims to decompose this function into the sum of a coarse approximation and a correction to the coarse approximation. Up to this point, the lifting scheme is, in essence, similar to the fast wavelet decomposition algorithm. The particularity of the lifting scheme is that the decomposition is carried out by filtering the function alternatively at odd and even locations. In its simplest version, a decomposition with the lifting scheme is carried out by cascading a prediction and an update stage. The prediction stage estimates the value of $f(x_n)$ at odd locations ($n = 2k+1$ with k an integer) from the points at even locations ($n = 2k$ with k an integer). The correction to the predicted values furnishes the output of the prediction stage. The update stage modifies the values at an even location to preserve the average.

Let us take the example of the Haar wavelet decomposition. A function $f(x)$ can be estimated at an odd location from its value at the previous even location:

$$\hat{f}(x_{2k+1}) = f(x_{2k}) \tag{A1}$$

The correction to this prediction is given by

$$\Delta f(x_{2k+1}) = (f(x_{2k+1}) - \hat{f}(x_{2k+1})) = f(x_{2k+1}) - f(x_{2k})) \qquad (A2)$$

Introducing the notation $Odd_k = f(x_{2k+1})$ and $Even_k = f(x_{2k})$, (A1-A2) can be put under the form

$$\hat{f}(x_{2k+1}) = Even_k \qquad (A3)$$

$$\Delta f(x_{2k+1}) = Odd_k - P(Even_k) \qquad (A4)$$

with $P = f(x_{2k})$ a lazy function of the points at even location.
The wiring diagram in figure A1 summarizes eq. (A3-A4).

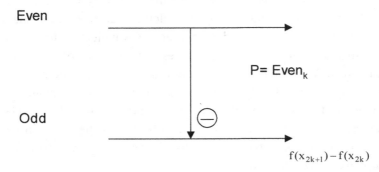

Fig. A1. The wiring diagram schematically represents the transform given by equations (A3-A4).

The second part of the algorithm consists of updating the points at even locations so that the average value on the points at even locations equals the average value of the function f(x):

$$\sum_{k=0,1...n} f(x_{2k}) + U\big(f(x_{2k+1}) - f(x_{2k})\big) = 1/2 \sum_{k=0,1...n} f(x_{2k+1}) + f(x_{2k}) \qquad (A5)$$

This condition is necessary as a wavelet decomposition must preserve the average of a function. The average is preserved with the following update function U:

$$U = 1/2(f(x_{2k+1}) - f(x_{2k})) \qquad (A6)$$

Setting $Even_k = f(x_{2k}), Odd_k = f(x_{2k+1})$ and $Oddp_k = Odd_k + P(Even_k)$ the wavelet decomposition with the Haar wavelet is given in the lifting scheme framework by the wiring diagram in Figure A2. The output points at odd locations correspond to the detail coefficients, while the output points at even locations are the approximation coefficient. Wavelet decomposition is carried out by cascading several diagrams, using the output even data points as input to the next decomposition level at each level.

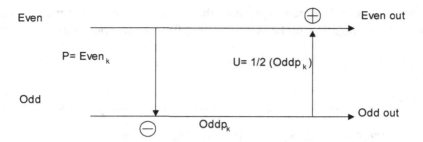

Fig. A2. Wiring diagram in the lifting scheme corresponding to a one-level Haar decomposition. The output points at odd locations correspond (to a factor) to the detail coefficients, while the output points at even locations are the approximation coefficients.

In the next example, we will show how to construct biorthogonal spline wavelets with the lifting scheme. The wavelet obtained with this construction corresponds to a Cohen-Feauveau-Daubechies biorthogonal wavelet [Cohen, Daubechies, and Feauveau, 1992]. This example will show the usefulness of the lifting scheme to construct wavelets, and it will also make clear that the lifting scheme is also an efficient algorithm for multiresolution analysis. In many cases, the lifting scheme is even more efficient than the fast wavelet algorithm.

Biorthogonal spline-wavelets constructions with the lifting scheme

The lifting scheme associated with biorthogonal spline wavelets bears many similarities to the lifting scheme for Haar wavelets presented in the introduction. In the first stage, the $f(x)$ values are estimated at odd locations from the points at even locations, and the difference between the true value and the prediction corresponds to the detail coefficient. The value at an odd location is predicted by taking the average of the two values of $f(x)$ at the two neighboring location points (see Figure A3-A4). The corresponding wiring diagram is given by

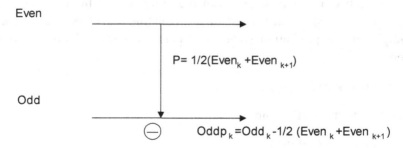

Fig. A3. Prediction stage for (2.2) biorthogonal spline wavelets.

The update stage is designed to preserve the average value of the function after the decomposition stage. An update operator that fulfills this condition is

$$U = 1/4 \cdot (Oddp_k + Oddp_{k+1}) \tag{A7}$$

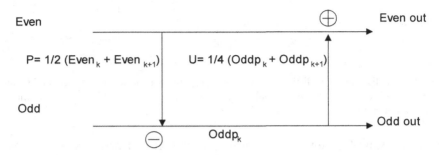

Fig. A4. Wiring diagram for (2.2) biorthogonal spline wavelets.

By substituting the operator P in the above expression, one obtains the approximation coefficients in terms of the input signal:

$$Evenp_k = -1/8 \cdot (Even_{k-1}) + 1/4 \cdot Odd_{k-1} + 3/4 \cdot Even_k + 1/4 \cdot$$
$$Odd_k - 1/8 \cdot Even_{k+1}. \tag{A8}$$

Similarly, the detail coefficients are

$$Oddp_k = -1/2 \cdot Even_k + Odd_k - 1/2 \cdot Even_{k+1} \tag{A9}$$

Equations (A8-A9) correspond to the filter coefficients of the biorthogonal (2,2) spline wavelets. The reconstruction algorithm is obtained by inverting the wiring diagram in Figure A5.

The ease with which one can invert the wiring diagram from the reconstruction to the decomposition algorithm is certainly one of the strong points of the lifting scheme. This property is intrinsic to the lifting scheme, as, at each step, one-half of the coefficients are recalculated from the other half of the coefficients. This very construction makes each stage of the construction invertible. Let us take the example of the prediction stage. The prediction stage corresponds to the operation:

$$Oddp_k = Odd_k + P(Even_k) \tag{A10}$$

This stage is inverted quite simply:

$$Odd_k = Oddp_k - P(Even_k) \tag{A11}$$

As the even coefficients are not modified during the operation, the expression P(Even) can be computed and the operator inverted. Similarly, all other stages in the wiring diagram can be inverted, making the wiring diagram perfectly invertible.

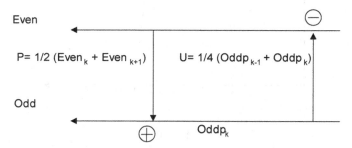

Fig. A5. The wiring diagram in Figure A4 is inverted for reconstructing the original signal losslessly from the transformed data points.

One constructs the wavelet function by putting all zeros but a one in the reconstruction diagram at the odd wire. A good approximation of the wavelet function is obtained by cascading several reconstruction diagrams. Figures A6-A8 illustrate the procedure for biorthogonal (2.2) spline wavelets.

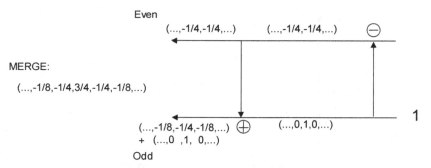

Fig. A6. The (2.2) biorthogonal wavelet is constructed by cascading the above wiring scheme corresponding to the reconstruction diagram.

After merging, one obtains the coefficients $1/8(-1,-2,6,-2,-1)$, which corresponds to the filter coefficients in the reconstruction algorithm with the fast wavelet reconstruction algorithm for the biorthogonal (2,2) construction, an example of the equivalency between the fast wavelet decomposition and the lifting scheme.

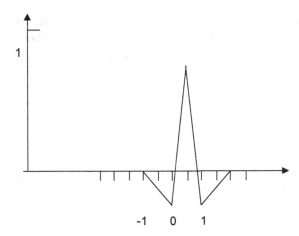

Fig. A7. Cascading the wiring diagram in Figure A6 to compute the (2.2) biorthogonal wavelet.

The choice of the scaling function does not determine univocally the wavelet function. Different wavelets can be obtained by changing the update in the wiring diagram. The scaling function can be obtained with a similar procedure, putting a one in the *Even* wire as shown below. The reconstruction coefficients for the scaling functions are obtained: (0.5, 1, 0.5).

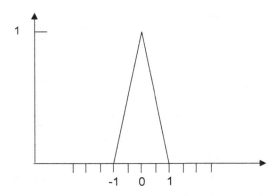

Fig. A8. Scaling function associated with the (2.2) biorthogonal spline construction. The scaling function is obtained by putting all zeros but one 1 in the even wire of Figure A6.

Annex B: Nonlinear wavelets

The decomposition of a function in a sum of wavelets is a linear method- The wavelet coefficients result from a cascade of linear filters. Wavelet theory is a linear method, even if some wavelet-based methods, for instance, denoising, may use nonlinear aspects. In the linear case, the above reconstruction stage is of the form:

$$x[n] = H(\{d_{m,n'}\}) + G(\{c_{M,n'}\})$$ (B1)

Nonlinear wavelet decompositions, or critically decimated nonlinear filter banks, as there are sometimes called in the filter literature, have been proposed by many authors [Egger, Li, and Kunt, 1995; de Queiroz, Florencio, and Schafer, 1998; Heijmans and Goutsias, 1999; Claypoole *et al.*, 2003]. A reconstruction stage of the form characterizes nonlinear wavelets:

$$x[n] = R[\{d_{m,n'}\}, \{c_{M,n'}\}]$$ (B2)

We will limit the discussion to giving some nonlinear constructions.

Said and Pearlman wavelets

We will first examine the nonlinear wavelet construction based only on the so-called S transform. In the first step, the average of two successive values is computed and rounded off to the next integer:

$$l[n] = \left\lfloor \frac{x(2n) + x(2n+1)}{2} \right\rfloor$$ (B3)

The high-frequency part of the signal is given by

$$h[n] = x(2n + 1) - x(2n)$$ (B4)

The inverse transformation is given by

$$x[2n] = x_1[n] + x_h[n]$$ (B5)

with

$$x_l[2n] = l[n];$$

$$x_l[2n + 1] = l[n] ;$$

$$x_h[2n] = \left\lceil \frac{h[n]+1}{2} \right\rceil;$$

$$x_h[2n + 1] = -\left\lceil \frac{h[n]}{2} \right\rceil$$

The rounding off is a nonlinear operation, and it has the great advantage of requiring only integer values. Therefore, the S stage is well suited to an efficient computation in a microprocessor. Due to aliasing, the compression of an

S-transformed image does not give convincing results. For that reason, [Said and Pearlman, 1996] did introduce a first transform, the P transform, to suppress aliasing. The P transform is also invertible.

Morphological Haar wavelets

The morphological Haar wavelet uses the max operator [Heijmans and Goutsias, 1999]. The wavelet decomposition uses two operators. The first operator corresponds to the approximation stage in the linear wavelet. It is given by

$$\chi_1[n] = \boldsymbol{max}(x[2n], x[2n + 1]) \tag{B6}$$

The second operator is the equivalent of the high-pass filter for the nonlinear case.

$$\delta_1[n] = x[2n] - x[2n + 1] \tag{B7}$$

The decomposition stage is invertible, allowing a lossless signal decomposition. Morphological Haar wavelets preserve the edges of objects better than Haar wavelets. The Haar wavelet tends to smooth out edges, while morphological Haar wavelets preserve the edge, as the max operator preserves the maxima. Global maxima remain, while a higher local maximum may remove local maxima at a lower resolution. The morphological Haar wavelets can be generalized to higher dimensions, and also the procedure applies to more complex decompositions. The general max-lifting scheme is such a method, a promising method for segmentation problems in combination with thresholding methods.

Wavelets constructions for genetic algorithms

The wavelet-based genetic algorithm in part 10 is specific to binary coding, and this annex shows that one obtains similar results without assuming binary coding using a slightly modified genetic algorithm. Let us start by describing a single stage of the nonlinear wavelet decomposition.

Consider a string $(a_1,...,a_n)$ with $n=3^J$. The nonlinear wavelet decomposition transforms a triplet (a_1,a_2,a_3) according to Table BI.

The approximation coefficients relate to the number of *0* and *1* in the triplet. If there is a majority of bits set to one, the approximation coefficient is one, while if the majority of bits is zero, the approximation coefficient is zero. The detail coefficient indexes the position of the minority bit. The wavelet decomposition is invertible, as seen in Table BI. Further, if all detail coefficients correspond to $(0,0)$, then the original signal is given by the string $(1,...,1)$.

Table BI

triplet	Approximation coefficient	Detail coefficients
(0,0,0)	0	(0,0)
(1,0,0)	0	(1,0)
(0,1,0)	0	(0,1)
(0,0,1)	0	(1,1)
(1,1,1)	1	(0,0)
(0,1,1)	1	(1,0)
(1,0,1)	1	(0,1)
(1,1,0)	1	(1,1)

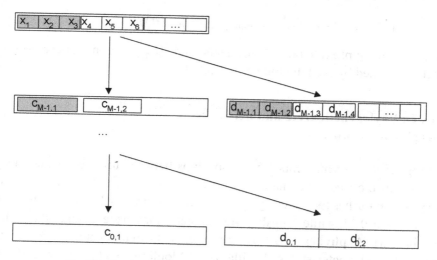

Fig. B1. Nonlinear wavelet decomposition defined in Table BI.

Figure B1 shows the nonlinear wavelet decomposition obtained by cascading the nonlinear wavelet decomposition (Table BI).

The wavelet-based genetic algorithm works similarly to the wavelet-based algorithm in part 10. Strings are reproduced according to their fitness. The operator O transforms the strings according to the following scheme: A string is kept unchanged with probability P_{Le} with Le corresponding to the number of decomposition levels. With probability P_{Le-M}, the low-resolution part of the string at level P_{Le-M} (Le ≥ M) is preserved, and the wavelet coefficients at levels Le,...Le-M are randomly chosen. The new string is obtained using the wavelet reconstruction algorithm defined in Table BI. Figure B2 illustrates the algorithm.

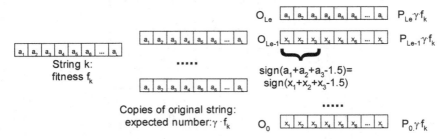

Fig. B2. Wavelet-based genetic algorithm based on the wavelet decomposition in Table BI.

After the first generation, the expectation of a string is

$$E^{(1)}(a = a_1, \ldots, a_k) = \gamma \cdot \left(\sum_{m=0}^{L} c_{m,n} \cdot P_m \cdot H_{m,n}(a) \right) \tag{B8}$$

with $c_{m,n}$ the approximation coefficients and $H_{m,n}$ the nonlinear low-pass projection defined by the left column in Table BI.

Annex C: Phylogenetic trees and networks (Outerplanar Networks)

A phylogenetic tree represents the relationships between taxa represented by the end nodes of the tree. The characters on each taxon can take several states. A **binary character** has two states (yes/no, present/absent, black/white) or translated in binary form 0/1), while a **multistate** character may have several states (blue, green, brown). A **phylogenetic tree** represents the relationships between taxa based on their character states [Thuillard and Moulton, 2011]. An edge of a tree splits the taxa into two subsets, A and B. A split is defined by at least one character with the same state on each element in A (see Figure C1). All taxa in B have the complementary state. A **circular order** on a phylogenetic tree corresponds to indexing the end nodes according to a (clockwise or anticlockwise) scanning. One observes in Figure C1 that in a circular order, all ones and all zeros are consecutive. This property is called the **circular consecutive-one property**, shared by both perfect trees and phylogenetic networks (or, more precisely, a particular type of phylogenetic network called outer planar networks). Let us note that the consecutive-one property was suggested by the famous archaeologist Flinders Petrie's work on pottery seriation.

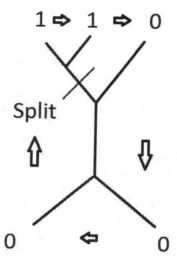

Fig. C1. Two complementary subsets of taxa define a split on a tree; the first subset has state '1' on a given character and the complementary subset with all taxa with state '0'.

Outerplanar networks permit the simultaneous representation of alternative trees and are thus generalizations of trees. All characters in a perfect outerplanar network and a perfect phylogenetic tree fulfill the consecutive-one conditions. The difference is that a phylogenetic tree meets the so-called 4-gamete rules. The **4-gamete rule** states that for each pair of binary characters, at least one of the four possible gametes (one gamete among (1,0), (0,1), (1,1), or (0,0)) is missing. Neighbor-Joining is the most common algorithm to search for the best ordering of the taxa in a phylogenetic tree defined by binary characters. NeighborNet is an extension of the Neighbor-Joining searching for the best phylogenetic network. The first step of both algorithms is identical:

With $Y_{i,j}^{l} = 1/2(\delta(i,l) + \delta(j,l) - \delta(i,j))$. The contradiction equals zero for any quadruple (i, j, k, l) different from (1,0,1,0) and (0, 1, 0, 1). The consecutive condition does not hold in these two instances, and the contradiction equals one. (For the last two clusters, take $(i < j < k < l \in C(i) \cup C(j))$)
Repeat the algorithm till one becomes a single cluster with all ordered taxa □
Let us show a useful connection between phylogenetic trees and networks in the case of lateral transfers between consecutive taxa. Step 1 corresponds to a tree-building algorithm. Lateral transfers between consecutive taxa preserve the circular order of a tree (see main text). It follows that the circular order of the outerplanar network corresponds to one of the circular orders compatible with the tree (after removing lateral transfers).

References

Claypoole, R.L. *et al.* (2003). Nonlinear wavelet transforms for image coding via lifting, *IEEE Transactions on Image Processing*, 12(12), pp. 1449–1459.

Cohen, A., Daubechies, I. and Feauveau, J. (1992). Biorthogonal bases of compactly supported wavelets, *Communications on pure and applied mathematics*, 45(5), pp. 485–560.

Daubechies, I. and Sweldens, W. (1998). Factoring wavelet transforms into lifting steps, *Journal of Fourier analysis and applications*, 4(3), pp. 247–269.

Egger, O., Li, W. and Kunt, M. (1995). High compression image coding using an adaptive morphological subband decomposition, *Proc. IEEE*, 83(2), pp. 272–287.

Heijmans, H. and Goutsias, J. (1999). Constructing morphological wavelets with the lifting scheme, *Proc. Int. Conf. on Pattern Recognition and Information Processing, Belarus*, pp. 65–72.

de Queiroz, R.L., Florencio, D.A. and Schafer, R.W. (1998). Nonexpansive pyramid for image coding using a nonlinear filterbank, *IEEE Transactions on Image Processing*, 7(2), pp. 246–252.

Said, A. and Pearlman, W.A. (1996). An image multiresolution representation for lossless and lossy compression, *IEEE Transactions on image processing*, 5(9), pp. 1303–1310.

Sweldens, W. (1995). Lifting scheme: a new philosophy in biorthogonal wavelet constructions, in *Wavelet applications in signal and image processing III* (International Society for Optics and Photonics), pp. 68–79.

Thuillard, M. and Moulton, V. (2011). Identifying and reconstructing lateral transfers from distance matrices by combining the minimum contradiction method and neighbor-net, *Journal of Bioinformatics and Computational Biology*, 9(04), pp. 453–470.

Index